REGIS ON KATHIE LEE

"She is irrepressible, indefatigable, unsinkable, ambitious, a whirl-wind, and frankly, she is the one who's really out of control!"

"Kathie Lee and I never speak unless it's on the air. Our stories stay fresh that way."

"Kathie Lee and Frank have a new house. Of course, her idea of a house is my idea of a compound."

REGIS ON GELMAN

"Can you believe it? Gelman profiled in *People*? It took me forty years to get into *People* and Gelman is doing it in twenty minutes. Maybe it's a slow week for *People*."

"Gelman may be the best-known executive producer on television, thanks to me. I need somebody to blame when I'm on the air."

REGIS ON JOY

"My real first love is Joy, of course."

"Joy generally joins me in Atlantic City on the day of the pageant and has never exhibited jealousy. . . . She knows she's my permanent Miss America!"

"She remains the greatest thing that ever happened to me."

I'm Only One Man! ☆

I'm Only One Man!

REGIS PHILBIN

with *BILL ZEHME*

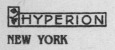

HYPERION

NEW YORK

ISBN 0-7868-8911-X

Design by Helene Berinsky

First Mass Market Edition

10 9 8 7 6 5 4 3 2 1

This book is for any of you who have ever wanted to do something but feared you might not be good enough to do it. This is to tell you to go for it. You might surprise yourself. Look what happened to me.

Acknowledgments

☆

People who seem to know about such things started asking me to write a book several years ago. But I never took it seriously. I've been talking to a camera for all these years and have told you practically everything that ever happened to me. I certainly didn't want to write the old "I was born in . . ." autobiography. You'd never sit through all that. And I've already lived through it, thank you. Maybe just a year would be easier on you—and on me. Besides, every day I'm reminded of something that's happened before, anyway. And then I met Bill Zehme, a brilliant writer for *Esquire* magazine, who did a whirlwind profile of me last year and proved to be something of a Regis Philbin aficionado—as well as a coach and clean-up hitter for this project. He knew more about my life than even I cared to remember. And we both thought that a day-by-day account of a daily talk show—and all of the problems that fall my way—might be interesting. And even pretty funny.

The good news is that I survived the process. And I want to thank some of the people who saw me through it. Naturally, I'm indebted to my indomitable cohost,

Kathie Lee Gifford—an unpredictable powerhouse of a woman—for her stamina, her presence, and her Introduction to this book. And also to Michael Gelman, who is the Gelman no one else could be, for his Foreword. You will see how closely our lives are intertwined in the following pages. And to my agent, Jimmy Griffin, who thought about a book before anyone else and wouldn't let me forget about it. To my editor, Leslie Wells, and my publisher, Bob Miller, at Hyperion, for their patience and expertise. To Genelle Izumi-Uyekawa, who transcribed all the words; and my assistant, Jennifer Sacca, who kept the pages landing on my desk. And to Neal Barr, our photographer, for capturing that elusive cover picture. And, finally, of course, to my Joy, for her wit and wisdom and sensitivity.

Foreword ☆

A woman screamed at Regis, as we walked up Columbus Avenue to have lunch at one of our favorite haunts, *Weren't you on The Joey Bishop Show?* After more than thirty years and eight thousand hours on television, fans recognize Regis from a number of different shows. I first remember seeing him when, as an underemployed college graduate in between jobs as a freelance production assistant. I would sit at home and watch TV, and as I was flipping through the channels looking for entertainment and employment ideas, I noticed a program called *The Morning Show* hosted by two people I was unfamiliar with—Regis Philbin and Cyndy Garvey.

I could tell that I was not one of the show's target audience, but there was something about it that kept bringing me back. Sometimes I would belly laugh at Regis's stories of woe about his transition to New York living after twenty years in Southern California. I felt Regis was talking directly to me—he literally jumped off the screen and into my living room. He was definitely not your average, everyday homogenized TV personality.

In January 1984, after months of freelancing, I received a call from a producer I had worked with when I was an intern at WABC. *The Morning Show* needed a production assistant and I was hired. That's when I first met Regis Philbin. Now, eleven years later, we're still working together.

To most people Regis is only one man—he's the talk show host they watch religiously every weekday morning. To me he's much more than that. Regis is my workmate, my lunchmate, my friend, my mentor, my almost-brother, my sort-of son, and my quasi-father. He's one of the first people I talk to in the morning and the last I call at night before I go to sleep.

In the eighties and nineties, critics have applauded modern day storytellers like Spalding Gray, Eric Bogosian, and Garrison Keillor for continuing the lost art. I concur with these critics, but many have missed the boat. They're overlooking a talent right in front of their faces—a man hidden in what could be called a talent wasteland—daytime television. What makes Regis such a great storyteller is his unique ability to remain down to earth and in touch with the people who watch him.

His obsession with nicknames is how he started calling me Gelman, but his generosity as an on-air personality is how the rest of America started calling me that too. Regis didn't mastermind the "Gelman" character just to create a straight man and get some more laughs; I think he also did it as a way of sharing. Many celebrities hoard the spotlight, but Regis has always felt secure and generous enough to share some of his fame with me.

However, the king is not without a few faults. Regis does have a mischievous, bratty, bad-boy side to his personality. He is the master of teasing and creating tension. After years of being kidded about my love life, I discovered an unusual yet effective defense—whenever he starts giving me too hard a time, I feign romantic interest in one of his daughters. But, for the record, I've never chased Jennifer or Joanna.

When I first heard that Regis was writing a book chronicling a year in his life, the blood drained from my face in fear of what he might include about me. You see, what makes many of his stories so funny is the particular version of reality in which Regis views, interprets, and sometimes exaggerates his world. When he tells his version of a story on the show, it dissolves instantaneously into the airwaves. To have those same stories now written down in a book is a different matter. I'm a bit afraid that readers will take these stories as fact. Just remember, this is only one man's version of history. But when I think about it, if history was left to only one man, I can't think of anyone else I'd rather have write it.

—Michael Gelman

Introduction

Regis. Just the name alone makes me laugh. And after ten years with the man I've laughed a lot.

When I first saw Reege on TV in Los Angeles twenty years ago I couldn't figure out if he was adorably obnoxious or obnoxiously adorable. I still can't. I just know that he is the absolute best at what he does. Nobody tells a story better than Regis. Nobody works an audience better than Regis. And nobody puts more of himself into what he does. Whether he's sumo wrestling, throwing a pass on Columbus Avenue, or just describing a torturous cab ride through Central Park—it's all done the same "Out Regis" way.

The charm of Regis is: (1) he is still the same scared and shy little Catholic boy afraid to knock on the door of the radio station at Notre Dame to ask for a job (even though he's now known all over the country by his first name alone); (2) he's still the same awestruck young performer singing "Pennies from Heaven" to Bing Crosby (even though he sings to sold-out crowds nationwide); (3) he's still the same kid who got dumped after the prom (even though Susan Lucci can't keep her hands off him);

(4) he's still the same sports nut who, as a kid, played stickball on the street (even though he catches passes from Steve Young, sinks baskets with Shaquille O'Neal, and works out with Cindy Crawford); (5) he's still the same insecure young man from the Bronx whose mother used to tell him, "The poorhouse is just around the corner, Mr. Big Shot" (even though a street is now called Regis Philbin Avenue). In other words, he's still a kid and he's still a fan.

People always talk about our "chemistry," and Regis and I just look at each other and roll our eyes. There's no formula for what we do. We just enjoy each other's company and we respect each other's ability and we crack each other up. It's really simple. We have fun, and fun is contagious.

Now, after all these years and all these shows together, you'd think I'd be sick to death of him, but the truth is I still miss him on weekends. I miss hearing him come down the hall singing "Sunset Boulevard" or "Lady of Spain I Adore You" or "Day-O, Day-O." I miss picking lint off his jacket and I really miss telling him he's a jerk.

Please don't tell him any of this, because it would spoil everything, but the fact is I love him to pieces.

—Kathie Lee Gifford

Part I

Anyway, here goes: Take my life, please. This will be a year of it, more or less. A diary. A record of what it's like being me. It's not always easy being me. I joke about living under a permanent dark cloud. (Of course, anything is dark compared to the blinding halo of a certain co-host!) And sometimes it does seem like everything happens to me. But I must confess: I'm just a guy like any other guy. Except that I get to prove it in front of a live television camera every morning.

I host for a living. I got my first talk show before talk shows became important. Now talk shows make big headlines. Ratings wars. Life after Johnny. Late-night thrones. Daytime sleaze. And then there's me. I started small and learned to keep it small. Small is friendlier and more real. Small lasts longer. It wears well. I guess that's why I'm still around.

What can I tell you? I will tell you everything. Whatever happens. Whenever it happens. All of the new adventures and old memories and little irritations—blow by blow, day after day. Kind of like our show openings—but without somebody always interrupting, if you know what I mean.

☆　　☆　　☆

I'm right back where my career started. Back in Los Angeles. To be exact, I'm on the CBS lot in Studio City. It's a warm summer afternoon and I'm here to do some acting. I'm here to play the role of Regis Philbin, co-host of *Live! with Regis and Kathie Lee*. (I've already done all the research for the part, thank you very much!) I have some pages from a script in my hand. The latest episode of HBO's *The Larry Sanders Show*—the acclaimed no-holds-barred spoof of a television talk show. Created by and starring Garry Shandling. *Larry Sanders* imitates the dark side of talk-show life. The back-biting. The feuds. The deceptions. The intrigues. And despite all of this chaos, Larry gets his show on the air every night. Okay, it's a fictional show, but he still gets it on! Guests who appear on Larry's talk show play themselves—both on-stage and backstage—and often get involved in the many twisted plots. And that's why I'm here. This week, I try to steal away Larry's great oafish sidekick, Hank Kingsley. According to the script, I've been hired to host my own late-night twelve-thirty show and I want Hank to be my announcer. Great. I've only been back in California for a few hours and already I'm a villain!

Anyway, it's good to be here. There isn't a cloud in the sky. Just a gentle breeze blowing between the huge soundstages on the lot. And there isn't a soul in sight, either. So quiet, it's kind of spooky. Of course, inside these big tombs there's a lot going on. But out here— nothing but the breeze. What a difference from New York City where I awoke this morning. Manhattan: the traffic, the tourists, the rhythms of the city, up and down Columbus Avenue. That's been my street for the past eleven years. It took me a long time to get back there.

When I first arrived at WABC-TV in New York, I remember looking down Columbus Avenue and beyond—where it becomes Ninth Avenue at St. Paul's on 59th Street. I remembered my mother telling me that I was baptized there. And I was born only a few blocks farther—at Childs Hospital, which was torn down to become Power High School, which was torn down to make way for a high-rise apartment house. But that church remains as it has for over a hundred years. I see it every day. A reminder that my life began on the West Side of Manhattan. I used to kid that I had come home to die. Just like an old elephant. That was eleven years ago. I don't kid about that anymore.

☆   ☆   ☆

My parents were a typical New York City couple. First-generation American. Her parents came from Italy and settled on 59th Street. My father's father came from Ireland, married an American lady and lived on the Upper East Side. My dad attended Regis High School for a couple of years. (I guess he liked the name.) Then, according to family gossip, he got involved in an altercation and was ejected from school. He continued his education elsewhere, finally receiving his master's degree from NYU in labor relations. We moved to Brooklyn for a year or two before moving up to the Bronx. And there we lived in a two-story house on Cruger Avenue with my Italian grandmother and uncle. The house was owned by my great-aunt who lived on the second floor. The rent was thirty-five dollars a month. And even on the coldest day of the year, I could hear my great-aunt walking down the stairs at exactly nine P.M., heading into the bowels of the cellar—a place I feared even in the daylight—to turn off the heat. It was a humble life, I guess. But you want to know something? I never noticed. I loved it. I loved everything about it.

And, all these years later, I still love the city. Coming back to New York was the smartest thing I ever did. My years on the West Coast were nice. All that peace and sunshine—and tremendous local ratings. But it was an impossible place to do a live national morning show. Wrong coast. Three-hour time difference. The rest of the country eats lunch while you're sipping your second morning cup of coffee. So I came back east. And I got lucky. After a long climb, my life is pretty darn good. I'm married to a beautiful woman who is smarter than me. And I'm working with a beautiful woman who is richer than me. We have a show that is more popular than I ever could have imagined. In fact, I couldn't have predicted any of this. Wouldn't have dared. But now I'm out in California again—on the CBS lot with all of these television soundstages hulking around me. Again. Just like in the beginning.

☆ ☆ ☆

I started as a Hollywood stagehand. My first real job in the business. I worked on the lot of KCOP-TV, a local station. There were two huge soundstages that surrounded a Mexican-type courtyard and wishing well. It was the mid-fifties—a quiet, unrushed time in Los Angeles. I had come to this place the day I was discharged from the navy. Drove up Highway One in my old Hudson convertible. I had a dream. Everyone does.

Mine seemed unlikely, but I would try. I wanted to be a broadcaster. All through my childhood, all through college at Notre Dame, all through the service, I had thought about it. Could I really be part of this business? Or was television just like any other naive dream—leading straight to disillusionment and heartache?

On the day before my discharge, I was confronted by a tough marine major named Kiegler Flake. I was a navy man, but had made two good marine friends. Flake was one of them. And he was imposing. That day, he leaned hard on me. Got right into my face. He demanded that I tell him what I wanted to do with the rest of my life. Sheepishly, I mentioned my television dream. But I said I wasn't sure if I had the talent, if I could actually look into a camera lens and talk. Flake moved in even closer, looked me right in the eye and yelled, *"Don't you know you can have anything you want in this life?! You've just got to want it bad enough!"* He thundered at me like I was a fresh recruit. *"So—do you want it?"* he screamed. And, for the first time, I heard myself say it and mean it. *"Yes, sir!"* I cried. Yes. I wanted it.

Next morning, I got into the car with a plan. I would drive to Hollywood to try to see the program director of KCOP-TV, a former marine named Al Flanagan. You couldn't get to him without an appointment. But somebody suggested that I tell a small lie. I would have to convince Flanagan's secretary that I was a personal friend of his. So I got there and gave it a try. It worked. He burst out of his office, and I knew immediately that this was not the kind of guy to fool around with. Flanagan was tall and angular. A severe-looking man with glasses and a crew cut. A true marine. His eyes landed on me and narrowed with suspicion. "Who the hell are you?" he glowered. I nervously spat it out: "Look, I don't know you, but my name is Regis Philbin. I'm looking for work." I handed him my two-line résumé that simply stated: "Sociology Major, University of Notre Dame. Lieutenant. J.G., LST Squadron, based Coronado, California." That was it.

Flanagan was a real no-nonsense type. He said only this: "What do you need?" That confused me. "What do you mean?" I asked. Now he was really getting steamed. "Look, kid," he barked. "If somebody offered me a job at thirty-five bucks a week, I couldn't take it!" I shot back: "I could." He liked that. He said, "Look, I don't have anything right now. But I'll call you when I do." I told him I hadn't been home in two years. Could he call me in New York? He said yes. And I walked out of his office and across that courtyard, past those big soundstages, feeling like I had just conquered show business.

Back in New York City, I recounted the adventure to my parents. They were slightly disappointed by my career choice. So many odds against success. My uncle Mike Boscia was a CBS radio press agent for Arthur Godfrey. He knew the ropes. And even he was very suspicious. "That's the oldest line in the business," he said, shaking his head. "Don't call us, we'll call you. You'll never hear from this guy." So Mike pulled some strings and got me a job as an NBC page. I was well suited for the task. Back then, the page department was run almost like a military unit. There was even a full-dress inspection before every shift. Television was still in its infancy, but there at Rockefeller Plaza things had truly begun to come alive. Sid Caesar was already a giant with his legendary *Your Show of Shows*, staged right in the building. Some nights, Imogene Coca would even join us for a drink downstairs at Hurley's on 6th Avenue. And those great live dramatic shows were all done in the eighth-floor studio that now houses *Saturday Night Live*. It was a thrilling time—even if you only got to sit at a desk outside the studio door.

My first assignment was Steve Allen's *Tonight Show*, which broadcast from the Hudson Theatre on 44th Street. I would seat people up in the second balcony. And, from there, I could look down at Steve in awe. Plus, he had assembled a tremendous cast of regular performers. All of them were kids with huge futures: Steve Lawrence and Eydie Gorme were there, falling in love. Then there was Andy Williams. Louis Nye. Bill Dana. Tom Poston. I knew that I was witnessing broadcast history. In fact, I had almost forgotten about Hollywood and that television station. I had finally come to my senses: Don't call us, we'll call you! How could I have been dumb enough to fall for that one?

Then it happened. A telegram came from the KCOP personnel manager. They wanted my phone number. My résumé was so incomplete, I was lucky to have included my address, much less my phone number. I called them back immediately and, sure enough, they had a job for me. A stagehand–stage manager job. I would carry the props, set the stage, wear the headsets, cue the talent when to speak, and hold the cue cards. My mind raced. I wrestled with that timeless show business debate—New York versus Hollywood. (It wouldn't be the last time I'd tackle that one.) Do I stay on as a page in New York? Or do I risk everything and go to Hollywood as a stagehand? I couldn't make up my mind. I was driving myself crazy. I couldn't sleep at night. I prowled the hallways of NBC asking perfect strangers what they would do if they were me. But, at the same time, I had noticed that big television shows had begun to move west. New York was unwilling to give the networks incentive to remain. Space was at a premium. It was cheap and easy to make shows in Los Angeles. New York was on the verge of losing billions and billions of tax dollars by allowing this new burgeoning industry to slip away. Years earlier, the city had lost the movie business for the same reason. Now it was happening again.

But forget about that. What about me? I had become a pest. People were starting to avoid me. Then I had an idea: Why not go to a fortune-teller and see what she says? I found a reader on 42nd Street, near 5th Avenue. A one-flight walk-up. The lady at the table said she would read my cards for one dollar. For two bucks, she'd read the tea leaves. I put a dollar on the table and said, "Deal 'em." She flipped the cards. Then stared at them. Finally, she said, "You're taking a trip." Well, that was my answer! I was going to Hollywood! I stood up and started to leave. She yelled after me, "Don't you want to know what else is going to happen to you?" I was halfway down the stairs and yelled back, "No! No thanks. I know now!" I should have stayed and listened to her, come to think of it. What was the rush?

☆　☆　☆

Back to the present: The *Larry Sanders* soundstage is dark. I flip through the script, going over my scenes. First one: I burst into Larry's office and make him uncomfortable. Okay, I can do that. Then: I find Hank wandering their studio and plant the idea in his head. I pull him aside and whisper my plan. I want him to leave Larry. Become the announcer for my new twelve-thirty show. This is very confidential information, I stress. I beg him to tell no one. Funny thing is, there *has* been a lot of idle talk about me taking the twelve-thirty slot following David Letterman on CBS. And I know how it got started. I was spotted one afternoon leaving Letterman's office building and the automatic assumption was that Dave was seriously considering me for that job. The speculation raced around the business. Critics and media reporters announced it as if it was a done deal. Actually, I just happened to be in Letterman's neighborhood, so I went up to visit my dear friend, Peter Lassally, the executive producer of David's *Late Show*. We had a few laughs and I left. But it created a storm of gossip. (For the record, if anyone gets that job, I predict it'll be Tom Snyder.)

But anything that happens in our business is fair game for *The Larry Sanders Show*. So here I am—on the verge of leaving Kathie Lee and stealing Hank from Larry. Big, bald, mustachioed Jeffrey Tambor—who plays Hank—is the first cast member I meet. He's a fine actor who goes deep into character. In fact, he rarely leaves character throughout the day. He's making me nervous! But here's what I'm not supposed to know: Hank gets an idea after I take him aside. He decides he doesn't want to be a sidekick, anymore. He wants my job with Kathie Lee. He puts his agent to work and gives Larry his notice—only to find out that Kathie Lee hates his guts and would never work with him. Hank's got no place to go. So he takes my offer. I tell him great. We'll go on the air in 1997. After I finish out my contract with the morning show! Very funny stuff. And so we start shooting.

During our breaks, everyone is talking about only one thing: Murder in Brentwood; early Monday morning; a gruesome slashing. Two victims. The estranged wife of

O.J. Simpson—Nicole Brown Simpson—and a young friend of hers named Ronald Goldman. It happened in front of Nicole's home. Local news coverage is nonstop. It's a high-profile story. And shocking. I hear a lot of whispering on the set. Lots of theories about what happened and who did it. Everyone is wondering about O.J. Who knows?

Friday ☆ June 17

I wrap up my bit on *The Larry Sanders Show* this morning. Joy, the beautiful redhead who married me twenty-four years ago, has flown to town. Most of our life together took place here in Los Angeles. The jobs. The children. The homes. The hard knocks. So many memories. I leave the Valley, drive over the hill, and check into our suite at the Century Plaza Tower this afternoon. We have a spectacular wraparound view of the city—the downtown skyscrapers, the houses along the Hollywood Hills, the Pacific Ocean to the west. Tonight Joy will visit her mother. But I have plans of my own. I've been looking forward to tonight for a very long time. Finally—finally!—I get to see a special hero of mine again. A guy who was better at being a guy than any other guy. A guy other guys only wished they could be. I'm talking about Dean Martin.

For years, I've been wondering about Dean. Where is he? How is he? Why doesn't anyone talk about him? I guess I'm not alone in my curiosity. I found another giant

Dean fan in Bill Zehme, the writer who profiled me for this month's *Esquire* magazine. (The piece was titled "It's Reege's World. We Just Live in It!" Yeah, right. If it's my world, how come I didn't make the cover?) Anyway, in the course of our many interviews, Dean's name kept coming up. For Zehme and me, it's *Dean's* world—and *we* just live in it. Zehme informed me that Dean eats dinner every night—usually alone—at Joe Patti's restaurant, La Famiglia, on Canon Drive in Beverly Hills. (They even have his records playing softly when he's eating.) Dean—a man of habit! Dependable. Easy to find. I just want to see him. Be near him. Make sure he's okay. Maybe even say hello and shake his hand again. So that's where Zehme and I are going for dinner.

Of course, Dean Martin is near to my heart for so many reasons. On my high school prom night, I saw Dean and Jerry Lewis at the Copacabana. They were fabulous. Screamingly funny. And then Jerry would take a break and Dean would sing in that mellow romantic voice of his. That night, he was concentrating on a pretty young blonde who sat ringside. A few days later, I read in the papers she was Jeanne Bieggers, a former Miss Miami who would soon become Mrs. Dean Martin. I collected his records. Knew the story of how he got out of Steubenville, Ohio. Made it to Cleveland. Then hooked up with Jerry Lewis in Atlantic City. And finally superstardom. Years later, I met him briefly when he popped onto *The Joey Bishop Show* one night. I even went to see tapings of his popular variety show over at NBC Burbank. Always marveled at his ease. You couldn't rattle old Dean. Nothing shook him. Not even Frank could intimidate him.

Once when I was working as a local Los Angeles entertainment reporter, I did a story about the all-star cast Burt Reynolds assembled for his *Cannonball Run II* movie. I spent a few minutes alone with Dean in his trailer. I wanted him to know what a fan I was. So I sang him "One Foot in Heaven"—one of his earliest recordings with the Sammy Watkins Band. He made that record in Cleveland, Ohio. Dino sat there watching as I did my best Dino impression—complete with a little dance step and that inimitable easy croon. And when it was over, he said patiently, "That was nice, Regis. But I don't remember it." I was shocked. He didn't remember. Now I realize how stupid I was. When people come up to me with their memories of something I once did on a show, I often draw a blank. Don't remember what they're talking about. How could Dean remember that song—after singing hundreds of others over the years?

But now I would see him again. Since he quit the business, he's been living very quietly. I've heard the stories about his ill health. About how he's never fully gotten over the death of his son, Dean Paul Martin, in that jet crash years ago. But he still gets out every night. A very good sign. Before heading to the restaurant, I flip on the TV in the hotel room. Every channel blares with the latest development in the Simpson murder story. This morning, it turns out, O.J. slipped out of a house in the Valley, along with his pal Al Cowlings. For hours, both men were missing. But now, Simpson's white Ford Bronco has been sighted on a Los Angeles freeway. The police are in pursuit, following the Bronco at a respectable distance. O.J. is in the backseat holding a gun. What a story. Every television station in town has a helicopter hovering above the Bronco as it cruises the now-empty freeways. No one's ever seen anything like this.

But wait a minute! I've now waited a couple of years for this night and the prospect of seeing Dean Martin again. Forget about that Bronco! I have to see Dean. Zehme picks me up and we drive through the empty streets of Century City and Beverly Hills to the restaurant. The whole town seems desolate. Everyone is watching the O.J. story unfold on television. And I would have liked to watch as well—but not tonight. I'm not even sure that Dean isn't at home watching this spectacle. But we walk into La Famiglia—and there he is. In that first booth on the left. All by himself. Wearing a windbreaker. A short glass of whiskey over ice in his hand. His records are playing softly on the restaurant's stereo. And the place is far from empty. Customers are clustered around a TV set on the bar. Every eye in the joint—including Dean's—is riveted to the bizarre picture. The lonely Bronco. The low-speed chase. An emotional moment. What will O.J. Simpson do? A few women are sobbing at their tables.

We take our table across the room from Dean. Right away, I can see that those grim tabloid reports are wrong. He looks spry as ever. Yes, he's well into his seventies. He wears a big pair of glasses that slide down his nose. And that great shock of black hair is now sprinkled with gray. But what presence he still has. Proud. Content. Never lonely, just alone. The way he likes it. After a while, I ask the headwaiter if I could go over to say hello. He says Dean would love it. I have him go ahead of me to remind Dean who I am. If he didn't remember that song, why in the world would he remember me? As I approach Dean, I see the Bronco approach its Brentwood destination. O.J. is going home. The waiter whispers to Dean. I step forward and shake his hand. It's warm and brief. "Regis!"

he says softly. His handshake is firm. I wish him well and tell him that he's still the greatest. He chuckles out a few more words and it's time for me to retreat. Now I know he's okay, and I feel better, too. Now O.J. is emerging from the Bronco. I return to my table to watch this chapter of the sensational story come to an end. O.J. gives himself up to the police. When I look back at Dean's booth, he's gone. And his records are no longer playing.

But when I get back to the hotel, there he is again. On TNT. Playing sexy secret agent Matt Helm. Wearing that turtleneck. Looking like a million bucks. Girls draped all over him. I lay on the couch watching the movie until it ends. Time can be a real killer. But Dean will always be timeless.

Saturday ☆ June 18

Joy and I drive around Hollywood. Things here sure have changed dramatically. We pass the old Brevoort Hotel on Lexington Avenue, my first stop in Hollywood back in 1955. The Brevoort was a small, charming white stucco hotel surrounded with colorful flower beds. Now the flowers are gone. The white stucco has turned to gray. Saddest of all, the front door is locked—even in bright daylight. Crime is rampant. No more innocence. But I spot that first-floor corner window of the hotel, and remember it all so clearly. Why am I so fascinated by the past? Joy can let go of things, but I'm always remembering . . .

So I took the words of that fortune-teller to heart. I did take a trip. Went west. Arrived back in Los Angeles on a late summer Sunday morning. I felt the sun and the promise. I hailed a taxi. Told the cabbie I had a job at KCOP-TV, at 1000 Cahuenga Boulevard. Asked him to take me to the nearest hotel. So he dropped me off in Hollywood at the Brevoort. The elderly lady behind the desk gave me what she promised was a great room. It had two windows. One facing east and the other facing south, which meant cross ventilation. A big plus. She charged me twelve-fifty a week. And I was only two blocks from the station.

Even as a stagehand, KCOP-TV was a colorful place to work. The station had a peaceful hacienda courtyard setting. The afternoon movie host would sit outside near the wishing well and talk about his film for the day. Seemingly a relaxed atmosphere. The truth is, we had a grueling schedule. Other than those movies, everything else was broadcast live. Including the commercials. And what commercials! The outlandish cowpoke Cal Worthington was selling cars. Charlie Stahl hawked Vic Tanny gyms. Sam Benson would blast through what seemed like twelve rooms of furniture—in two minutes flat. And we had to lug every stick of that furniture from the prop house over to the soundstages, where it was all set, shot, then struck—and hauled back to the prop house. Meanwhile, Hollywood's favorite prognosticator, Criswell, made his predictions every night on his own fifteen-minute KCOP show. I remember how we would torture Criswell by holding his cue cards just a little too far away—so he'd have to strain to see them. It drove him nuts, but we thought it was a scream. Then there were travel-adventure shows with Bill Burrud and Jack Douglas. Betty White had her own comedy show—the beginning of her on-camera career. Film director Sam Peckinpah was a stagehand in our prop house. Legendary newsman Baxter Ward did two newscasts a night. And Tom Duggan came from Chicago to do a late-night show. Even the great pianist and raconteur Oscar Levant had a much-talked-about show of his own. And Liberace launched his television career on our station with an afternoon variety show.

In the midst of all this activity, I knew it wouldn't be easy to get noticed. Unless you thought of a gimmick—which I did. I began writing a series of anonymous comic critiques of our shows. I'd compose them late at night in the prop house—then go tack them up all over the station. I intended them to be funny, but the management thought they were a little too sarcastic. And before long, I was discovered as the mysterious author. Station manager Al Flanagan read me the riot act. But something good came of it. He liked my writing style. Suddenly, I found myself with two jobs. He said I could work as a newswriter—as long as I also fulfilled my duties driving a film-delivery truck around Hollywood. In the morning, I would wrap up film that the station had run the day before. Then load the film into the station's van and return it to the various distribution centers around Hollywood. On Tuesdays, I would drive down to the Wiltern Theatre on Wilshire Boulevard and change Liberace's name on the marquee, as he finished his show. Every week I watched from the back of the house as he closed his broadcast, singing "I'll Be Seeing You." Even then, I knew he was going to be a big star. Once I made the mistake of entering a bathroom backstage to wash my hands. Liberace was also in there using the facilities. His manager practically threw me out. Liberace didn't like company in the bathroom. Who knew that Liberace would one day be a guest on every show I ever hosted? He also became a friend. And, ironically enough, the manager who kicked me out of the john—Seymour Heller—later became my manager.

But my favorite duty was writing news stories for Baxter Ward. He had a wonderful voice and a great delivery. During the newscast, I would stand in the darkness at the back of the studio, watching and admiring him—quite proud that he was reading what I wrote. Because Baxter was a superb writer himself, he wanted his news to sound different from anyone else's in town. The stories had to be punchy with a sense of humor and style. Here's an example of a 1956 story I wrote for him, which I recently pulled from an old trunk in my Connecticut garage:

"Justice has prevailed. Law and order have been restored to Beverly Hills. . . . One of our community's most notorious fugitives turned herself in today. Miss Marilyn Monroe showed up in a Beverly Hills Municipal Court to answer a long overdue traffic citation. It was issued in November of 1954. The blonde beauty, dressed in a tight-fitting long-sleeve black dress, paid her $56 fine for driving without a license and failure to appear on a citation. It happened on Sunset Boulevard. She had a week to appear in court. The week went by. No Marilyn. Judge Griffith set a February 1 deadline. Again, no Marilyn. Another deadline, this one April 7. Still no Marilyn. That's when the judge had enough. He issued a warrant for her arrest. Now Marilyn was a fugitive. Did that bother her? Apparently not. She was in New York studying *The Brothers Karamazov* and tying up traffic wherever she went. Saturday, she returned to Los Angeles. Today she visited Judge Griffith, looking great in that dress, but still had to pay her fine. Tonight, she is no longer a fugitive from justice, and Beverly Hills is a lot safer."

Back then, it was just Baxter and me alone in the newsroom. And we would break ourselves up laughing over how to put our distinctive spin on the news. Meanwhile, Tom Duggan, a tall, smiling Irishman from Chicago, had arrived in town for his late-night talk show. Duggan made quite an entrance on the lot with his gorgeous teenage Indian bride—and his so-called bumbling producer, Irwin Berke. (Rumor had it that Tom was forced to leave Chicago by the mob.) It didn't take long for Duggan to make an impact on Los Angeles. He'd interview celebrities on the show, take on-air phone calls, and conduct a running tongue-in-cheek feud with Irwin, his fastidious producer who could do nothing right. I enjoyed watching that ongoing battle every night and filed it away for possible future use. (Little did I know that somewhere in heaven, a yet-to-be-born Gelman would come to earth and become my favorite foil.) Duggan got so popular that Al Flanagan gave him a fifteen-minute sports show to follow the Baxter Ward early evening news. And because I was the only one in the newsroom, I inherited another job: I would cull the sports wire, assemble the film and pictures, write the copy, and also produce the Duggan sports show. For all that, Duggan paid me five dollars a week. And I took it. Gladly. Then one day, the big guy was too hung-over to come in for his sportscast. Irwin was frantic. Since I was the only one who knew what would go on the show that night, he decided that I should pinch-hit. On camera.

Here was my chance. I had dreamed about it for years. I'd finally gotten the call. I borrowed Irwin's tie, got a jacket from the prop house, and climbed behind the sports desk. My knees were actually knocking. My heart began to beat so fast, I thought I would have a heart attack right on the set. This was what I had wanted all right—but now I wished I had more time to prepare. Too late now. One of my stage manager buddies cued me, the red light came on, and I started to read the sports so fast, the words cascaded out of my mouth. There was no stopping me. I was ripping through story after story like a locomotive. I had gotten so good at producing the show that I knew exactly how much copy it would take to fill fifteen minutes. Finally, I got to my last story, still talking a mile a minute. I glanced over at the big clock under the monitor. It said six twenty-six. I had four minutes to fill and had already read everything. There was nothing left to cover—except maybe a Chinese table tennis match in Beijing. But I didn't even have that. So I launched into my first spate of ad-libbing. Later, my whole career would be ad-libbed. I have no idea what I talked about to fill out the time. I just knew it was fast. Too fast. Probably pure gibberish. But it must have made for fascinating viewing. Irwin congratulated me after the show. I recovered slowly, thinking the worst about my appearance. But by the next day—human nature being what it is—I wanted more. I wanted to do that again. Only there didn't seem to be a next time. Baxter never missed a newscast. And Duggan made up for his hangover by showing up every night from then on.

So I was back to my daily routine of film delivery and news and sports writing. The morning delivery work was beginning to wear me down—it made for a twelve-hour shift and I began to resent it. One day, I was particularly down in the dumps, sorting and wrapping the big reels.

Flanagan walked by. I knew he liked me—even though he loved to needle me. "How's it going, kid?" he yelled. I must have been terribly bugged. Because I looked at him and yelled back, "I'll tell you how it's going! You could train a gorilla to do this job!" Flanagan was never one to back away from confrontation. So he walked over to me, gave me his sternest look, and said, "Want to see me get one?" I didn't back down. "Yeah, why don't you," I said. He said, "You want to leave now—or do you want to give me two weeks' notice?" That's when I came to my senses. "Two weeks?" I answered, realizing the finality of the situation. This was happening so quickly. Within two minutes, we'd gone from "how's-it-going-kid" to "good-bye." Those final two weeks went by fast. I hated to leave Baxter and all the laughs in the newsroom. The satisfaction of having my words spoken on TV. I had no idea what the future held, but it looked pretty bleak. This would be the first—but not the only—time I'd be between jobs. And it's always terrible. Your self-confidence erodes. You can't believe that you've got no place to go every morning. Time moved slowly. A few months went by. Finally, the phone rang. It was Flanagan, who always had a soft spot under all that gruffness. He had heard about a job at a radio station in San Diego and urged me to apply. I thanked him profusely and left for San Diego. And I never once asked if he ever got that gorilla.

We're off to San Diego for a week. Right back to where Flanagan sent me. Where I would work for several years and build a reputation. Where I got my first talk show on Saturday nights, which led me to a life of talk shows. Everyone has to go someplace to hone their craft. For me, San Diego was the place. Ironically, it was also the place where I'd left the navy to pursue my dreams. And I was back in no time flat. Anyway, Joy and I fly down this afternoon. Next Saturday night, I'll host the local Emmy Awards here and, in between, probably drive everyone crazy with all of my San Diego memories. I guess there aren't too many of us left from those days. But tonight we'll have a reunion dinner with my good friend Tom Battista, Jay Grill, my old sales manager at KOGO-TV, and Jeff and Lisa Clark, two of the station's personalities when I worked there. Already, I can see how much the town has changed since it was my home. We've checked into the Sheraton Harbor Island Hotel and, from the window, I see the bridge that connects San Diego with Coronado, my old navy amphibious base. Before that bridge was built, I would go back and forth on a ferry boat. Seven minutes each way. It was a wonderful respite, drifting across the bay. Always with my cantankerous old Hudson convertible. The ferry boat hands dreaded the sight of me. They never knew if the car would start again whenever we landed. I stopped counting the times they reluctantly pushed me and the lemon I loved off the boat and onto Orange Avenue on Coronado Island.

Directly opposite our hotel is the North Island Naval Air Station. That was the site of so many great Friday night happy hours at the Officer's Club with my close friend Major Bill Rankin. A marine jet pilot, Rankin lived in the same BOQ as me at the amphibious base. He and Keigler Flake were my two marine buddies, both of whom outranked me, but got a genuine kick out of my misadventures. Both had enlisted before the Second World War and earned battlefield commissions on Guadalcanal. Rankin had gone into Marine Corps aviation and was part of the group that bombed the bridges of Toko-ri, which James Michener later wrote about. I first met him outside the BOQ where I would endlessly work on my Hudson's temperamental engine. I can't remember when there wasn't some problem with it. Anyway, I would always hear somebody lifting weights on the second floor. Turned out to be Rankin—trying to build up muscles in a leg that had been severely wounded on a mission over Korea. Now he'd been temporarily stationed on Coronado in some kind of air-support job. This tough, brusque marine major began teaching me the finer points of weight lifting. And I probably needed all the help I could get. I was an ensign —more naive than anyone would believe—assigned to an LSM squadron staff, headed by a commodore who hated my guts. He made that clear. He'd tell me that there were four things in life he hated most: ensigns, reserves, college graduates, and supply officers. And he would say to me, "Philbin, you're all four!"

I guess it didn't help when I reported to duty at our Quonset on the base and promptly forgot the combination to the safe I was in charge of. We had to blow the lock off. And the commodore just shook his head in disgust. I was totally humiliated. It got worse. But then came a reprieve: The commodore went off to sea for a couple of weeks. I couldn't have been happier. And while he was away, I used the time to pull a prank that makes me cringe every time I think of it. How it began: I had borrowed a copy of *Saga* magazine from Rankin. It contained the story of Rankin's bridge bombing and also a story about the terrific boxer Kid Gavilan. Anyway, I had the magazine on my desk, where it was spotted by a Filipino steward assigned to our squadron. His name was Lopez. I always had a good time with him. Turned out Lopez was a huge fan of Kid Gavilan. So he asked if he could borrow the magazine. I let him—but pointed out that it belonged to this fearsome marine major. "So don't lose it," I told him. Well, you know what happened. Lopez took it to lunch and we never saw it again. I was upset, but Rankin told me to forget it. He was never one to save his press clippings. But I decided to have some fun with Lopez. The commodore was gone and I needed a few laughs. So I told Lopez that Major Rankin was fuming about the lost magazine. Lopez was unfazed. He joked that if the major came around, he would just give him one of Kid Gavilan's bolo punches. No skin off his nose.

This gave me an idea. What if the major did show up at our hut and confronted Lopez? What a riot that would be! I devised the whole plot. Rankin would barge over when Lopez was outside watering our flowers and go ballistic! As a marine, he had no authority to come inside our navy hut. But outside he could make all the noise he wanted. Rankin, however, wanted nothing to do with the plan. But I pleaded. "You've got to!" I said. "I just want to see Lopez's face when you confront him." Rankin finally agreed—against his better judgment.

Next day, I suggested Lopez go water the flowers. He got out the can and I called Rankin to come over. But then, something happened. Lopez was distracted. He was taking too long inside the hut. When Rankin didn't see him outside, he came inside, and just as I'd planned, he thundered: "I'm looking for a man named Lopez!" He was intimidating as hell. A huge marine firmly gripping his ominous swagger stick. Rows and rows of medals up and down his chest. Even I snapped to attention. And Lopez? He jumped so high, he practically ricocheted off the ceiling. He hit the floor saluting. Rankin eyeballed him and growled, "Where's my magazine, Lopez?" Lopez babbled broken English. He didn't know where it was. Someone had stolen it at lunch. But he would get it back if it took him the rest of his life. Rankin told him to see that he did. Then he was gone. Lopez fell into a deafening silence. My practical joke had worked. In fact, it had worked too well.

Later, back at the BOQ, I howled over the episode. A classic prank! The best ever! Rankin even smiled a little. Then we forgot about it. But Lopez didn't. The commodore returned from his tour and, as he entered the hut, Lopez threw himself at him, raving about this marine major who was after him. My heart sank. He gushed out all of it with new embellishments. "You mean this major actually came inside our hut?" said the commodore. "Who was the officer on duty?" Lopez pointed to me: "Mr. Pillbin!" He always called me Pillbin. Commodore's back arched: "Mr. Pillbin was here?" His gaze burned a hole through me. This thing was backfiring in a big way!

He went on: "You were here, Philbin? And you let this marine major push one of our men around?"

Let him? I had begged Rankin to do it! My head spun with visions of my court-martial and execution at dawn. I couldn't believe it. "Don't worry, Lopez," the commodore said. "I'll get to the bottom of this!" I already knew who was at the bottom of it. Me! What a dope. How would I get out of this alive? While the commodore was unpacking his bag, I slipped out and raced over to Rankin's hut. I blurted: "The commodore's back and Lopez is crying to him. They want an apology from you." Rankin laughed. "Apology? Are you kidding?" The phone rang. It was the commodore! Rankin answered and said, "No, Major Rankin isn't here right now. He's up flying." I wanted to kill myself. But this went on for days. Commodore calling. Rankin lying: "The major is out for the day." "The major had to fly to Dallas to attend a conference." Every night, I'd pray that the commodore would forget. And every morning he would make the call again. One day, he finally slammed the phone down and announced that he was going to Rankin's hut to hunt him down. He stormed out. I immediately called Rankin and flashed an SOS. The commodore was coming. He should leave. Please leave. Rankin left. But the game wouldn't end. A meeting was arranged. I told Rankin that I should just give myself up and face the commodore's wrath. But no. Rankin wanted to finesse it for me.

Their meeting was set for noon the next day. I was a wreck. The commodore had even broken out all of his medals for the showdown. Promptly at noon, the major entered our hut. Lopez threw himself against the wall, as if he was still terrified. And I stood by, ready to be sacrificed if need be. It started quietly. Strictly business between two military officers. Then it got hot. And hotter. There was yelling. It was all about territory. Rankin had invaded our space and had threatened one of our men. Or so the commodore thought. I was about to give myself up, turn myself in. But it had gone too far. So I hung back during the fireworks. Rankin was smooth. He gave no apology, but an explanation. And it ended. Thank God. The commodore claimed victory. Lopez felt vindicated. And I swore to myself that would be my last practical joke. Ever. Or at least until I left the navy. Anyway, things would never be the same in that hut.

Wednesday ☆ June 22

Showing Joy around downtown San Diego. I take her to the old U. S. Grant Hotel, which was the hub of the city. Visiting celebrities and local big shots all ate at the Grant Grill. This was the mecca for every big shot in town. And radio station KSON broadcast out of the hotel mezzanine. I had hired on as a news reporter, thanks to Flanagan's recommendation. My shift ran from six A.M. to two P.M. I would drive around town at dawn in the KSON news wagon equipped with a typewriter and microphone to call in my stories. The boss insisted on a fresh story every hour. He wanted it late-breaking and urgent. Of course, realistically, he would settle for anything I could find that early in the morning. So I'd hang around the San Diego police station, checking reports as they came in. But in the late fifties there was no city more docile than San Diego. Not much ever happened. Especially at dawn. I had to make the most of the least. And I relied on every trick I had learned from Baxter Ward at KCOP. I'd make it different. Make it fun. Make it interesting. Even the smallest story.

Like this one, pulled from my old trunk, dated March 29, 1958. There had been a piggy bank theft in the town of Vista! My late-breaking report: "The piggy bank situation in Vista gets more serious every hour. There's someone in this town with a tremendous fascination with piggy banks and their contents. This morning, on KSON's seven A.M. newscast, this unit reported a theft of two piggy banks from the home of Wilson Perry. The take came to seventy-five cents. But this was only the beginning of what looks like a menacing wave of thefts. Mrs. Waldo Roberts has just reported that someone has taken her piggy bank with fifteen dollars in it. She said it happened last Friday. She said she is reporting this now only because she heard three other homes had lost their piggy banks recently. In all cases, nothing else was taken. Just the piggy bank. As these reports continue to mount, piggy bank manufacturers are stepping up production in a desperate attempt to supply the demand for piggy banks that seem to vanish daily in Vista."

Talk about your quiet towns. But that's the kind of paradise San Diego was. The Chamber of Commerce called it Heaven on Earth. They weren't far from wrong. So I'd wait and wait at the police station. My expectations couldn't have been lower. Any other place would have been bursting with corruption and mayhem. Any other place would have hardened cops who lived and breathed danger and violence. Any other place. At noon, on April 29, 1957, I reported this story from my news wagon:

"Thanks to the ever resourceful Police Chief Elmer Jansen, our policewomen have a new look today! It was last November when the Chief thought he'd perk up everybody's morale. Including his own. The Chief called in seven female police officers for a consultation. Something had to be done about their uniforms. They agreed. Those drab whites would have to go. After several months of reviewing the latest fashions, the Chief made his decision. Today, it became reality. The ladies are now wearing tailored white cotton blouses, wide black leather belts, and slender black skirts. And the morale boost has been amazing. Sergeants are now smiling. Lieutenants are laughing. Even the prisoners seem to be happier."

Hey, I did what I could—*all right?*

Friday ☆ June 24

In the rental car, Joy and I drive around the city I'd known so well. Then we cruise around La Jolla. Past my parents' home there. My father had worked for Sperry Gyroscope Corporation in Lake Success, Long Island. When I went off to Notre Dame, they left the old Bronx house and moved to Long Island so he could be closer to work. Once I left for California, he was transferred to North Carolina. Then finally he came to General Atomic, just outside of La Jolla. I was just next door in San Diego and they could watch all my local shows. Of course, my sainted mother lived and died with all of my professional struggles. Whenever one of my shows faltered, she'd always suspect a hidden conspiracy or plot. Ratings meant nothing to her. She was fiercely protective. And she truly loved my father. Once, during an October heatwave, he plunged into the ocean in La Jolla after doing some serious beach jogging. The extreme temperature change caused his heart to fibrillate. Eighteen months later, he passed away. My mother missed him terribly. During her last years, I was able to bring her back to New York several times. And it was always a thrill for me to show her the wonders of the city. Plus all the places she remembered as a little girl. Now both of them have been gone for years. And I'm sitting in this car in front of their home. That house. With the addition they put on. And that garage they built out back. All quiet now. So sad to see this place but not see them. They loved their La Jolla years. Thought they could live there forever. But now somebody else lives in their house. It seems like yesterday when we drove the kids down from Los Angeles to visit them. But it's not yesterday anymore. I swallow hard. We drive away.

Saturday ☆ June 25

Tonight I'll emcee the local Emmys. Joy has just left for home, where I'll return tomorrow. Before heading to the airport, she gave me her usual warnings about not losing my reading glasses or sunglasses or wallet. Yeah yeah yeah. Of course, I won't lose anything! Come on! Give me some credit here. Anyway, I decide to return the Hertz rental car this morning. I'll be rehearsing all afternoon, emceeing all night, and leaving early the next morning. And the rental return is less than a mile away. Why not get it over with? I'm wearing jeans and they're a little tight. Can't get my wallet in the pocket without bulking. So I put the wallet on the car seat and drive over to Hertz. Done. Back to the hotel. An hour later, I reach for my wallet—and can't find it. I turn the room upside down. No wallet. I get that sinking feeling. I retrace my steps. Of course, it's in the rental car! I rush back to Hertz. But not fast enough. The car has already been rented! It's now on its way to Los Angeles. The Hertz people look through trash bins, check the grounds. Still no wallet. Joy has been gone two hours and already I'm in trouble! What a nightmare. Forget about the cash in the wallet—it's the credit cards, the pictures, the driver's license. Oh, dear God. The driver's license! That's a day and a half of waiting in line in New York City. A fate worse than death. How stupid can I be! My only consolation is that somebody is bound to find the wallet. Someone's bound to recognize my name—the same Regis from *Regis & Kathie Lee*! They'll mail it to me in New York. Everything will be all right. Won't it?

My friend Tom Battista joins me for the Emmy show tonight. Of course, Tom has been through everything with me. My lifelong pal. We met here, put my first talk show together, and have never lost touch. But all of our contemporaries from back then have left town. One will never leave. Longtime weatherman Bob Dale is still here making the most of local weather that never really changes. And I even worked with Bob at one point. I was hired away from KSON radio by KFMB-TV, where I kept doing my quirky feature stories. And my nightly spot on the eleven o'clock news preceded Bob Dale's weather report. I knew how popular Bob was—so I would always throw it to him with a funny line. I was hoping some of his popularity would rub off on me. And it did.

A year later, the rival station in town, KOGO-TV, offered me a job doing features at six and anchoring at eleven—and, most importantly, the promise of my own talk show down the road. With that schedule, my days were full and hectic. For my three-minute feature at six, I'd work for hours shooting, writing, editing. Then I'd start gathering up the news, film, and pictures for eleven. It never stopped. And, like Baxter Ward, I wanted the news to sound special. Every sentence. Every story. One night, a new stage manager came on duty to work the show. Tall, good-looking guy. I've always noticed stage managers—how they work, how they cue me. After all, I started out doing the same thing. So, in the middle of the newscast, my sequence of pictures came up, which I complemented with all the spiffy writing I could muster. But to stay in sync with each story, it was imperative that I see the pictures on the monitor. Only this big stage manager had moved directly in front of the monitor. Totally blocked my line of vision. I fumbled through the stories and went to a commercial. Then I got up from the desk and walked over to him. To this day, there are two versions of what happened next. In mine, I politely explained that I needed to see the monitor to get through those pictures. According to his version—well, sometime if you meet him you can ask him. But I don't think I could have really said all those shocking things. Anyway, that big guy was Tom Battista and we became the best of friends. When I finally got that late-night show on Saturday nights, Tom became my director. That was the beginning of it all for me.

Now, thirty-four years have passed and we're sitting together at a dinner honoring the stars of San Diego television—yesterday and today. I should be having a perfectly happy time. But I keep thinking about my wallet. Then I get that pang in my heart.

Monday ☆ June 27

Back in New York. Back on the air. Still no wallet. So I make an open plea to America! What better use of the airwaves? Joy is pinch-hitting for Kathie Lee, who's off this week. Nothing like humbling yourself in front of your wife and millions of viewers at the same time. And she just sits there shaking her head at me. But I give the details. It was a cherry red Cadillac, I say. The wallet was either on the seat or the floor. Rented in San Diego. Driven to Los Angeles. And, in my mind, someone is out there watching, listening, saying: "Hey, that's the car I rented! Let me go look. And look! Here it is! Here's Reege's wallet! Let's call him at ABC in New York and tell him the good news!" But that call would never come. So I make another open plea. To the New York Department of Motor Vehicles. Why not? *Please!*—I beg—*Don't make me have to come down there and wait in line for another driver's license!* I can't take the torture! It's inhuman! Have mercy! Joy, of course, just keeps shaking her head.

Then, to make matters worse, I have to watch her tango with Kirk Douglas. He's our first guest and is as suave as ever. Kirk's always been a great storyteller and now he's turned into quite a writer. His latest novel is called *Last Tango in Brooklyn* and the lead character is a crusty, sixtyish trainer who's in terrific shape and isn't afraid to punch out the bad guys and romance the young ladies. Sounds like Kirk himself. In fact, it sounds like he's written himself a movie role. Anyway, we conclude the interview with the two of them doing a tango, while I contort my face and perform my prized Kirk Douglas impression. I growl, "It's me! I'm Kirk Douglas!" Kirk pays no attention. He's busy flinging Joy around. Then he goes for a passionate dip, which doesn't thrill me—but has Joy blushing happily. It's all a bit much, but what am I going to say to Kirk Douglas?

Fortunately, the Department of Motor Vehicles contacts us after the show. The legislative liaison, Mary Fasoldt, is eager to improve the department's image. She arranges for her commissioner to come on the show and explain how much easier it is to renew with the new license express office. No waiting! No suffering! What service. Only one problem: It's still the worst picture I've ever taken. Guess there's nothing they can do about that.

A s usual, my day at work starts with Gelman. Gelman may be the best-known executive producer on television, thanks to me. I need somebody to blame when I'm on the air. And I can blame Gelman for anything. In fact, I do blame him for everything. Everyone ought to have a Gelman. Anyway, I get to the station every day by eight-thirty, a half-hour before showtime. And every day Gelman slips into my office a few minutes later, helps me pick out what I'll wear on the air, then he watches me get dressed. Gelman doesn't understand privacy.

He also tells me about any last-minute crises. We always have last-minute crises. That's live TV. And that's life with Gelman. Then, we head to the men's room, where I brush my teeth (for Kathie Lee—no bad breath, all right!) and Gelman relieves himself. A few months ago, we walked in there and found David Letterman. He was going to storm onto our show that morning and make trouble, then use the segment for his show. Anything for Dave. Anyway, here's Dave checking himself out in the men's room mirror, while Gelman does his thing and I brush my teeth. Dave starts getting nervous. He shifts uneasily. Doesn't know what to say. He hates small talk. Finally, he makes a tortured face and sighs, "I think this room might be a little small for all of us boys." And he flees for his life. That's how exciting my morning ritual with Gelman can be.

People ask me, "Where did Gelman come from?" I

usually say, "It happened one Christmas morning. I opened my front door and there he was, lying in a manger. So what could I do? I had to take him in." But the truth is, Gelman was born in New York, has real parents and also a first name. Michael. But he'll always be Gelman to me. It sounds funnier. Gelman was here at this show before I was. Back then, this was a local show with another name and Gelman was a college intern, doing all kinds of office jobs. Then he left to continue his education and that's when I came to start *The Morning Show*, as it was called. Gelman came back and got a job as a production assistant. But I don't really remember seeing him around much. We had a rather large staff and Gelman was just another face. My co-host then was Cyndy Garvey, followed by Ann Abernathy, and, finally, Kathie Lee Gifford. As the show progressed, my producers were being picked off by other shows like Sally Jessy Raphael and Joan Rivers. Gelman, meanwhile, rose through the ranks until he was one of the few people left who knew how to do the show the way I wanted it.

But then he left again. He couldn't get along with our producer, so he went off to work on *Hollywood Squares*— for my very first talk-show producer, Rick Rosner. (I'm not sure whether Gelman was responsible for the Xs or the Os.) When that assignment was over, he came back to New York and I gave him the job of producing my Lifetime cable show. He did a terrific job and understood my loose format perfectly. So when the next *Morning Show* producer left, Gelman applied for the job. Station manager Walter Liss had his doubts, but I went to the mat for him and got Gelman instated at the helm. He was only twenty-six, but I knew he had the right stuff.

Until just a few years ago, Gelman still looked like a

baby. This show has aged him. He operates under a lot of pressure and can gracefully withstand all of the daily problems. Thousands of guests are offered to us each year—some of them friends of ours—and Gelman is the only one who can say no. I couldn't do it. But he does it without impunity if he thinks they're not right for the show. I admire that quality in him. Besides that, he thinks he knows everything in the world. And to tell the truth, he damn near does! Sometimes he even thinks he's my father. Ever since my heart procedure last year, I have to watch what I eat. Except Gelman does most of the watching. Like a hawk. Every day as we peruse a luncheon menu, Gelman will point out a nice salad to me—or something equally healthy and boring—and say, "Yum-yum-yum." Like I'm eight years old!

Anyway, Gelman is thirty-three now, living out his prized bachelorhood, making the most of his on-air presence. You put a guy on camera and, all of a sudden, his whole persona changes. He used to wear glasses, get regular haircuts, and fade into the woodwork. As soon as I started teasing him on the show, he turned into Steven Seagal. He ran out and got contact lenses, grew a ponytail, bought a new wardrobe, and started striking heroic poses on the sidelines. For some ungodly reason, women in the audience began treating him like a sex symbol! They're always trying to set him up with daughters and nieces and cousins. I won't do it. In fact, I tell him to stay away from my daughters! But he doesn't seem to need any help. His relationships usually last for years. And he guards his private life zealously. I know more about it than anybody, but he doesn't like me talking about it on the show. So I keep him a shadowy figure, a mysterious bachelor. But I don't think Steven Seagal is too worried.

Wednesday is my piano lesson day. Every New Year's Eve, I make a resolution to master some new skill or another. The one I've yet to give up on is learning how to play the piano. And the main reason I've continued is my teacher, Stanley Yerlow. He's persistent, encouraging, and on time every Wednesday right after the show. We use the piano on the *Live* set, but only after the studio is empty and no one can be offended by my occasional mistakes. (Well, maybe the mistakes aren't so occasional, but I'm trying!) Yerlow has peppered my repertoire with such crowd-pleasers as "Moccasin Dance," "Für Elise" by Beethoven, and my current jazz favorite, "Boogie Bent." Whenever I play them at concert appearances, a reverent hush always falls over the audience. At least, it *seems* reverent. Maybe they're all just using the time to get a nap. The truth is, I'm a little afraid to look up and see for myself.

By coincidence, our guest today is Marvin Hamlisch. How I would love to confidently sit at the piano like Marvin and be charming and bright and witty and play all those wonderful songs. Marvin's an old friend and, in his heart, I think he's proud of me for trying to master the piano at this stage of my life. As a matter of fact, Marvin Hamlisch was instrumental in organizing my first nightclub act. It was 1984 and I'd been booked to play the Club Bene in South Amboy, New Jersey, so I went to Marvin for help. He lives right across the street from us on Park Avenue. Here's this man who wrote Academy Award–winning songs for Barbra Streisand, and I'm bothering him about a date at the Club Bene. But he was nice enough to at least get me started with a great rousing opening number that he arranged himself. Ironically enough, it was "If They Could See Me Now," which is Kathie Lee's theme song for her Carnival Cruise Line commercials. But this was before Kathie joined me on the show. I had seen Shirley MacLaine perform the song in Las Vegas and thought it was a terrific opening number. Marvin changed the first lyric to: "If they could see me now, my friends at ABC, they'd see me being just what I'm supposed to be." And we were off.

I was scared stiff that first night at the Club Bene. It's a place where the audience can be—shall we say?— demanding. They like to bring their own vegetables, if you know what I mean. But it was a packed house full of fans. Still, this wasn't a TV show and I had to prove myself onstage. On TV, you never know what your audience is thinking; at the Club Bene, you know instantly. Fortunately, I passed the test.

From there, my agent Lee "Love Ya Baby, Love Ya Baby" Salomon booked me directly into Atlantic City. Opening for Steve and Eydie at the Atlantis Hotel. My knees were knocking, but they made me feel right at home. Then I would open for Tony Bennett and Don Rickles and Sergio Franchi. The Tony Bennett engagement was unforgettable. Tony's only accompaniment that weekend was thirty violinists. Only nobody told Love Ya Baby or me. I found out when I took the stage for rehearsal and found no band at all. Just thirty violinists. I mean, it's nerve-racking enough to open for a superstar— but no band? Anyway, the hotel rustled up some musicians for me and we got it done. But for a minute there it could have been Regis Unplugged—not a pretty picture.

For sentimental reasons, though, I always returned to the Club Bene. I love the Bene family and their audiences. Eventually, I even took Gelman there to break him in as my opening act. It was time for him to spread his wings and make a few extra bucks. My pal Tom Battista drove us over that first night and Gelman was in the backseat. Just before we entered the Lincoln Tunnel, Gelman insisted on previewing his act for us. I've always felt that this is bad luck and tried to stop him. But Gelman, who was incredibly nervous, could not be stopped. He began talking fast, then faster, then even faster. And then he became almost indecipherable. Gelman was speaking in tongues! I became alarmed and thought about leaping from the car, but it was going too fast. But even Gelman was a hit that night, and to this day, he occasionally shares the bill with me in nightclubs. He still likes to rehearse everything he's going to say—and I still have to listen to him!

Friday ☆ July 1

After the show, we leave for a July Fourth weekend at Claudia Cohen's house in the Hamptons. Claudia is our entertainment reporter. But she's also the best hostess in the world. She fills the weekend with aerobic training, tennis lessons, massages, wonderful food. You can't beat it. Before we leave, Alec Baldwin guests on the show. And he picks up where Kirk Douglas left off with Joy. Alec is such a great-looking guy. Which doesn't escape Joy. During the interview, she and Alec engage in a little meaningful eye-locking—with me sitting there between them. They don't think I notice. But I do. Only they don't see me notice. In fact, I don't think they see me at all. Alec's new movie is *The Shadow*, in which he plays the legendary crime fighter who happens to be invisible. Which is exactly the way I feel right at this moment.

Sunday ☆ July 3

Party time in the Hamptons, one of the most beautiful oases left in the world. The homes, the grounds, the views—unmatched. It's gorgeous. Claudia is such a gracious hostess, you never have to leave her house for anything. But I'll usually sneak away in the morning for a workout at Radu's Hamptons gym. I jump into Claudia's Range Rover and take off. Once, after a workout, I stopped in at a local deli store. When I came back out, I couldn't get the Range Rover started. In fact, I couldn't even turn the ignition key. It was jammed. Or I had jammed it. Okay, I admit it—I'm a mechanical dope! I can't even figure out a coffee-maker. Now people surrounded me, offering suggestions. Even a woman on crutches tried talking me through it. But I never did get the car going. Finally, I had to call Claudia and say, "I give up! Send somebody out to get me!" So I became a helpless Hamptons spectacle. Very embarrassing.

Tonight at a party I'm seated next to Martin Bregman, who is coincidently the producer of *The Shadow*. He is very nervous about the opening-weekend grosses. Have you noticed lately how everybody writes and talks about the grosses? Nobody cares anymore about how good the movie is—just how much money it makes. I can understand why Bregman is concerned. But when my Bronx boyhood pal Freakin' Finelli stays up nights worrying about movie grosses, then you know this trend is getting to be a problem.

Friday ☆ July 8

The city is at its best on these perfect summer days. What a pleasure. Gelman and I eat lunch al fresco practically every day. Right out on the sidewalks of New York—where anything can happen. I remember a sidewalk lunch outside The Saloon on Broadway. A rollerblader raced up to our table and hit the brakes. I had to look twice before recognizing actor Tony Danza. He was out having a ball by himself, blading around the West Side. That's something you just can't do on Hollywood Boulevard. Tony's a former boxer and true athlete. But last winter he had a terrible ski collision and broke his back. It was a slow, painful recovery for this happy-go-lucky guy who hardly ever stops moving. Today, we welcome him back on the show after his long convalescence. He looks great and sounds very happy to be back on his feet. I hope he stays off the skis now. I'll be thinking of him next time Joy tries to get me to go skiing. I'd rather die a natural death, thank you.

Kathie Lee and Frank have a new house. Of course, her idea of a house is my idea of a compound. And this new one already sounds like her version of the Kennedys' Hyannisport digs. She tells me that she's now got her own peninsula, jutting into the Long Island Sound. Yes, the woman has a peninsula! Anyway, the Giffords invite us out to take our first look today and then stay, as usual, for tennis and a barbecue. Joy and I have no idea what to expect, but we're prepared to be awestruck. Redoing houses may be Kathie Lee's greatest thrill—after singing, that is. She's the queen of renovation and redecoration and, just like everything else she does, she's not big on showing any restraint. As long as I've known her, she's been redoing her places. When she first came into my life, she had a Manhattan brownstone in the West Seventies—the only one on the block with a painted exterior. Who else would paint a brownstone? Hers was coated in a pretty beige. But she knows exactly what she wants. She's the kind of woman who falls in love with something right away—whether it's Frank Gifford or wallpaper or a house.

Next, she found a small weekend house for herself on Long Island and redid that beautifully. Refurbished, redecorated, then planted flowers everywhere. Then she married Frank and they bought another place in town, a co-op on 57th Street. This is one of the greatest New York apartments you've ever seen. Like something out of a forties MGM musical, full of Art Deco furnishings, all white, with a two-story living room and a balcony where they can play Romeo and Juliet love scenes to each other. Then they bought a Connecticut farmhouse and proceeded to build its equal right next to it, then connected the two. Enormous space. I loved that house. In fact, whenever we went over for parties, I conducted official tours of the premises, leading guests into every corner of the place. Water ponds all over the property. The gorgeous pool. The perfect tennis court. The ten bedrooms—including the master bedroom that overlooked the living room. (Another balcony! More love scenes!) I'd even walk people through their private bathroom and point out, "Frank Gifford takes his shower there and Kathie Lee luxuriates in her bathtub over here." Everything had been redone because that's what she's got to do.

One day, it's time to move again. This was a couple of months ago. She finds this island property surrounded by water. Long Island Sound. Her own peninsula with a spectacular view of the New York skyline. She says this house is so perfect, the only thing she plans to do is change the drapes. But I guarantee that she'll find a hundred things to do before the year is out. She's happiest when workmen are crawling all over her property, ripping things up and spreading around all that testosterone she loves so much.

Anyway, we drive over and immediately realize there isn't a house in sight—hers or anyone else's. You see only water. Water on all sides. We keep driving and finally spot the tennis court, then the pool, then a large, imposing

Mediterranean house—all perched on this island. We're knocked out. The fluffy dogs are romping across the vast lawn. Cody and Cassidy's playthings are scattered here and there. Flowers and trees and ocean everywhere. It's all absolutely perfect—just like its occupants, who give us their usual warm greeting. Kathie and Frank are truly great hosts. Tennis, food, relaxation, sun—anything you want you get. Frank is the master outdoor chef, always flipping the grilled steaks and swordfish. And the new place has a grill the size of a car, facing the ocean, so Frank can cook and watch sunsets at the same time.

People are sometimes amazed that the Giffords and the Philbins spend any off-time at all together. And, in truth, during the work week, Kathie and I almost never speak unless it's on the air. (Our stories stay fresh that way.) But, in the summer especially, we've had some terrific weekend times. Except when Cody is showing off his latest karate moves. He's enrolled in a martial arts class for little guys. Takes it seriously, too. Likes to practice on old Uncle Reege. And it can be cute. But once, not too long ago, he got himself into position. I smiled and said, "Go ahead, give me your best shot!" And I kept smiling. And he made his little combat cry. And I kept smiling. And he lifted his little foot. Like a lightning bolt, he jabbed it deep into my groin. I stopped smiling. And stopped breathing. My face turned blue. And Cody laughed his little head off. Cute kid. I wonder if he notices today that I always protect myself whenever I see him coming.

Joy doesn't understand it. Neither does Kathie Lee. But I can't help it. I have acute wrestlemania. I love wrestlers, love the noise they make, venting and spewing and challenging their opponents. (I've had to master many of these techniques just to keep up with a certain co-host.) They turn confrontation into a circus act. So, naturally, wrestlers have always been among my favorite guests. And, over the years, all of the stars of that world have done the show. During my San Diego days, it was classy Freddy Blassie and the Destroyer and ex-Charger Ernie Ladd who came by to wreak havoc. I worked with Gorilla Monsoon and Bobby "The Brain" Heenan. I know them all!

When I first returned to New York, Freddy Blassie had begun managing great wrestlers like the Iron Sheik. Always a showman, Blassie would put a burnoose on his head and even kneel in sacred prayer with the Sheik. (The Sheik, as far as I knew, was probably from New Jersey, but Blassie never let anyone break character.) The eighties quickly became the golden era of wrestling. Vince McMahon was producing World Wrestling Federation matches with the flair of Florenz Ziegfeld. He had a stable of the most unusual, incredible wrestlers imaginable. And he maneuvered them beautifully through their matches, which always ended so outlandishly, you never knew what to expect. But, most probably, it was Hulk Hogan who reinvented the sport and made the world take notice. The Hulk was unbelievable. No one could rile up a crowd like him. With his hand cupped to his ear, egging on all comers and spectators, he would ignite that mob and bring them to their feet cheering. He could make Madison Square Garden rock like few athletes in the world.

As it happens, Hulk is back on the show today and I'm ecstatic about it. Lately, he divides his time between wrestling and his television series. Hulk's got the acting bug. If he can do onscreen what he does in the wrestling ring, he'll be a movie champ as well. So out he stomps and, right away, I rip off my shirt to engage him in a physique contest. I always try to torment him, to push him as far as I can to get his juices flowing. But today I notice that the Hulk is more reserved than ever. The more acting he does, the less animated he's become as a wrestling persona. Now he's just sits there talking politely. I'm wondering, Where's my old Hulkster? So I take a chance. During the commercial break, just before we get back on the air, I slap him hard on the face. Finally, the Hulk reacts! He goes for my throat. He knew what I was doing and it worked. He came alive and launched into a classic Hulk Hogan spiel, growling and intimidating. For a minute, I thought he was about to crush me and, frankly, I couldn't have been happier. A host has to do what a host has to do. Even if it means risking instant death.

Kathie Lee, meanwhile, kept a safe distance. Wrestlers could not interest her less—although I think she has a soft spot for the Hulk. But there have been some truly tough moments. Like the time Ravishing Rick Rude came on the show. Rude's gimmick was to have his pants monogrammed with his opponent's face—sometimes on his rear end, sometimes above his groin. On this day backstage, he wore a full-length, white bathrobe—which is standard issue for any wrestler. But then on camera he peeled off the robe and there on the front of his pants was my face—and on seat of his pants was her face. Or was it vice versa? Anyway, it turns out that Frank was watching the show that day in the office of an important ABC-TV station boss and he sees this guy strutting around with his wife's face on his pants. Frank was mortified. And Kathie was offended. As for me, I figured it was just another day at the office. Besides, such crazy stunts are exactly why I love these guys. I only wish he'd given me those pants.

Sunday ☆ July 17

Connecticut bedroom farce. It happened last night in my house. Thank God I slept through it. This morning I get the shocking details. Joy's mother, Ethel (also known as "Well Hello, Let's Eat!"), has been with us all week, both in town and now in Greenwich. J.J. is here, too, with her boyfriend, Will, a nice fellow who's captain of the Notre Dame lacrosse team. Everyone had a great Saturday, swimming and relaxing. Then night fell. Time for sleep. Will takes the guest room, where Ethel usually stays. Ethel takes Joanna's room. J.J. goes to her own room. Sometime during the middle of the night, it happens: Ethel, whom J.J. has always called Gams, gets up to go to the bathroom. It's dark and she's a little confused. She's used to sleeping in the guest room, not Joanna's room. She's all turned around and groggy. She finds the bathroom, then wanders back to bed. Her usual bed. In the guest room. Where Will is asleep. He feels something nudge him. Opens his eyes. Realizes that Ethel is getting into bed with him. He's kind of a reserved, quiet guy, so he speaks gently. "Gams?" he says, tentatively. Ethel is half-asleep. "Gams?" he says again, louder. She leaps out of bed. She's mortified. Apologizes profusely, then scurries back to Joanna's room. Will sleeps the rest of the night with his eyes open. I doubt he'll ever be able to sink another lacrosse goal. Poor guy.

Thursday ☆ *July 21*

A first. We're going to play Las Vegas. Kathie Lee and I are here to do two shows in the big room at Bally's—and also make the rounds at the annual video convention. We both have exercise videos to promote. Mine's been out for a few months and hers will be in stores by fall. It's been a while since I've been to Las Vegas. During my Los Angeles years, we made the trip quite often. We even took *A.M. Los Angeles* to Caesar's on remote for a few weeks. Tom Jones was appearing there at the time, and one night after his late show, we did a backstage interview with him. I decided to play a joke on Joy. A few weeks earlier, Angie Dickinson had come on our show to plug her special on great movie kisses. One thing led to another and, before I knew it, she took advantage of me by demonstrating a kiss. With me. I tried to resist, of course, but she overpowered me. (Well, maybe I didn't try all that hard.) But Joy didn't like it. And I never heard the end of it.

So my plan now was to get Tom Jones talking about his female fans and how they all yearn for his kiss. Joy was standing in the back of the room, and I surprised her on camera by asking her to come meet Tom Jones. "Would you give her a little kiss, Tom?" I said. "You know, just a little one." I thought this would put Joy on the spot and make for some fun. Of course, Tom didn't mind at all. And, as I sadly found out, neither did she. They locked in an embrace that went on for what seemed like an hour. As the cameras rolled. I guess I had never seen Joy in a clinch like that before with another man. It left me a little shaken, which had been her intention all along—she was out to teach me a lesson. And it took me a long time to get over it. And I wondered, When am I going to learn to stop these stupid practical jokes that always seem to backfire on me?

Kathie Lee and I are amazed at the growth of Las Vegas. The airport, once removed from the city, is now surrounded by the city. On the escalator to the baggage area we encounter a huge sign that rises up in front of us. It's a picture of us! Emblazoned with the words *Regis and Kathie Lee!* Followed by the only true magic words in our business: "Sold Out." The couple standing down on the step in front of us see it, too. "Regis and Kathie Lee!" the woman groans. "I wouldn't spend a dime to see them." We tap her on the shoulder and say, "You don't have to. Here we are!" We think this is funny, but the couple immediately goes into shock and says nothing.

On the Strip, it's a thrill to see the marquee at Bally's

blaring the same words. Appearing in the hotel's other showroom is George Carlin. Regis and Kathie Lee *AND* George Carlin! Bally's is covering every taste base. Rehearsal goes smoothly that afternoon. Still hard to believe we're appearing in Las Vegas. The performers' dressing rooms are housed in one central area. So it's easy for me to run over and do George Carlin for George Carlin. I figure it'll get him up for his show. George is not the snarling, growling guy you see onstage. But it's fun to be backstage with him. During Kathie Lee's portion of our show, I come out and tell her that Cody and I have just been over to see Carlin's act. We'd had a couple of drinks, smoked cigars, and now Cody has a brand-new vocabulary. She gives me quite a look. I'm not sure she's amused.

Saturday ☆ July 23

Before heading home, we appear at the video convention. Everybody, it seems, has an exercise video on the market: Angela Lansbury, Jaclyn Smith, Joan Lunden. I can hardly believe I have one, too. I only wish it had happened under different circumstances. After I returned to work last year from my blocked artery episode, I was told to include some aerobic work in my regular exercise routine. I talked on the show about the warning signs I'd previously ignored—those chest pains—and the public reaction was phenomenal. I received so many letters from people who had similar pains but didn't go to the doctor until they heard me talk about my incident. So they'd sent me thanks for helping to save their lives. It was very touching. Until then, I had turned down all offers to do an exercise video. But I thought, well, maybe this was the time, maybe it would do some good. And now, months later, I've already run through David Letterman's audience several times, tossing out those tapes in a frenzy to everyone in sight. Dave thinks it's a funny gag. But I think he might be trying to induce another heart seizure in me. Think of the ratings!

Finally, we fly home, which is a problem in itself. Getting to Las Vegas from New York City isn't easy, but it's even worse going back. There's only one direct flight, on America West, and it's packed to the gills. Plus, there's an hour wait and then another delay once we get on board. Shortly after midnight, we land in New York. Passengers are putting on their jackets, reaching for their bags, getting ready to depart. On my way out with my arms full, the flight attendant—who talked and laughed with us for six straight hours—now decides to ask for an autograph. And she doesn't have a pen. I set down my bags and give her the autograph, but some people behind me are not too happy about it. I hear a lot of grumbling. But it's not over yet.

As we walk through the terminal, two women catch up to Kathie Lee. A few days earlier, she'd gotten her hair cut, which was a big topic of conversation on our show and even made news in *USA Today*. One of the women says to Kathie, "So how do you like your hair?" Kathie says, "I love it." The woman says, "Really?" She doesn't believe her. "Who did it?" she asks next. Kathie says, "The same gentleman who's been doing my hair for ten years now." Kathie, at this point, is getting a little steamed. It's been a long weekend and now this. But the lady isn't through yet: "Was it his idea or your idea?" she asks. And now her friend chimes in: "You know, when you came on the show with your haircut, my friend called me and said, 'Turn on the TV! Wait until you see what Kathie Lee has done to herself!'" Poor Kathie Lee. Dead tired and put on the defensive, but she doesn't stop smiling. With good reason. The woman who is doing all the inquiring is dressed, top-to-bottom, in fluorescent purple. She looks like Barney the dinosaur. And you should have seen *her* hair.

Tuesday ☆ July 26

Now Gelman wants to kill me. He wants me to die on camera. He's declared this week to be Daredevil Week on the show. That means a stunt a day, usually with me participating, hanging on for my life, while some brave guy does something dark and dangerous. Why do I go along with these ploys for ratings? Where will I draw the line? This afternoon, for instance, I head over to the Hudson River to take a powerboat ride with Bruce Penhall, the champion motorcyclist who now wants to be a speedboat demon as well. Bruce and I don helmets and life vests, get strapped in, and we take off. Bruce opens it up and I'm watching that speedometer climb to 50, 55, 65, 75, 85 miles an hour. The boat is literally leaping out of the water, crashing down hard, dislodging my intestines and moving them into places they've never been before. We go faster and faster. The skyline of the city races by me. So does most of my life. But it's a thrill and it gets even better when we hit 100 miles an hour. On the Hudson River. I feel like I'm on *Miami Vice*. Is it possible to get seasick and whiplash at the same time? I only wish we'd strapped waterskis on Gelman and brought him along for the ride.

Tonight, after I regain consciousness, we go to the premiere of *It Could Happen to You*, a sweet movie based on the true story of a New York cop who split his Lotto ticket with a coffeeshop waitress, as sort of a tip. Afterward, we make our way to the postscreening party at the Boat House in Central Park. (I could have lived without seeing another boat for awhile.) Both of Joy's sisters—Janet, whom I call The Winds of War, and Marilyn, alias The Gentle Breeze—are in town and they meet us at the party just in time to see Gelman arrive with his girlfriend. It's a beautiful night in the park with the big moon shining on the lake. But Gelman says he has to leave early—so he and his friend go. And that's when the sisters begin speculating about the girlfriend's age. An argument breaks out. The sisters unanimously decide that she's too young for Gelman. It's up to me to defend Gelman. Why do I always have to defend Gelman? Afterward, during our usual late-night phone call, I ask him just how old she is. And I turn out to be right. Gelman is too young for her.

It's Gelman's turn to risk his neck. Daredevil Week continues. I have a notoriously bad back and have learned the hard way to say no to stunts that aggravate this condition. And that's exactly what I say to Gelman when he suggests that I be shot out of a cannon today. "No, you do it," I say. Although he doesn't look it, Gelman is quite a daredevil. A few months ago, he showed me what he's made of by taking a perilous bungee jump. So it doesn't surprise me when he says yes to the cannon. We go outside to do it on 67th Street. The cannon is bigger than I expect and, when Gelman presents himself in a cape and tights, I know why he wanted to do this so much. He loves his new look. Gelman is actually preening and posing in his costume. The cape and tights are making a big difference in his personality. He feels bigger, stronger, better. Suddenly, Gelman becomes one of the Flying Wallendas! He climbs into the cannon, waves goodbye to us, and disappears deep into the barrel. Then, bang! Gelman is flying. He's airborne. Not high, not far, not pretty—but he does it. And I'm proud of him. So proud, in fact, I let him wear the cape and tights all day.

Kathie Lee and I finally sleep together. Now before anyone starts having gamey thoughts, I can explain. But first, let me set the scene: This will be the beginning and the end of our summer tour. These summer tours have gotten shorter and shorter over the years. Now we've reached an all-time low: Two nights! How hot can an act get? But that's largely because of Kathie Lee's responsibilities at home. Still, there's nothing like the thrill we get doing our concerts together. Not to sound too corny or showbizzy, but fan reaction to these appearances is nothing short of phenomenal. Always has been—from our first concert at the Westbury Music Fair back in 1988, right on through our engagements in Las Vegas and Atlantic City. At first, we thought, "Well, they love us because we're a home product here in New York. And they're a hometown audience." But, then and now, it's always been screaming, yelling people grabbing at us as we come down the aisle. Sheer pandemonium. And it reaches a peak tonight at Buster Bonoff's Warwick Music Theater, outside of Providence, Rhode Island.

It's a hot, steamy night. Fans are lined up, clamoring to be entertained, sounding very, very vociferous. Sometimes, in the middle of it all, I wonder, What's going on? What's the big deal here? All this for a mother of two and a guy bravely marching through his middle years, entering his final glide path. These crowds carry on as though we were a red-hot rock group. A successful television show can give you satisfaction. But being onstage surrounded by all that love and affection is something else. Jack Paar once said to me, "Nobody knows what you do in your act." But what I do onstage—besides sing and tell stories—isn't too different from what I do on television. For instance, in the act I always invite some of the ladies in the audience up onto the stage to audition for Kathie Lee's job as co-host (should she ever leave). It's a challenge to turn these women—and sometimes men (this is an era of equality, isn't it?) into co-host material. Over the years, we've found some great talent.

Here in Warwick, at the first show, only three ladies. dare to come up onstage. But with the first one I strike gold. I always ask what they do. And this one is short, plump, and unafraid. "I'm a corrections officer," she says. "I work nights and I put ninety minimum security prisoners to bed every night in a dormitory." She puts ninety guys to bed every night!? Imagine where we go with this! And that's where I'm leading you now.

For this engagement, Kathie and I are sharing a mobile home dressing room. Kitchen, living room, two dressing areas, and a bathroom in between. The afternoon rehearsal is short, so we have a couple of hours to kill before getting dressed. It turns out, this is the first time we've ever been all alone before a show. Or sharing quarters, no less. So Kathie puts on her robe and curls up on one of the couches in the living room. I get comfortable on my couch. And we both watch television without saying a word. If Gelman were here, he'd be thinking "sexual tension." Gelman, who thinks he knows everything, says the subliminal reason for our success together is sexual tension. I keep telling him he's nuts. There is no sexual tension. At least, not on my part. When I think it over, though, I realize that maybe once in a while she wonders about it. But probably not.

Anyway, we finally doze off on our separate couches. Which I guess technically means that we are sleeping together. So around six o'clock, it's time to get ready for the first show. She gets up, wanders into the kitchen, and offers to make me a sandwich! I decline. God forbid she should break a nail making that sandwich! I would never hear the end of it. I insist that she use the bathroom first. Now the shower is running. It's just like home. I'm sitting on the couch. She's in there taking a shower. Suddenly, the phone rings. Guess who? It's Frank! Yes! Frank Gifford looking for his wife!

"Why, Frank," I say, gleefully, "she's in the bathroom taking a shower!" Long, long scary pause. I should have explained we were sharing a dressing room, but why go into all of that? I just yell through the door, "Darling! Your husband's on the line!" Okay, it's a little strange. And funny, too. But at least he can't punch me through the phone.

Later when I use the bathroom, I notice she's left it in perfect condition. Even her washcloth is neatly folded. And not a spot or drop of water anywhere. The woman is on her very best behavior. Obviously, she's trying to impress me. So when I finish my business, I rehang my towels very carefully and leave my toilet kit at attention. No sloppiness. No whiskers in the sink. We're both being very, very considerate.

Then showtime. As we reach the stage, she whispers, "I want to say something to you." But the noise becomes too loud and she says, "I'll say it onstage." I detect a certain playfulness in her eyes. She's behaving *very* warmly. My mind is racing. I'm panicking. So we get out there and she tells everybody that we had finally shared a dressing room together. Then she pauses for a moment. Lets everybody conjure the image. Lets them think the worst. Then she blurts out, "*Regis is very neat.*" And, just for that moment, I think, "Well, maybe Gelman's right. . . ."

Saturday ☆ July 30

Second and final night of our punishing summer tour. Wallingford, Connecticut. Flew back last night. Got in around two in the morning. We're exhausted, but too exhilarated to sleep much. By afternoon, we're headed up to Wallingford's Oakdale Theater. We've played here twice before and know the premises well. I've invited Jack and Miriam Paar to the first show. We've become friends since we moved to Connecticut for the weekends. Jack now watches our show once in a while. But, as he made clear, he has no idea what I do onstage. He even said to me, "I know what she does, but what is it that you do out there?" Usually I answer, "You know what Sinatra does? That's what I do!" (Only kidding, Frank.)

Sell-out crowds again. They're noisy and loving, which makes us feel like the luckiest people in the business. During my portion of the first show, I introduce Jack Paar, who gets a wonderful hand. I explain to the crowd that even though I started my career as a page, worked as a stagehand, then wrote the news and finally got into radio and onto San Diego television to read it—I still wasn't entirely sure what I was cut out to do as a broadcaster. Until I saw Jack Paar. Saw the way he opened his show, sitting on his desk, sharing little anecdotes about what was going on in his life. Jack never opened with a song or a joke monologue. He simply told a story—always in a humorous, entertaining, personal way. And it occurred to me that this might be something I could do. Back then, of course, I had never met Jack Paar. But I would come very close a couple of times, which is how my luck goes. . . .

My first chance came after Jack had retired from television. This was in the days of *The Joey Bishop Show*, my sidekick period. Joey had learned that Jack was vacationing in Beverly Hills and successfully persuaded him to appear on our show. It happened to be a week when Johnny Carson was bringing the *Tonight Show* out to Los Angeles from New York. So Joey was hoping to counterstrike by getting Paar. Finally, I would get to meet Jack and maybe tell him how much I admired his work. Or so I thought. A half-hour before the show, Joey's producer, Paul Orr (who was also once Jack's producer), told me that both Jack and Joey were extremely nervous about the show. He said maybe it would be best if I didn't sit on the couch with them. I was slightly heartbroken, but I asked Paul to at least introduce me to Jack after the show. "No problem," he said. The show began. And the two hosts were very good together. The audience loved seeing Paar again and I quietly watched from the sidelines, patiently waiting for my introduction. Suddenly, it was over and Joey said goodnight. And, as the credits rolled, Jack got up, bolted off the stage, and disappeared. I was terribly disappointed and never had another chance until I returned to New York years later.

This time, in 1984, I'd been invited to watch Jack tape a special at NBC Studios. After I took my seat in the audience, an attractive woman turned from the row in front of me, smiled warmly and nodded hello. I couldn't place her, but someone next to me said, "That's Jack's wife, Miriam." The show was warm and wonderful, as Jack brought us all up to date on his life and retirement. Witty and classy as ever. He told those anecdotes just the way I remembered when I watched him twenty-five years before. He had great excerpts from old shows: A conversation with Richard Burton about Winston Churchill. Great moments with the Kennedys and Richard Nixon. Exchanges with his regulars, like Alexander King and Charlie Weaver. As the show ended and the audience applauded, Jack made his way up the aisle. *Wait a minute*, I thought. *This may be my chance to meet him*. Closer and closer he came, shaking hands with audience members. He looked great. I got very excited. I was ready to extend my hand when he stopped at the aisle in front of me, took Miriam out of her seat, then both of them walked back down the stairs and left the studio. Once again I was foiled. Every fifteen years I got close, but no introduction.

Word got around about how disappointed I was. So my producer Steve Ober decided to surprise me one day. He booked Jack on the show. Without any warning, Jack simply walked out. How great it was! He sat on the stool next to mine and I could see he was very excited about being there. And a bit nervous, too. In those days, our program was called *The Morning Show*. Some days our studio audience was so large, their seats were moved up to within a few feet of us. But finally we were together. Only Jack began looking and playing to a group of women to his right—and I was sitting to his left. He rarely looked at me! I had a tough time getting his attention. But he did get laughs—especially with those women to his right. And, in a few moments, he was gone again. A few years later, Frank and Kathie Lee ran into the Paars at New York's "21." She reminded Jack how much I admired him. Soon after, Jack organized a dinner party at his home and included Joy and me. And there, I finally got to explain to Jack Paar what he meant to me. This time I had him trapped in his own home. And though he may have wanted to, he simply could not escape.

Flash ahead to Wallingford: Now I'm standing in front of him onstage. And I can't imagine what he thinks of the show. Kathie rejoins me for our final number, but first I say to her, "You know who's here tonight?" "Who?" she asks. "Jack Paar!" I say. "And he's sitting right over there!" And I point to the spot where Jack is sitting. Except he's gone. Just two empty seats staring back at us! Was it something I said? Does he hate my singing? I had asked his wife, Miriam, to bring him back after the show. But now there's no trace of them! What have I done?

Then I remember a funny story Jack once told me about how he hates backstage visits. He and Miriam had gone to see David Mamet's *Speed the Plow* on Broadway. And, ironically, they ended up sitting next to Steve Allen and Jayne Meadows. All that talk-show history in one aisle! Steve suggested that the two of them give the actors a little thrill and go backstage after the show. Jack was terrified. What if they didn't recognize or remember him. He's a very shy man. But Steve insisted and they did it. Against Jack's instincts. But the two lead actors—Joe Mantegna and Ron Silver—couldn't have been more pleased to meet these two talk-show legends. Then it was time to go see Madonna, the female lead in the show. They climbed a winding stairway up to her dressing room and Steve knocked on the door. A voice inside said, "Who is it?" Steve announced, "Jack Paar and Steve Allen here to see Madonna!" The door cracked open about two inches. An eyeball stuck out. A voice said, "Thanks for coming." And the door slammed shut in their faces. "See," Jack said, "we shouldn't have gone backstage." And tonight, I'm sorry to say, he doesn't.

Sunday ☆ July 31

Early Sunday morning. We're home in Greenwich. Phone rings and it's Jack. He's resurfacing after his mysterious disappearance. And he's nothing if not enthusiastic about the show. I tell him, "Jack, I introduced you again at the end, so Kathie could wave hello!" He says, "Oh no! You didn't!" Then he explains what happened: "You know, I couldn't believe the traffic going into this place. I thought you were talking about a theater where the capacity was two hundred seats! But it took us forty-five minutes to inch into the parking lot. Then I realized that these people were all coming to see your show! And to sit there among three thousand people, not a vacant seat anywhere—well, I had no idea, dear boy!" And that's why he left early. Didn't want to fight the traffic again. Besides, Jack never goes backstage!

Wednesday ☆ August 3

The Yankees clinch the pennant. It's a terrific team this year. Finally, they have the right manager, Buck Showalter. So it looks like a World Series in New York this fall. Unless, of course, there's a strike. I liked life better when the only strikes in baseball were caught by the catcher and called by the umpire.

Saturday ☆ August 6

I become a maestro today. I'm off to Hyannis, Massachusetts, where tomorrow I will be the guest conductor for the famed Boston Pops Esplanade Orchestra. They sent me a little baton and a tape of the "Washington Post March" and I've been practicing in front of my stereo all week. It's a great sense of power, waving that baton and making all that music. I'm determined to do as good a job with the actual orchestra. Joy is with me for support and so are Peter and Alice Lassally. (Peter almost never leaves New York when the Letterman show is in production, so this is a rare pleasure trip.) My old friend Jack Hynes meets us at the airport with the ladies in charge of the Pops event. Hynes, a Notre Dame graduate, is the son of the former mayor of Boston and one of the most popular newscasters in Boston television history. Then we all check into one of those charming but quaint tourist inns right off the highway near Hyannis, which turns out to be a little too quaint for Joy. The Lassallys get their own guest house, which is private at least. Our room in the main house is a bit on the Spartan side—not exactly spacious and no TV. But we spend a peaceful night, pretending we're early Americans.

Sunday ☆ August 7

We make a morning tour of the Kennedy compound at Hyannisport, including the house where Rose Kennedy still lives. It's a place full of history and nostalgia. We cross the lawn where the Kennedy boys played touch football, the ocean just a short pass away. The house is filled with mementoes and pictures of a family that has grown together through so many triumphs and tragedies. All of this has a very sobering effect on each of us. And upstairs, away from view, Rose Kennedy sits quietly while these strangers prowl through her home.

Later this afternoon there's an enormous turnout on the village green for the Boston Pops. Even Maria Shriver and husband, Arnold Schwarzenegger, have come out to witness my baton wizardry. We visit briefly backstage and Arnold reminds me of his last appearance on our show. He had requested a taping rather than doing it live—anything to keep Arnold happy. But then, we had trouble getting ready for tape. Somehow we just can't tape something without a problem. Of course, we also have problems doing things live, but at least we can play those moments for laughs. But Arnold was getting tense backstage, waiting for the taping. He wanted to get started and we were still hung up. He threatened to walk off and, just before he did, the tape finally rolled and out he came breathing fire. Kathie Lee and I know when a guest is not happy about being there, especially when the guest is as big as Arnold Schwarzenegger. So we poured on the charm and Arnold began spinning stories. He was getting laughs, suddenly having a great time with us. He left to a big hand from the audience. And now, in Hyannis, he's telling Maria it was the best interview he did on the media tour for his hit movie *True Lies*. I'm thrilled that the big guy has a selective memory. Gotta keep that Terminator happy!

Now it's time for my turn in front of the orchestra. Eighty-five-year-old conductor Ellis Dixon introduces me. He's one of those old dynamos who could be here for another hundred years. With a gesture Ellis taught me moments earlier, I bring the musicians to attention, and we commence. I wave my baton. I work with them. We soar together. And the music is magnificent. I am in full command and it feels terrific. Only I notice that the musicians rarely look up at me and my vigorous baton strokes. But they must be paying attention, since they're playing so well. I mean, they must have seen me up there. Well, anyway, I like to think they did.

Flying home, in a chartered light plane, we almost die. The weekend skies are full of light-plane traffic, with people flying themselves to and from vacation homes along the East Coast. At one point, we seem to be flying directly into the sun. All of a sudden, another light plane looms right up, out of the sun, in front of us. Our pilot banks sharply to the left and the other pilot veers to the right, and if but for a few seconds, we could have been in a midair collision. Joy screams. The Lassallys go white. We're all a wreck for the duration of the flight, which is blessedly uneventful. In fact, I try to amuse myself by picking out Kathie Lee's peninsula home off Long Island, but have no luck. You'd think you could at least spot her halo from up here.

Tuesday ☆ August 9

A Host Chat oddity: For no reason at all, Kathie Lee tells me there is no soap in the soap dispenser over the left sink in the ladies' room outside the studio. For the past eight years, she says, it's been soapless. This reminds me that there's never been soap in the soap dispenser over the right sink in the men's room I use on the fifth floor in all of the eleven years I've been back in New York. All of a sudden, we're arguing over the number of sinks in each rest room. The women have two and the men have three and she wants to know why. "Because Gelman needs one and I need two," I tell her. She's not through yet. She asks how many toilets. "Two," I answer, hoping that she might eventually remember we're on the air. "We have three," she says, once again feeling superior. I offer my congratulations and move the conversation out of the bathroom.

I take the mound today against singer Michael Bolton. I am pitching and he will be denied! Our big charity softball game is slated for this afternoon, out in the Scranton–Wilkes Barre area of Pennsylvania. It will be Michael Bolton's Bombers against the Regis Montage All-Star team, featuring Gelman. The site: Lackawanna County Stadium, a beautiful minor league ballpark that's home to the Phillies farm team. And most of the 12,000 seats will be filled. I'm ready for combat. The arm is primed.

Because our show is shut down for summer vacation, Gelman is already out in the Hamptons and I'm in Connecticut. To reach Scranton, we've rented a light plane that will depart with Gelman from the Hamptons, pick me up in White Plains, and then it's on to the game. Our pilot is Gelman's friend Mitch Baker. Also on board is Gelman's tennis pro, Jimmy Saladino. The skies are ominous and we land finally in a light drizzle. Our Scranton affiliate, WNAP-TV, sends a car for us at the airport and we're treated to a nice lunch back at the station. Afterward, they transport us in the station helicopter for the ride to the stadium where we land majestically at second base. What an entrance. The crowd is roaring. Let Michael Bolton beat that. And he does. In a mile-long white limo, out from which pours the entire team. They are dressed in Yankee pinstripes and are all business. His Bombers play softball all year round and they've got a solid team. They lunge right into batting practice, with Michael leading the way, pounding ball after ball out of the park. He must derive strength from that long, flowing hair of his. I'm impressed. And a little worried. In fact, the Bombers all show awesome power at the plate. But then they aren't hitting against me. Not yet, anyway. We hang around the batting cage watching, trying not to look too intimidated. Among my teammates are Joe Klecko, a huge former defensive tackle for the New York Jets who lives in the area, and Bill Hunter from our WABC-TV sales staff, who once actually pitched for the New York Yankees. We've also recruited some local Scranton guys who look powerful enough.

But the game gets off to a rather ugly start. Gelman is at second base, where he feels he will be the least problem. Second base usually is nice and safe. Except for today. The first guy up for the Bolton team gets a hit. He's on first. The second batter hits a ground ball to our shortstop, who grabs it and tosses it to Gelman to start a double-play. Gelman collects it and tags the runner right smack in the groin. The runner doubles up in pain. Gelman, that beast, has thoroughly incapacitated this guy and Bolton's team immediately tears out of the dugout, looking for revenge. A lot of them are muttering snidely and some just curse. Gelman is mumbling, "What did I do? What did I do?" We finally get out of the inning, holding them scoreless, and it looks like it could be a decent game.

Well, it wasn't. It wasn't even close. These guys are unstoppable. Homeruns all over the place. They were shelling me mercilessly. My only consolation was Michael Bolton couldn't get a hit against me. He looked great in his skin-tight uniform. He has a beautiful swing. But the man can't hit me! He can't hit my stuff! But that was a small consolation. We lost 22–3, in a driving rain that increased along with our desperation. At least part of the proceeds from the game went to a charity headed by my cousin Betty Bellantoni. Years ago, her husband, Michael, a high school football coach, suffered a paralyzing injury in a car crash but found recuperative support from an area facility, Allied Services. Now they are trying to launch a foundation for wheelchair athletes. These two have been through a lot and I hope they succeed.

As though the beating we'd just endured wasn't bad enough, we couldn't get out of town. We were stranded at the airport, waiting for the heavy rain to pass. Even when we took off, that storm wasn't finished yet. Up in the air, the clouds and the thunder took on frightening dimension. Lightning crackled all around us. We tossed in the turbulence. Nobody said much in that little plane, but I think we were all thinking that maybe this flight wasn't such a good idea. Fate's a strange thing, but I hate to think that the last face I'll ever see will be Gelman's.

Sunday ☆ August 21

Joanna and J.J. have reached an age where the last place on earth they want to be is cooped up on a ship with their parents. They would rather do anything but stare at us for five days straight. Nevertheless, the four of us are about to board the *QE2* for a transatlantic crossing. Weeks ago, I began preparing them. I sat the family down for a meeting. I told the girls that they could choose not to come and I would understand. But if they did come, I didn't want to see them with long faces, wishing they were home with their friends. I can't live with the long faces. I'm particularly concerned about J.J., who can go south at any moment and become downright mournful, missing friends. But they decided to come, promising no long faces. Their summer break from school is almost over, and a cruise would be a nice way to top it off. On our way to the Westside Pier in Manhattan, however, I can tell the girls are thinking *three meals a day together for five full days and nights*. Nobody is saying anything, but I can sense they are beginning to feel trapped. No long faces yet, though.

The QE2 is one of the great old-timers of ocean liners and also an interesting venue for entertainment. Every night there's a new show. I'll be performing my act aboard ship on Thursday night, which gives me time to size up the passengers, so I can include ship-related stories in the show. In our room we find a warm note from Vic Damone, who stayed here on the cruise that just ended in New York. It unnerves me when I realize I'm following the great Vic Damone as a headliner onstage. (There are other reasons the name Vic Damone haunts me, which I will share later.) Of course, the passengers who saw his show have now left the ship and the new crowd will never know he was there. That's good.

The girls are situated in a room three decks below us, which gives them a little privacy and might keep those long faces from overtaking them. At dinner, we see a debonair bald-headed gentleman at the adjoining table and realize it's Patrick Stewart, alias Captain Picard on *Star Trek: The Next Generation*. The girls are happy to meet him. He's handsome and urbane, an Englishman who bought an English country-house two years ago and has yet to spend a single night there. So he's returning to make his first stay. He's been a guest on several of my shows and it's nice to know he is equally charming both on and off camera. Incidentally, his is just one of many internationally flavored voices I'm hearing aboardship. I'm trying to think of why that's giving me pause.

Monday ☆ August 22

I've figured it out. And I'm worried. I've been prowling the decks, soaking up color and studying the passengers, and I've found the mix here distinctly international. In fact, all I'm hearing are foreign languages: French, German, Spanish, Italian. It's dawning on me that this crowd has never heard of Regis Philbin, much less Gelman or Cody or anyone else I talk about in my act. I'm beginning to sweat. I'm foreseeing a miserable death onstage. It's always nice to have die-hard fans in the audience, but right now I'd happily settle for Americans. As if that's not enough, I see that Frank Rich, the most feared theater critic ever to write for the *New York Times*, is also on board to give a lecture. Not only that, but his equally terrifying wife, *Times* writer Alex Witchel, who once did an unforgettable piece on Kathie Lee, will be lecturing as well. (Kathie Lee still has bruises from that story.) This gig is becoming tougher by the moment. On the bright side, J.J. has so far remained her sweet self and not sunk into homesickness. But that could change any moment.

Tuesday ☆ August 23

We attend Alex Witchel's lecture about women in the media. The girls are very interested in the topic and learn that, especially in the print media, getting ahead is still quite a struggle. After the lecture, we introduce ourselves to Alex and Frank, who tell me they are planning to see my act Thursday night. I smile like I'm thrilled, but it's intimidating news. I feel a wave of anxiety come over me. I'm thinking about offering them a couple of hundred bucks to stay in their cabin that night. Meanwhile, there's a veritable chorus of foreign tongues all over the ship, getting louder and louder. They'll never get my stuff. All that and the Riches, too. It's much too late to throw myself overboard and swim for shore, but I still give it some thought.

Wednesday ☆ August 24

It's Frank Rich's turn to talk. He lectures about the state of the theater in New York and London, and the news is not good. The expense of mounting a show on

Broadway and the West End has become prohibitive. Rich, who now writes political opinion columns for the *Times*, paints a depressing picture of what's happening onstage in both countries. Afterward, I offer my congratulations on his talk and then once again try to convince him to stay in his cabin tomorrow night. "Read a book!" I tell him. But no. He insists on coming. He wants to be there. Just my luck. The toughest critic of them all wants to show his support, I guess, for his fellow passenger. One of the reasons I've never done my act in New York City is to avoid getting my brains beat out by the critics, and now here I am trapped on a ship with Frank Rich. Where did I go wrong? The good news is the girls are still cheerful as ever. I'm the one who's wearing the long face.

Thursday ☆ August 25

Okay, it's my birthday. Too many candles, too little time. I'm aging at sea. At least I'm surrounded by my loved ones—and also by hundreds of foreign people who have no idea who I am. Why am I so gloomy? Let me count the ways. First, it's another gray day. Haven't seen the sun since we left New York. White caps out there are tossing. I'm rapidly losing my tan and also the will to live. I can't sleep at night. I can't sleep during the day. And tonight's the night. I'm full of dread, but must press on. I have two shows to do. Rich is coming to the second one. Some birthday present. Too late to stop him now.

Stanley Yerlow, my piano teacher in New York, has come along as my conductor tonight. He opens the show with his piano wizardry. The Europeans are wowed. Then the timpani drum beats (or is it my heart?) and the announcer introduces me. I swear that I hear people in the audience murmuring, "Who? Who?" And I'm on.

Well, it wasn't so bad. The reaction is better than I expected. Some people just sat and stared, so I convinced myself they didn't understand English. Mostly, however, they all seem to enjoy the show, even if they've never heard of Regis and Kathie Lee. One show down, one more to go.

This time Frank and Alex are in the audience with their two handsome sons. Joy and the girls are there, too. The show goes very well. I do my usual search for a co-host among audience volunteers. Then I crown one woman Miss America and tears well up in her eyes. Unfortunately, they're not tears of happiness. She looks panicked and whispers to me as I place a crown on her head, "No, please don't! I'm a feminist!" But it's too late and she stoically accepts her coronation. I feel terrible as she walks the stage without smiling. I see Frank lean forward straining to hear what she was saying to me. But by now I'm singing, "Here she is . . . Miss America!" I dodge that bullet, finish the show, and get a thumbs-up from Joy and the girls. Frank and Alex come backstage and couldn't be more complimentary. Except Frank wants to know about that tearful Miss America. I shrug and tell him, "What can I say? I have a powerful effect on women, Frank. They melt around me." I'm not sure he's buying. But the shows are over and I couldn't be more relieved. I don't mean to be paranoid, but I plan on scouring the *New York*

Times for the next month, just in case they have a change of heart.

The journey is over. We pull into the pier at Southampton just as the sun finally comes out. Only now, once the cruise ends, do we get sun! When I boarded this ship, I was young and rested and tan. Now I arrive in England old and haggard and untanned. But the girls held up beautifully and we had a nice family time, with lots of talk about the past and their future. We're packed and ready to go ashore, but suddenly Joy can't find her wallet. After all the lecturing I received when I lost my wallet in San Diego, she's now missing hers. And she never used it once on the trip, never took it out of her carry-on bag. I feel badly because I know how frustrating it is. We start to think that maybe she never brought the wallet to begin with, that it's at home where she left it. We'll see. Meanwhile, I've got about four dollars left in my pocket after all the tipping on the ship, then tips for the limo driver who brings us to Heathrow Airport and for the curbside baggage handlers. That means I've got four bucks to get home on. At the ticket counter, we're told that the first-class seats we'd been promised on British Airways have been downgraded to business class. Joy is not happy. To her, a deal is a deal. The Furies are building within her. We call my William Morris agent, Kenny De Camillo, to see if he can straighten things out. He can't. We'll fly business class, which is fine with me but less fine with Joy. But we can't even get on the plane, because the air-conditioning is broken. We're delayed. So much for British efficiency. So much for this trip. Get me home. Please. Just get me home. (Fortunately, home is where we find Joy's wallet, right where she left it. Then we collapse.)

Monday ☆ August 29

I am Net Man. Net Man marauds over tennis courts. Net Man cannot be denied. Today, Net Man welcomes back tennis star Chris Evert, who possesses a healthy respect for the Net Man's prowess. Chris comes on the show and immediately reminds me of our last meeting on the court. She had invited me to a tennis tournament last October in Florida. I rarely play in these tournaments, but she's persuasive, so I grabbed my sneakers and my big Weed racket and went to Boca Raton for the big match. My partner was the great Billie Jean King. Chris had President George Bush as her partner. Yes, Net Man did mixed-doubles battle with the past leader of the free world! Everybody says George Bush is a terrific guy. And when Bush told me that—out of friendship for Chris—he flew all night to be there, even I was convinced. He's a pretty good athlete, too. ESPN was taping the match so they miked me for my comments. The crowd really got into it and, of course, I couldn't resist having some fun with the former president. If he slammed a shot past me, I'd yell, "That's it! I'll never vote for you again!" It was a fairly close match, too. I love playing with pros because they force you to be so much better than you are. That's when it occurred to me that it must be Joy and our weekend opponents who have been holding me back on the courts. I could be so much better. But now I was playing against the former president of the United States. And I thought, Come on! Come to your senses! Let the guy win! He flew all night to get here. Don't let him face the wrath of the big Weed. No one should have to go up against the big Weed, as wielded by Net Man!

It was close. It was tenacious. But now I am ready to tell the truth: I let him win. Why not? It seemed like the politically correct thing to do.

Wednesday ☆ *August 31*

Kathie Lee does the Letterman show tonight. This morning on our show—for fun—I try to shake her up a little bit. After all, sitting next to Dave is a tough enough seat, but then his writers sometimes like to make matters worse by springing surprises on you. "I just want you to be cool," I tell her, "in case anything weird happens with Dave tonight." Of course, I have no idea whether anything is planned for her. I suspect, in fact, that it'll be a very straight interview, but I can't resist throwing a scare into her.

Then around one o'clock this afternoon, my phone

rings. It's Maria Pope, the Letterman segment-producer whose job somehow includes calling me almost every week, whenever Dave wants me to barge onto the show and run around his aisles like a mad man. Rob Burnett, Dave's head writer, likes telling me that I'm known over there as The Show Saver. Of course, I think he's just sucking up, but Show Saver does have a nice ring to it. Anyway, when Maria calls it usually means it's another job for The Show Saver. So today she says, "Kathie is coming on to promote her exercise video and Dave thought it would be funny for you to come out carrying a basket of your own exercise videos and do the usual thing—run down the aisle distributing your tapes to the crowd, give one to Kathie, then run back out the aisle again." I say, "Well, all right, if I have the time—maybe I'll do it."

But, of course, I go down there and put on my workout clothes. I'm supposed to be part of a convoluted plan: At the top of the show, Dave makes one of his prank calls to the pay phone out on 53rd Street, brings in the guy who answered, locks him behind one of the theater side-doors, where he's supposed to think of a question to ask Kathie Lee. Then during her interview, Dave pulls this guy out to ask his question. Naturally, it's a Cody question. Then he sends the guy back to the door and tells him to wait. That's when I sneak in and wait with the guy, so that the next time Dave opens the door, I burst out with my videotapes, throwing them everywhere. Last time I did this, I stopped in front of Dave's desk and performed some simple push-ups. This time, I up the ante. I explode from the door, run over to his desk, prop my feet on a guest chair, position my hands below the rise on the actual stage floor and, at this perilous angle, start doing push-ups. Jack La Lanne, eat your heart out! The crowd goes crazy. Then I get up, throw out the rest of the videotapes, and leave. Poor Kathie. After the show, she tells one of the talent coordinators, "He was on longer than I was." And I really didn't mean to be. She probably thinks I knew all along that I was coming on, but I had no idea until that call for Show Saver.

Doing the Letterman show is always a terrific jolt of adrenaline. Part of the excitement for me, anyway, is seeing the technical things his staff can do. The simplest things are done so well. The lighting, for instance. Their lighting makes Kathie look absolutely fabulous. I know she's a good-looking lady, but maybe I'm used to seeing her in our lighting, which is spotty and a little dismal. With Dave's lighting—wow! What a knockout. (And that skimpy little wisp of a dress didn't hurt, either. How did *that* get past Frank?) Then there's the sound system, which allows the studio audience to actually hear everything Letterman says. In our studio, I have to yell in order to be heard by the audience. (And you thought that was just my temperament!) As a matter of fact, I've made these key points in my current contract renegotiations. These technical problems really drive me crazy. And it's the technical expertise that makes the Letterman show so irresistible to me. It's an electric show. I'm jealous.

It happens every autumn: For me, the opening of Notre Dame football is when my new year begins. Everything is fresh. Anything is possible. All summer long, I go to Radu's gym on 57th Street, always with the team in mind, working hard on my own body, getting ready in case Coach Lou Holtz needs me. Last Saturday, the season officially got started in Evanston, Illinois, where Notre Dame crushed Northwestern 42–16, stoking my expectations to the heavens. After a year of injury, Ron Powlus threw four touchdowns in his very first game! It was more than I expected. It was awesome. What a season we're about to have. But tomorrow is the real beginning—the first home game of the new season against a tough opponent—and I'll be there where I have to be, on those God-kissed pastures of South Bend, Indiana.

It's the big Michigan game. A key meeting of two legendary rival teams. (Lou, I'm coming!) I've already called my friend Dick Ebersol, president of NBC Sports, who assured me that a seat is waiting for me on the NBC private jet bound for South Bend. We'll leave at ten-thirty this morning, right after the show. So I jump in a cab, race out to Teterboro Airport, where we take off and climb into the skies. I'm full of anticipation.

That's when my heart plummets. I don't much believe in omens, yet I'm instantly overcome with dread. Why? I suddenly realize I'm aboard the very same plane on which I had flown back to New York after the last game of last season—Notre Dame's heartbreaking loss to Boston College. I'll never forget it. The pain! The anguish! The whole season destroyed on the final play of the year! Now it all comes rushing back. And I'm exactly where I left off last year. I'm even staring at the same carpeting. The same fixtures inside the same cabin. I say to myself, "My God, is this déjà vu? Am I jinxing the team by flying on this thing?" Please, don't make me relive that horror!

Yes, I'd been there for the B.C. game, witnessing the devastation from the skybox: B.C. starting out fast, racking up some early touchdowns. In that last quarter, Notre Dame—coming back, fighting furiously—went ahead by a point in the last minute of play. B.C. had less than a minute to get down field, and they did it. Scored a last-second field goal, winning by two points. Notre Dame was deprived of the championship. Everything turned black. We drove to the airport in the NBC van and I couldn't speak. The flight home was the longest and the worst I'd ever made.

And now I'm back in the same plane! I yell, "Stop this thing! I gotta get off!" But it's too late. An hour and a half later, we're gliding over the Golden Dome. There's the campus and my old dorms, the Convocation Center, the football stadium, the two lakes—all of it absolutely majestic. I lead the NBC guys through a chorus of the Notre Dame fight song—"Cheer, cheer for old Notre Dame!" And my spirit soars again, as it always does every time I come back here.

I remember coming back in 1974. That trip simply saved my life. It was early fall, and I had been out of work for nearly a year. I'd been trying to make ends meet with a variety of jobs around the country. My first boss, Al Flanagan, who gave me the stagehand's job at KCOP-TV in Hollywood in the fifties, hired me that summer to do sports on his Denver station. Afterward, I had also filled in for several months as host of *A.M. Chicago* and gotten a very good reaction. In the fall, they would name a permanent host. I felt confident. I needed that job. And Chicago was Joy's hometown. Hollywood had become a dead end, and real-life responsibilities were closing in from all sides. Joy and I already had Joanna and were expecting Jennifer. Bills were mounting. Money was tight.

I worked in Chicago for the rest of the summer and into the fall, getting closer all the time to that permanent job, which I felt would be mine. Ironically, my producer at WLS-TV in Chicago was Rick Ludwin, now the director of entertainment for NBC and my boss on the Miss America Pageant. My co-host was Sandi Freeman, who went on to have her own CNN talk show. Brandon Tartikoff was the WLS promotion director. And Lew Erlich, who like Tartikoff would go on to network hierarchy, was the station manager. One day, Lew decided to check out some other hosts—just to make sure I was the right one—and he brought up a young fellow from Houston. I knew this guy. In 1968, he had done a radio interview with me when I was appearing in town in *A Funny Thing Happened on the Way to the Forum*. His name was Steve Edwards. He looked familiar to Lew Erlich when they met. He looked familiar because he and Steve were boyhood pals from the Bronx. Even went to the same grammar school. Funny, I was from the Bronx, too, but I went to the wrong school. Steve got the job. (A decade later, when I finally moved to New York, he would take over my job on *A.M. Los Angeles*.) Anyway, I was devastated.

It was a shocker. I left the station, totally unglued. I needed that job, wanted it, and now it was gone.

I was supposed to fly back to L.A., but I couldn't. Everybody knew I was out auditioning around the country. I kept coming back empty-handed. It was embarrassing. My confidence was destroyed. I didn't have the heart to tell Joy, one more time, that I didn't make the cut. So I got in my rental car and started to drive aimlessly around Chicago. I got on the Skyway, going east, which led to the Indiana Tollway. I just kept driving. A million things were racing through my mind. Suddenly, I realized that I was heading to South Bend. To Notre Dame. Why not go back? Give yourself time to think, to sort things out, get your spirits up.

Ninety minutes later, I swung off the tollway onto the Old Dixie Highway, turned left at the golf course, and there was the campus: the Sacred Heart steeple, the Golden Dome looming above it. How I wish I could have started all over again. I turned left again on Notre Dame Avenue. Went up that famous road heading straight for the Dome, rising over the trees. . . . The old cemetery on my left, the stadium on my right. . . . It was all coming back. . . . All those great years of spirit and tradition and discipline. I turned right again and headed for the football offices at the ACC Building, behind Notre Dame Stadium—the House That Rockne Built. I went past the door to the team's dressing room at the stadium. And there was that tree standing there, all alone, by the door. Oh, that tree . . .

How well I remembered a dark, dreary day in 1950. The second game of that season. Purdue stormed into the stadium with Dale Samuels at quarterback, passed the Irish silly, and handed us our first loss in five years. Five years! It had been so long since Notre Dame had lost a game, the whole student body had no concept of defeat. We'd never experienced it or considered it an option. Loss. It was a shock, a real crusher. We all just sat in the stands after the game ended, rain pouring down on us. Stunned. The pain was enormous. Until then, every Saturday had been a celebration. For some reason, a bunch of us wandered over to the team dressing room near that tree—the tree that had stood firm during so many postgame celebrations. The tree now anchored this dreadful scene in the rain. The door opened and there was Coach Frank Leahy—this mythical coach, already a legend, whose teams knew only triumph. He had come out to talk to us. For the first time, he would explain defeat to us. How we should accept defeat on a football field and in life. How we should use it to make ourselves stronger, to face and overcome the next adversity. Because there was always going to be a next adversity. Leahy could make the hair on the back of your neck stand up when he spoke and, even in the gloom of that late afternoon, we were moved and strengthened. All of a sudden, it didn't hurt so much. Didn't feel so bad. I moved away from that old tree renewed.

And so here I was, twenty years later, staring again at that tree with a new emptiness burning in my gut. Nearly twenty years in the broadcast business and nothing to show for it. But that didn't matter to Coach Ara Parseghian and his great coaching staff—George Kelly, Joe Yonto, Tom Pagna. They gave me a locker, threw some Notre Dame sweats at me, and dragged me out onto Cartier Field. The old practice field. Nobody cared about *A.M. Chicago* there. "There are bigger things ahead," Ara said, always confident.

I jogged around the track, ran some wind sprints. (Maybe they weren't exactly sprints, but I ran as fast as I could.) I caught some passes and watched Ara and the coaches time the incoming freshmen. One of them was an eighteen-year-old quarterback from Monongahela, Pennsylvania, named Joe Montana. Joe wasn't very fast, but he sure could throw, and I made a mental note to remember that name. Of course, for the next twenty years, you couldn't avoid that name. Suddenly, the afternoon wasn't so bad anymore. Most of the anger and frustration of that morning had evaporated. I was back on campus, once again running like a colt and feeling like a freshman. That night I went to sleep in George Kelly's spare bedroom, near his pub room—the site of so many wonderful Saturday night victory parties. My legs were tired but my mind was clear. I wouldn't quit. I'd keep going. Just like Frank Leahy said—I would be made stronger because of the defeat.

And now twenty more years have passed. My daughter J.J. is a junior at Notre Dame and loves it as much as I did all those years ago. Now it's the eve of the first home game of the season. The lakes are shimmering in the sun. The campus is buzzing. And Lou Holtz has asked me to speak at tonight's pep rally. I'm ready! I'm always ready for Lou!

The crowd is big, noisy, hopeful. I get up, take a deep breath and holler: "In the last two years, we've had two fabulous teams, yet neither one of them could win the championship. They came close. They deserved it. They earned it. They didn't win it. So now we have this team and they know better than anyone else that this is their season! Their year! Their chance! Their turn to bring a national championship back to Notre Dame, where it belongs!" I've got the crowd roaring. "We have three things on our side," I keep yelling. "The greatest sports fans in the world! The greatest tradition in sports! And the best coach in college football! Let me tell you how good Lou Holtz is," I go on. "You could kidnap him on the day of the game. You could tie him up, blindfold him, hide him in a cellar in Goshen, Indiana! And he would still out-coach the other guy!" Crowd goes wild. Band plays the victory march. Lou speaks and brings down the house. We're all on fire.

But I'm not through for the night. The NBC guys ask me to talk to some of the game's sponsors after the rally. So I go to their dinner and try to explain how I feel about Notre Dame. "Once you are touched by that spirit," I say, "it becomes part of your soul. I've been to some of the great places in the world. But, for me, there is no place better than this campus. These fifteen hundred acres mean everything to me. You'll know exactly what I mean, as you walk around tonight and feel all those ghosts— Rockne, the Gipper, the Four Horsemen! You are on hallowed ground!"

Then on to another dinner: I sit with J.J. at the University Club, where the father of one of her classmates is hosting a reunion for a hundred friends. And, once again, I'm asked to get up and say a few words. My third speech of the evening! I'm getting exhausted! But I will never turn down an opportunity to talk about Notre Dame. And I can see J.J. looking so happy, loving this place. It makes my heart burst with pride. As much as she loves it now, she'll love it even more later. It's something no one will ever be able to take away from her. Anyway, when I finally get to bed, I'm almost ready to stop talking. Almost. And I've almost forgotten about that jinxed plane. Almost.

Morning is electric. I walk over to the NBC truck with Dick Ebersol and his network lieutenants. Tailgate parties are in full swing. Irish flags flap in the breeze. People yell, "Regis! Regis!" And my favorite question: "Where's Kathie Lee?" Ebersol and I take our places in the skybox. The game begins. It's close and hard, back and forth. Michigan ahead, Notre Dame driving back. "My gosh, isn't this what happened at the B.C. game?" I think. No, couldn't be. With a minute left, Powlus fires a touchdown pass to Derrick Mayes in the end zone. We go ahead by two points. Wait a second! There's a minute left! "My gosh, isn't this what happened at the B.C. game?" This time I say it out loud. But it can't be. They can't come back like B.C. It just can't happen again! And then I think of the plane and that sinking feeling I had when I got aboard. Am I jinxing the Irish? Please, don't let it be me! Suddenly, Michigan is in field-goal range. A few seconds left. No, no, no! Don't let it happen again! They kick, it's up, it's far enough—they make it. They win. I can't believe it. I can't talk. I may never talk again. Forty years later and I still have trouble with it. Nothing tears me up like a Notre Dame football loss. And the flight back to New York is longer than the one last year.

Thursday ☆ *September 15*

How exactly does Miss America get crowned by a guy like me? Even I wonder sometimes. I mean, it makes sense for someone like Kathie Lee—the human sunbeam—to take part in a coronation. After all, to hear her tell it, she's coronated every night by Frank the Human Love Machine. Anyway, we have the job together—following in the footsteps of legendary emcee Bert Parks. We're now in our fourth year as co-hosts of the Miss America Pageant—the biggest, most famous contest of beauty, brains, talent, and poise anywhere. It's also one of the few annual televised events left that involves the modeling of swim suits.

This year's big news: For the first time in pageant history, the ladies will do the swimwear modeling in their *bare feet*! No more of those traditional high heels. And this has caused shock waves? Beautiful women without shoes? Who cares? The real shame here is that the hosts don't get to emcee shoeless. I don't want to brag, but it's no secret that I was blessed with beautiful feet. Feet are my strong suit! Kathie Lee has a halo; I have spectacular feet. Perfectly smooth. Not a bunion or a callous. I've compared them with the best and prevailed every time. Julio Iglesias came on the show recently, wearing sandals and flaunting his handsome Latin feet. I had to remove my shoes and bring him back down to earth. Sorry, Julio. You're a nice guy and a great singer, but just keep your shoes on around me!

After today's show, we head for Atlantic City. I ride down there in a car alone. Kathie Lee gathers her entourage—Cassidy, the nanny, the live-in couple, the assistant—then commandeers a jet and they all fly down. That's how it goes with us: I'm the loner, out on the open road. She's flying high, with gang in tow. To prepare for the Saturday night show, we spend a good part of the day at the Convention Center, where rehearsals have been grinding on all week. Then, at dinner, we get to know the contestants, trying to put together the faces with the names with the states. As always, these girls are sweet and personable, but full of drive and huge career plans. They all desperately want to win the big scholarship prize money that comes with the crown. No timid little shrinking violets in this setting.

Later, we watch the final trials of the talent competition, along with Leonard Horn, the Atlantic City attorney who runs the pageant. Leanza Cornett, the incumbent Miss America, hosts these proceedings. At one point, I get up and go to the men's room. My first mistake of the weekend. Inside the bathroom, I suddenly hear Leanza's voice over the sound system: "Ladies and gentlemen, in our audience tonight are the stars of their own show and the hosts of our show for the last four years . . . How about a rousing hand for REGIS AND KATHIE LEE!" At this precise moment, I'm in no position to take a bow. I'm facing a wall. I'm as indisposed as a man can be, having started something I can't stop. If you know what I mean. Meanwhile, all alone in her seat, Kathie Lee rises and drinks in all of the applause. I hear Leanza say, "Where's Regis? Where's Regis?" Then I hear Kathie Lee shout with relish: "He went to the men's room!" What a classy guy I am. This never happened to

Bert Parks! I finish my business as quickly as my metabolism allows. Then I run back into the auditorium, where the show has resumed and, frankly, nobody cares whether or not I'm available to thank them for the nice hand.

Now for my early prediction: By now, I've gotten pretty accurate at picking winners. And tonight I immediately see sparks coming from Miss Alabama, Heather Whitestone. She's the young woman who's been hearing-impaired since she was eighteen months old. She performs an interpretive ballet (without actually hearing the music) and the crowd reaction is wholehearted and supportive. She's clearly the favorite—all of the contestants seem very protective of her. We'll know for sure Saturday night, but I've got a feeling that she'd make a tremendous impact as Miss America.

Friday ☆ September 16

Time to answer Bryant Gumbel's hard-hitting questions about the swimsuit competition. Because NBC broadcasts the pageant, we do a live on-location interview every year for the Friday morning *Today Show*. We get to do battle with Bryant, who can't wait to talk about the bare feet controversy. Please! When was the last time you saw high heels on a beach? What's the big deal? So, by eight-fifteen, Kathie Lee and I are in place at the Convention Center. We do a little tease shot at eight-thirty and then wait our turn. First, Katie Couric has to visit with a computer wizard, who never stops talking. And Katie keeps asking questions. She can't get enough of this guy. And we're still waiting. Finally, they throw it to us. We have exactly two and a half minutes! Then the Big Brush-Off! I complain: "Bryant, the computer guy was on forever! This is it for us? Come on!" And Bryant laughs and laughs and keeps saying, "Bare feet, huh?" Who cares?

All day, we rehearse and rehearse, working on intros and cues. I feel the anticipation heighten. Tonight, the ladies parade along the boardwalk and we sneak off to dinner. And what an unforgettable dinner it is. Gelman has finally arrived in Atlantic City. He comes down every year. Says he does it to give us support. But I know better. (It couldn't have anything to do with all of these attractive, single young women. Couldn't possibly!) Kathie Lee's parents have also come to town, as well as her secretary and Mary Kellogg, our liaison with Disney. Anyway, Kathie arranges for us to head over to a little restaurant a few blocks from Trump Plaza, where everyone is staying. "Meet us at seven-fifteen in front of the hotel," Kathie tells me. So I go down and wait. And wait.

People are yelling, "Hey, Regis! REGIS!" I wave back and continue to wait. Then a couple of guys come over to keep me company. One of them wants to know if I think he looks like Dustin Hoffman. I tell him Miss New Hampshire looks more like Dustin Hoffman than he does. (And, believe me, Miss New Hampshire does *not* look like Dustin Hoffman!) Meanwhile, nobody has come down to meet me. And that's because Kathie Lee changed our plans without telling me. It turns out that they're all upstairs at the hotel in Ivana's restaurant. And there's a lovefest under way at the table that might change the course of talk-show history.

Maybe it's because of the wine. Maybe it's just fate. But by the time someone comes to fetch me, a miracle has occurred. The rift of the century has been defused. Kathie Lee and Gelman have officially made up—ending a long, uncomfortable war of silences and dirty looks that's become part of my daily world. For my part, I've always enjoyed the tension between them. I figure that if everybody always gets along, our audience might fall asleep. Because Gelman is the producer, he decides who is booked as a guest and who isn't. Sometimes, though, Kathie Lee has disagreed with Gelman's ideas and it eventually created an icy wall between them. The breaking point, I think, came when Gelman refused to book Art Buchwald, an old pal of the Giffords. She pushed and pushed and Gelman wouldn't cave and it seethed in her heart and just kept festering.

But now suddenly all is forgiven! As I sit watching this, I feel my fun ending. Gelman is actually saying, "Kathie Lee, I love you!" And she's stroking his hand and saying, "Michael, I love *you*!" It's a terrible sight. Life is about to get boring. No more arguments. No more looks. No more daggers. How dull things are going to be! Now Gelman has her enraptured with stories about his organic garden! And she's going on about the joys of having children—while Gelman smiles and nods! Is this some kind of bad dream? Can somebody just wake me up! But no. It's actually happening. I can't take any more! I don't want to be here. Finally, when I can stand no more, I call for the check, pay it, and quickly make my escape. Love is in the air and my stomach hurts.

T he big day. A full day of rehearsing and nurturing my throat for the famous "There she is . . . " coronation song. Kenny Rogers will also sing to the ladies tonight, performing the old hit, "You Are So Beautiful." So all day, I take every opportunity to run up behind him and impress him with my best gravelly Kenny Rogers impersonation. "You are soooo beeeyoooteefulllll," I croon to him. At least he keeps smiling. Meanwhile, I spend as much time as I can in my dressing room, where I've got the Notre Dame game on. At halftime they're down, 20–7. But I go back to my hotel to see them win, 21–20, which gives me the strength to go on.

It's always interesting to experience the final moments before the show. The dancers are on the floor stretching. The judges are wide-eyed and slightly dazed. And the contestants are hopeful, pensive, and almost giddy. You get attached to these ladies. You'd like to see all of them win. Backstage, Kathie Lee and I watch the opening number. The crowd is all attention. Then, the announcer booms: "Ladies and gentlemen, your hosts for the Miss America Pageant—Regis Philbin and Kathie Lee Gifford!" I start to walk across the stage and she's heading toward me from the other side. I grab her hand and we walk together to centerstage. The contestants are flanking us, applauding—it's an exciting moment.

So I begin: "Hello, everybody. We're happy to be here!" And, at this exact moment, her earring slips off and falls to the floor. It's a whopper of an earring, too. Hits the stage like a boulder. She's panicked. She can't be here on live prime-time television—the most glamorous event of the season—with only one earring. Nothing else to do but get down on all fours and find it. Our big entrance—and I'm bent over on the floor like a dog! Would Bert Parks do this?

Anyway, I scoop it up, she clamps it back on her ear—and the pageant has officially begun! Just how difficult is it to do the Miss America show? Does the pressure get to us? Actually, after what we do day after day on our own show, the pageant is a comparative breeze. Our show is unscripted. But this night is timed to the letter. There's the teleprompter right in front of us with everything we have to say. It's quite a luxury. The competition winds down to the final ten. Then the final five. And then it's time to shut off the prompter and go to work.

This is my favorite part of the show—interviewing the five finalists. One question on any subject I choose and one focusing on their main interest or platform. Miss Alabama is among the finalists, of course, and I still think she'll win. But anything is possible. The ladies are visibly nervous. As it turns out, Miss Alabama is the first one I interview. I make it a point to look directly at her and not talk too fast. (At lunch yesterday, I was too fast for her. But no problem now.) She reacts beautifully and spontaneously—as do the other finalists—especially to my first question. The second question about their vital interests sometimes brings more of a rehearsed response. But you do root for them all.

And then that moment comes. The cards with the results are delivered to me. The first four runners-up (or is it runner-ups? We've never figured that out!), followed by the winner. There's a lot of lip-biting as they line up. And, one by one, I announce their names and states. Unfailingly, they react joyfully, even as they lose. When I used to watch the show at home, I always wondered how they managed this. And standing two feet away from them, I wonder even more. Maybe it's just relief. Finally, the winner: Heather Whitestone. Miss Alabama. The crowd goes crazy. She'd been their favorite all through the preliminaries. Now it is official. A good choice, too. She's down the aisle, waving to the audience. Kathie Lee and I do our chorus of that song, and it's over for another year.

But the toughest part of the whole night comes after the show. How to get back to my room? The audience spills out of the Convention Center in massive herds. I'm still wearing my tux, toting a garment bag. I weave through my gauntlet of shortcuts and slip into a side door of the Trump Plaza. So far, so good. Except now Trump's elaborate system of escalators has broken down. There's a monumental crush of people at the bottom waiting for the thing to start. I'm being swarmed. There's no air. "Where's Trump?" I yell. "Get him out of bed! What good are all those millions if he can't get his damned escalators to run!" The crowd laughs. I'm getting worked up. Please! Can't a guy just get to his room and collapse! Trump must have heard me. Just when I'm sure I'll be spending the night in the lobby, the escalators start. And I go to bed.

Up early. I board a little eight-seater plane bound for Westchester and fly home with Kathie Lee, baby Cassidy, and her assistant, Taryn. It's a bumpy flight. Kathie panics and shoots me a few of those "This could be it!" looks. I keep thinking: Maybe this is why God wanted her to make up with Gelman! But we level off and land at around ten-thirty. Joy and Frank have driven out separately to meet our plane and decide it would be funny if they climbed into the same car to wait. We're supposed to get the impression that they, too, had spent a lovely weekend together. (It's funny, all right, but I still wonder about those two.)

I take the wheel of our car and Joy asks the dreaded question: "Mind if I make one stop before we go home?" She says Joanna needs some shelving for her apartment at Brown. Here I am—fresh from Miss America, fresh from presiding in a tudexo on prime-time television— wandering around a furniture warehouse store in Connecticut on a Sunday morning. I'm looking at wooden planks. People are staring and asking, "Aren't you Regis? What are you doing here? We just saw you last night." For some odd reason, nobody expects to see me down at the local Pergament shortly after crowning a new Miss America. And they've got a point. I mean, it's not right! A man like me shouldn't be seen like this. Shouldn't I be lounging in a luxurious suite somewhere? I should try to create some mystique about living the good life, but reality keeps getting in the way! Anyway, we find a terrific shelf. I load it into the car and we drive home.

Monday ☆ *September 19*

Here she is: Miss America herself is our first guest today. Heather Whitestone from Alabama is about to begin the experience of her life, a yearlong reign as goodwill ambassador and role model. Meanwhile, I'm getting very nervous. The Kathie Lee–Gelman lovefest that began at dinner in Atlantic City the other night continues to blossom. When I recount that horrible episode during Host Chat, Kathie Lee suddenly jumps from her stool, walks over to Gelman, and plants a smooch on his lips. This startles me. And, of course, it startles him. What exactly is going on here? This is one dangerous, unpredictable woman. Later, I have lunch at the Russian Tea Room with my agent Jimmy Griffin and several people come by to talk about the kiss. I'll have to tell her about this tomorrow. Can she sustain what she's started? I wonder.

More about that kiss. From today's Host Chat, verbatim:

ME: Everywhere I went yesterday, people were talking about that kiss.

HER: Frank said he saw it and turned off the TV. It made him sick.

ME: And I don't blame him one bit. And all I said was, there was some bonding going on down there in Atlantic City. We were all at dinner—you and Gelman were making up and kind of slobbering all over each other, boring the heck out of everybody else there. There was no reason for you to get up and go over and do what you did to Gelman. A handshake would have sufficed. A kiss on the forehead would have been nice. But a kiss on the lips, please! So I stand firmly with Frank, coming down on this kissing on the lips. I mean, there was no reason.

HER: I was in a generous mood.

ME: Oh, were you ever generous!

HER: Well, they settled the strike in Atlantic City.

ME: And that's what made you feel so good? Very weak excuse. At lunch at the Russian Tea Room, everyone wanted to know, "Why?" I said, "I don't know. Leave me alone. I have no answer for you."

HER: [*sarcastic*] Oh, I'm sure they asked about it at the Russian Tea Room!

ME: As a matter of fact, that's exactly what they asked me about. That kiss!

HER: Oh, Reege. Don't make anything out of it. The truth is, Gelman and I have had a rough spell where we disagreed about a lot of things. We didn't have the same opinion of what should be on the show.

ME: And now that's changed?

HER: He's doing exactly what I want him to do and we're getting along extremely well.

ME: Well, that's what I thought. I knew you'd probably whip him into shape. And you did. You prevailed because you are woman! Hear you roar!

Wednesday ☆ September 21

Cindy Crawford, my partner in body-building, is on the show today. We've spent a lot of time perspiring together. Both of us work out at Radu's Gym, where you get to see people exactly the way they are. No frills. Just sweat. And, more than once, I've caught Cindy staring at me, admiring my Olympian muscles, my sheer masculine power. Who can blame her? She's only human, no matter how beautiful she is! We met at the gym about five years ago, shortly before she exploded on the national consciousness. Yes, she's a great beauty. But more than that, she's as natural and down-to-earth as they come and not afraid to work hard at the gym. She likes to challenge me to shoot hoops on Radu's basketball court. She's good, but I beat her every time. And she hates to lose. Just like me. Lately, I've noticed she's been a little quiet and pensive as the press scrutinizes her marriage to Richard Gere. But she doesn't talk about it. So we don't talk about it. I hope, for her sake, it will all work out.

Thursday ☆ ***September 22***

Ashley, one of my cats, has made the new issue of *Life* magazine. It's no big deal. The whole magazine is devoted to celebrities and their pets. There's a picture of me holding Ashley, with that goofy tooth sticking out of his mouth. What a strange cat. He has his own rhythm, his own agenda, this cat. For days, he will ignore me, simply disappear around the apartment. And then, on certain nights when you've forgotten all about him, he will stride with purpose into the bedroom. Usually I'm in bed when he comes in. Our eyes meet and, if I slap the bed, he will run over, leap onto it, and come directly to me. We both know what he wants. He wants his back scratched. In fact, I can scratch him into a semi-coma within seconds. His eyes glaze, his back arches, as my fingernails gently run along his spine. It's almost spooky. He'll be practically out cold. And there we are. A man and his cat. Then without warning, he'll get up and jump off and go about his business elsewhere. Next time I see him, he will look at me like I'm the devil himself and race away from me in a panic. I think he's nuts.

Our two cats entered our lives ten years ago. The girls just had to have kittens, just couldn't live without them, so we began a search for the perfect cats. We found Ashley in a very expensive home in Chappaqua. And Scarlett (the girls were going through a *Gone With the Wind* phase) was waiting for us in a Brooklyn tenement apartment. Joy walked up five flights of stairs to the apartment, where at least thirty cats were crawling all over the place. And, ironically, of the two, Scarlett turned out to be the healthiest and the least trouble. She's sweet and affectionate, never a problem unless we drive somewhere. On the other hand, Ashley, with his fancy pedigree, has had all kinds of problems and surgeries. No wonder he's different. Today he's the one who made *Life* magazine. But he doesn't care.

Friday ☆ September 23

Gelman is all excited. For today's show, he has booked what could be the world's biggest tomato. Yes, Gelman has now stooped to booking vegetables! He has quite a vegetable garden out in the Hamptons, so he knows what it takes to make a big, beautiful tomato. The record for the world's biggest tomato is seven pounds, twelve ounces. We found an Ohio farmer who has a contender in his own backyard. This guy nurtured his tomato in new and shocking ways: He spoke to it everyday; he hugged it; he kissed it; he loved it; he treated it like a baby; and at last he has grown it into something resembling a bowling ball. Gelman is beside himself with excitement over this tomato. And today we send a limo to fetch it and bring it over for its final weigh-in. Besides the honor of being proclaimed the World's Biggest Tomato, there's a $100,000 check from Miracle-Gro for the farmer—if indeed it makes the grade. If not, the farmer still gets $10,000. So we bring on the tomato with fuss and fanfare. Even I get a little excited, mostly for the farmer to get that hundred grand. The tomato looks awesome enough. Big and round, but at this point, also a little leaky. The trip from Ohio had apparently taken its toll. Anyway, we finally put the tomato on a strange contraption, a scale the likes of which I have never seen. We all hold our breath, but the scale registers only four pounds, five ounces. Far below the world record. I feel for the farmer, but he did get $10,000 for his trouble, plus a night in a luxurious hotel room with his tomato. Afterward, the phone lines to the show were jammed with irate viewers who figured we robbed the farmer by using that strange scale. I'll admit it *was* a weird-looking scale, the kind only Gelman could have found. But it's too late now.

After the show, I fly to Chicago where Joy is making an appearance to promote her syndicated home-decorating show, *Haven*. Or, as I call it, *The Red Hot Haven Show*. She does a terrific job as host, and has great rapport with the guests and a feel for the subject matter. Frankly, she's getting too big to pinch-hit on our show. We've made a plan to meet later in South Bend, where we'll see J.J. and attend Saturday's Notre Dame–Purdue game. Joy will fly to South Bend once her business is done for the day. Meanwhile, I'll rent a car in Chicago and drive directly to Notre Dame. Seems like a reasonable plan, even for us, but I should have known better. Nothing is ever easy for us. I made a reservation for a car at Avis. When I finally get to the car rental counter, after a torturous walk through the cavernous O'Hare Airport, I see Avis is the only rental agency with a long line of customers. No waiting anywhere else. This line, however, takes forever. Finally, it's my turn. I get the key and car assignment. The flight to Chicago took about as long is it does to rent the car.

I wait outside for the bus that shuttles you to the car lot. Here comes a Hertz bus. Then a National bus. Then a Budget bus. Then another Hertz bus. Then another National bus. Come on! Where's my Avis bus? I count six Hertz buses, five National buses, and five Budget buses before the Avis bus finally shows up. Now I am fuming. And guess what? The bus is packed. But I don't care. The doors fly open and I hit the crowd like a battering ram. I push my way on and find myself cheek-to-jowl with an elderly woman, who says, "Aren't you Regis Philbin? What are you doing here?"

What am I doing here? I'm trying to order a chicken salad sandwich, lady! What does she think I'm doing here? We stop at the Delta terminal, where two empty Avis buses zoom past ours. Just my luck. Timing is everything, I guess.

At last, I make the long drive to South Bend, and meet Joy and J.J., who looks as happy as ever. Somehow, that makes all of the hassle worth it.

We drive around the Notre Dame campus this morning before the Purdue game and, as usual, I'm overcome with nostalgia. My old dorms are there, just the way I left them. Only everything around them is even more beautiful. Dillon Hall, my junior-year residence. The dining hall, where I met and later dated a girl named Joyce, who worked on the food line. (Last year, she showed up at a signing party for our cookbook in South Bend. Still looks good.) Then, on the other side—Fisher Hall, my senior-year residence. I remember how my friend Frank Varrichione had to climb through Mike Tucci's first-floor window there when he'd returned to campus past curfew. I go on reminiscing aloud like this, until I realize Joy and J.J. are talking about something else. I'm consumed with all these memories, but they've heard them all before. Nobody is listening. Nobody cares.

It's odd to be back at Notre Dame just two weeks after the Michigan upset. Today, the Irish win decisively. They should—Purdue isn't much. This year's team is tough to figure out. They look so good on certain drives. Then, something happens, and they can't make a first down. It could be a long year.

Joy and I drive back to O'Hare after the game through a torrential thunderstorm. I drop her at the airport and return the car to the Avis terminal. And that shuttle bus is waiting—empty and ready to leave for the airport. I have to go to the bathroom, but I don't want to miss this bus. Who knows if there'll be another one. I ask the driver how long before he leaves. He looks at the big clock on the wall and says fifty seconds. I decide not to risk it. Where was this guy yesterday?

Sunday ☆ September 25

Driving to Connecticut, Joy and I listen to our favorite radio station, WQEW. One of the best things about living in New York, particularly on Sunday mornings, is Jonathan Schwartz's program. His radio voice is just above a whisper, but he's so knowledgeable about music. That comes naturally because he's the son of famous songwriter Arthur Schwartz. He's about to play a Mel Tormé rendition of an old Bing Crosby song and mentions how much he enjoyed Mel's appearance on our Friday show. As it happens, Mel's latest CD is a salute to Bing Crosby and the songs he made famous. I knew most of these songs when I was a kid and later I even had the opportunity to sing one in front of Crosby himself on national TV, which was both a thrill and an accident.

It happened on the Bishop show. Joey always used to tell me that, even as a kid, all he ever wanted to be was a comedian. And I'd tell him that, since I was five, my dream was to become Bing Crosby. (Hey, it was a *dream*, okay?) I would endlessly listen to Bing's version of "Pennies from Heaven" and sing along as best I could. Nothing made me happier. So now, years later in Hollywood, Bing came by to do Joey's show. I remember seeing him backstage, walking the hallways. I couldn't take my eyes off of him. Here was this legendary figure, standing around like everyone else. He had no plans to sing on the show and everyone was afraid to ask him. He agreed only to tell a few funny stories, then leave. But Joey had an idea. He would appeal to Bing on the show. He would ask him to sing for me. Except Joey couldn't get the words out straight that night.

He leaned over to Crosby, pointed at me, and said, "Bing, see this kid? He's your biggest fan. It would be the biggest thrill in his life if he could sing 'Pennies from Heaven' to you." I couldn't believe what I was hearing. *If I could sing to him!* Joey meant it the other way around. But it was too late. Bing flashed those steely blue eyes at me and smiled and nodded for me to go ahead. I had no choice. So I went for it. When was I ever going to have a chance to sing for Bing Crosby again? I launched into the obscure opening verse. I sang my guts out. I sang every line, every chorus, every penny in the whole bloody song. Right into Bing's face. But he kept smiling. It must have taken up four minutes of airtime. It even ate into time allotted for the next guest, Dorothy Lamour. When she finally came out, she gave me a sharp look and said, "*You had to sing the whole thing?*"

But something odd resulted from all of this. The next day, I got a telegram from Leonard Mink, the president of Mercury Records, asking if I would be interested in making my own album. I showed the telegram to Joey, who said, "Somebody's playing a joke on you." But, to my amazement (and Joey's), the offer turned out to be on the level. So, with the help of the great arranger Artie Butler, I recorded the album, which was called, *It's Time for Regis!* I probably own most of the copies that were pressed. Except that early this year the album was reissued on compact disc. I'm sure it's currently a riot on the party circuit. For some reason, my likeness on the cover seems to have been oddly retouched. Maybe I'm crazy, but I now bear a strange resemblance to Korean comic Johnny Yune. Of course, Johnny Yune could only dream of singing so well.

Saturday ☆ October 1

It's Fanfare Weekend. For the past few days, we've been at Disney World with seven hundred loyal fans. Once a year, we invite our viewers to join us at a special location for a few days of television shows, concerts, and other special events. It's the brainchild of Mary Kellogg, who is the Disney rep on our show. She used to be the program director for KNXT, the Los Angeles CBS station whose general manager was Jamie Bennett. When Jamie joined Disney's syndication wing, Buena Vista, he took Mary along for the ride, and the first project he proposed was to make our show national. That was in 1988 and, of course, I was all for the idea. And, fortunately, he didn't want us to change a thing, especially the Host Chats. After our successful launch, Jamie went on to other pursuits and Mary became our Disney leader. She's a real mother hen type, out to satisfy all our concerns, not the least of which is to see Gelman safely married. She's the one who makes these trips happen—whether we go to Hawaii, Detroit, Chicago, or Las Vegas. It's a logistical nightmare, but Mary makes it look easy. And now she's brought us to Disney World to meet the fans.

Among the perks for those who've made the trip here are a health-walk with me and a fashion show featuring Kathie and her line of dresses. I collect my gang at EPCOT for a walk around the world, which seems like a funny idea. I've been walking pretty regularly since my heart procedures and think I'm in pretty good shape. But some of these fans really impress me. I get going at a decent clip padding around EPCOT, but I still keep falling behind. How embarrassing. Especially since some of the ladies whipping by seem to have a few years on me. Here I am with my big-shot fitness video on the market, telling everybody to walk and walk and walk, and now these women are walking away from me. I've got to train harder!

Sunday ☆ October 2

Joanna's piece about our *QE2* cruise appears in the travel section of the Sunday *Daily News*. Both girls have now been published in the *News*. They're excellent writers, and it's a thrill for Joy and me to see their bylines. I thought Joanna really captured the essence of the cruise—without mentioning my irrational fear of Frank Rich, for which I'm grateful. And speaking of ships, we attend the Broadway opening of *Showboat* tonight. What a show! We love it. And every notable in New York— from Mike Wallace to Lena Horne—seems to have turned out. Believe it or not, Joy and I find ourselves seated next to Frank Rich and his wife, Alex Witchel. We haven't seen them since the cruise. Frank saw *Showboat* up in Toronto during its tryout period and was lukewarm about it. Tonight he doesn't seem to like it at all. I wonder what it takes to make Frank happy. I'm still reading the *New York Times* closely, fearfully, waiting for his hatchet job on my *QE2* performance. Apparently, his reviewing days are behind him for now—but for how long?

Monday ☆ October 3

I'm still singing the songs from *Showboat*. Especially "Can't Help Loving That Man." I try not to notice the funny looks I get when I do that one. Anyway, Gelman was also at the opening and I tell him that we should have Michel Bell come on the show to sing "Old Man River." It's one of the truly great moments in the theater. The guy has such an incredible voice. If I were the producer, I say, I would have had him on today. Gelman stuns me by saying, " 'Old Man River'? Nobody knows that song!" Art Moore rolls his eyes and I begin to feel like Old Man Talk Show.

Big news. Kathie Lee announces she's been asked to sing the national anthem at the Super Bowl in January. That's quite an honor. It's always one of the most watched televised events of any year. But that won't unnerve her. Nothing unnerves her, especially me. She'll be great, but I can't help making my bid. I explain to her I could learn to play the national anthem on the piano. I could accompany her! It would be great for the show. Think of the publicity value! But she doesn't buy it. "Think about it," I urge her. "I should be a part of this. After all, we're a team!" I'm kidding, of course. But I *could* learn it by January. I know I could.

We also talk on the show about Princess Diana and a new book that's exploiting her name. And I mention that I'm in the midst of writing my own book. This one. That's when she tells me about Cody's book. I should have known he'd write a book, too. First hers, then Frank's, now Cody's. The working title is *Conversations with Cody* and it'll be in stores well before mine. Of course it will. I'd just better hurry up or Cassidy and the family dogs will crank out theirs before I finish this.

Cabdrivers seem to know everything. They never fail to surprise me with their insights. This morning, my cabbie says, "I see you have Pamela Anderson on your show today." I confirm this. The beautiful blonde of *Baywatch* is our guest. The cabdriver then amazes me with the story of how she was discovered: "It happened at a football game," he says. "She was sitting at a Vancouver Lions game wearing a white LaBatts Beer T-shirt. They put her picture up on the scoreboard, the audience cheered, and, bang, she was discovered!"

How does he know these things? I share this story with Kathie Lee during the Host Chat. "And I had to do it the hard way," she grumbles. "Twenty-five years of one-night stands!" I say, "Maybe if you had a T-shirt that fit as well as hers, it wouldn't have taken so long." Then I catch myself: "On second thought," I say, diplomatically, "my co-host can hold her own with any woman in a T-shirt, dead or alive." But she has something else on her mind. She introduces her first love, who happens to be in our audience, Yancy the surfer. She met him years ago when they were kids. Nice-looking guy. Then she says, "Who was your first love, Reege?" Why does she do this to me? "My dog, Skipper," I say. "I miss him so much." But she won't leave it alone. So I cave in: "I guess my first crush was on Inez Brown, who went to Our Lady of Solace School with me in the Bronx. And then there was Phyllis Setzer, who I took to my high school prom at the Copa to see Dean Martin and Jerry Lewis. I've been around a little bit, you know. But my real first love is Joy. Of course." After all these years on the air, a guy learns how to dig himself out of trouble.

Friday ☆ October 7

I want blood. I want revenge. Notre Dame is playing Boston College this weekend in Boston. I've waited almost a year for this one. They ruined my life last year and now they must pay. All week long, ESPN has replayed the last-second field goal that cost Notre Dame the 1993 national championship. It's driving me crazy. Lou Holtz is taking the high road. He doesn't want this to be a revenge game. "A good Christian university doesn't believe in revenge," he says. He's right, of course, but in my heart of hearts, I have to admit I want revenge. They must pay!

Saturday ☆ October 8

I'm feeling sick. I sit in horror in front of my TV set, watching the B.C.–Notre Dame game. Notre Dame is being clobbered all over the field. I've never seen them dominated like this. It is terribly depressing. Thank

God I didn't go up to Boston for this one. I wouldn't have gotten out of the stands alive. Maybe a little revenge wouldn't have been such a bad motivation after all. Certainly they need more emotion, more passion. Every team they face comes into the game sky high, out for the kill. This, I know now, is going to be a long, hard season.

After the miserable game, Joy and I drive up to Providence, Rhode Island, with Tom and Elaine Battista to attend a benefit for physically disabled adults and children. I was hoping the trip could be made under happier circumstances, but on this late afternoon I am in shock as we drive. Once again, I am unable to talk. It's immature, I know, but I'm sorry. I can't overcome it. I sit in the backseat and try to sleep. Or pretend that I'm asleep. Joy is getting angry because of my stony silence. I'll be all right later but, right now, I'm deep in pain. And no one can feel my pain. Or wants to.

At a cocktail party we visit first, I quickly realize that Boston and Providence and all of New England is one world. Every guy there hits me with the same line: "Hey! What happened to the Irish today?" It's a tough crowd. We go on to the show and meet some of the kids this benefit will help. These are impressive kids whose happy faces belie their problems and make the whole trip worthwhile. Then I get the key to the city of Providence from the mayor, Buddy Cianci, who's quite a character. After dinner, we return to our hotel in time to see news coverage of the city of Boston going crazy, savoring their victory. People dance in the streets. Bonfires are raging everywhere. Late-edition headlines are glaring with today's score. I've never been to a city whose team had just defeated Notre Dame. I didn't realize it was such a monumental event. But now I know. So why don't I feel any better? Next year they die!

Monday ☆ *October 10*

The second Monday in October. Boy, does this day bring back the memories. Thirty years ago today I got my first big break in Hollywood—a break that came and went so fast, nobody ever remembers it. But, for me, it's tough to forget, no matter how hard I try. I had been selected by Westinghouse to replace Steve Allen as host of his late-night syndicated show. Steve was tired of the grind, but Westinghouse wanted the show to go on. And that particular show may have been Steve's best ever. Every night, he pulled crazy, wild, imaginative stunts. He stuck cameras out the windows of his theater on Vine Street to capture all of the lunacy of Hollywood streetlife. He'd pluck classified ads posted on the bulletin board at the Hollywood Ranch Market next door and make on-air calls to people who were selling their cars or dogs or ironing boards. It was great television and, in fact, a forerunner of many bits David Letterman does so well today. And there I was in San Diego, watching and loving that show every night. I was in my third year of doing my local Saturday night show and I yearned for Hollywood and the big time more than ever. Suddenly, my shot at the big time arrived, and this was how it happened:

My Saturday-night show had finally gotten a review in

Variety, the showbiz bible. The writer was Don Freeman, who was *Variety*'s San Diego correspondent as well as TV critic for the *San Diego Union*. I had always admired Freeman's writing. I remember discovering his column while I was stationed in San Diego in the navy. He wrote with style, insight, and elegance. I became a devoted reader. Near the end of my service days, I convinced myself to seek him out for career advice. I remember standing on a downtown corner in front of the *Union-Tribune* building trying to muster up enough courage to go see him when suddenly I spotted him walking up the street. He was going to walk right past me. I thought about stopping him but lost my nerve. He strode by and entered the building. I waited five minutes and then followed him. His desk was on the second floor. When I got up there, I saw a sea of desks, side by side, one after another. I caught sight of him down a long aisle, sitting at the next-to-last desk. I started walking toward him. But, again, my insecurity got the best of me. Closer and closer I came to his desk, only to find I couldn't stop. It was ridiculous to be so intimidated by someone's writing, but I couldn't stop. I walked past him and reached the only desk left before I would smash into the wall. There was nowhere else to go. I introduced myself to the man seated there and was relieved to learn he was the *Union* movie critic. I innocently told him that I was interested in finding a job in television and that I would be discharged from the service in a week. Did he have any suggestions? Amazingly, he did. He told me about KCOP-TV in Hollywood, owned by the Copley Press (which also owned both newspapers in San Diego). "See a guy named Al Flanagan," he said. "He might be tough to get to, but if you can get in to see him, he might like you enough to help out." I thanked him profusely and walked quickly and silently past Don Freeman's desk, hoping he would have given me the same advice. But now, years later, I had not only gotten Freeman's attention but also a terrific review from him in *Variety*.

Everybody in Hollywood read *Variety* and so, in no time flat, an agent named Max Arnow from GAC called me. He had remembered my name from a plug in Walter Winchell's column and now this review further piqued his interest. He hopped on a PSA plane to San Diego to come see me. Max was a rather well-known agent who had seen it all and had a wonderful flourish about him. I met him at the airport, drove him to the station, and showed him some tapes of my show. Max liked what he saw, signed me to a contract, told me to lose five pounds, and flew back to Los Angeles.

From the way he talked, I thought it would be a matter of hours before I'd be in Hollywood. But the phone didn't ring, which only compounded my frustration. Still, it turned out that Max had been thinking of me and spreading my name around town. In meetings with his junior agents, he would remind them of this young talent in San Diego, ripe and ready and anxious for Hollywood. Weeks later, at a restaurant across Vine Street from the Steve Allen Playhouse, one of Max's young agents, Bobby Levine, stood at the bar talking about this kid with the strange name from San Diego. Steve Allen's executive producer, Chet Collier, happened to be sitting on the other side of Levine, eavesdropping on his conversation. He jotted Levine's name in the palm of his hand because he knew he would never remember Regis Philbin.

When I learned, not long afterward, that I was being

considered to follow Steve Allen, I couldn't believe it. A week or so later, Chet Collier brought some Westinghouse executives to see my show in San Diego. Zsa Zsa Gabor was a guest that night and we had a very, very funny interview. When Zsa Zsa walked out of the studio, she blurted, "My God, he's as good as Carson." Zsa Zsa loved to exaggerate, of course, but that appraisal was pure gold for the Westinghouse guys. Things happened so fast, my head spun. Within a few weeks, I would do my last show in San Diego, then head out on a tour of the Westinghouse stations prior to starting my own national late-night talk show.

All of a sudden, I had gotten what I wanted. And I was scared to death. Reluctantly, I signed off on my last Saturday night show in San Diego—three years to the day since it had begun. In those three years, that show became a San Diego broadcasting staple. I didn't know how much I would miss my freedom and my friends.

Early the next morning, after a sleepless night, I was aboard a flight to Boston, home of Westinghouse's powerful WBZ-TV station. I sat with Jim Allen, one of the Westinghouse execs, worrying about the sudden turn of events. We landed late Sunday afternoon at Logan Airport and, out the window, I saw a Catholic high school marching band blaring triumphantly. I asked Jim who on earth the band was there to greet. He said, "You." And I froze. I wasn't expecting this. These kids had never heard of me. In fact, no one in the city of Boston had ever heard of me. Suddenly, I felt shaken and unworthy. That old complex was coming back to haunt me.

That night I attended a banquet, met all of the Westinghouse guys and their wives, and spent the night at the Ritz Carlton. Next day at the station, I appeared as a guest on several shows, explaining who I was, how I got the job, what my chances were of beating Johnny Carson in the ratings. God, it was heady stuff. I began to wonder what I had gotten myself into. These people were gambling lots of money on me. All of a sudden, I didn't feel so confident. When I visited the Cleveland station, I could tell that Mike Douglas, who did his show there, was annoyed because he didn't get the late-night call. (He had no idea how lucky he was.) Likewise, the receptions for me in Pittsburgh and Baltimore were loud and boisterous. But I knew everyone was mystified by my good fortune. "Why him?" they all seemed to be thinking.

The last stop was the San Francisco station, KPIX-TV, where finally I found myself alone in the Presidential Suite at the Mark Hopkins Hotel. Alone, and by now, scared stiff. I flipped on the Steve Allen show, which was one of his last. The laughs were fast and furious. Only eight years had passed since I worked as a page on the second balcony of the Hudson Theatre for Allen's *Tonight Show*. Now I was poised to succeed him. I was unable to sleep that night. Not a wink. At dawn, I watched the sun come up over the Golden Gate Bridge. The tour was over and the show loomed ahead. There was no turning back.

Life in Hollywood couldn't have been more different from life in San Diego. I was disoriented from the start. To begin with, I had a staff. A couple of writers were hired to write my material, one of whom had written for Groucho Marx. The great vibraphonist Terry Gibbs was picked as my band leader and among his players were such jazz greats as Herb Ellis, Ray Brown, and Colin Bailey on drums. In San Diego, I booked my own guests for the show. I would meet with my director, Tom Battista, for ten minutes in the station cafeteria on Thursday to tell him who was booked and what I planned to do. For the Westinghouse show, all of this was being done for me. I wasn't so sure that was good. Also, in San Diego I broadcast live. I could talk about what happened last night, whatever was in the news, whatever people were talking about. Now, I would have to contend with a two-week tape delay. Whatever I said about something current would be stale and dated by the time we aired. And those writers were writing me jokes. I had never told a joke in my life. I used to just sit on a stool and talk. But no more. And if that wasn't enough, we had a grand total of thirteen stations airing the show. That meant we didn't really have a chance. Only we didn't know it at the time.

When it came time to book our first guest, I had one request. I wanted an astrologer to come on and forecast the future of the show. The idea was risky, interesting, and daring. So they booked noted astrologer Sydney Omarr, who seemed harmless enough. On opening night, he came out to give us a reading. I had given him all of my birth data to work with. And now he was sitting next to me—my very first guest on my first national show. "So tell me, Sydney," I said, "win or lose, how are we going to do?" Sydney fixed his eyes on me and said, "This show will fail. There's a fight going on right now behind the scenes as to what direction the show should go. It will not become your show. Others will take it from you. You won't make it."

Well, this had to be an all-time first for an opening segment of a brand-new show. I was, to say the least, humbled. And, in my heart, I knew he was probably right. On this show, I wasn't allowed to do what I did best. They wanted me to be an altogether different personality than the one they had found in San Diego. Sydney was exhorting me to take control, make the show mine, but I didn't know how. During a commercial break, he asked if he could see me alone after the show—as if what he had already said wasn't enough. He told me the next few years would be the worst period of my life. There would be drastic changes all around me. In fact, he said, the earth would literally move under my feet. I simply could not comprehend what he was telling me. But that's exactly what happened.

We were renewed after our first thirteen weeks, which came as a surprise. Chet Collier, my executive producer and Westinghouse's key man on the show, remained patient and loyal. He had seen my show in San Diego. He understood my potential. With the renewal, my confidence soared. I felt like maybe we did have a chance. The shows were getting better and better. I even asked for Omarr to come back. I wanted to hear what he thought now. So he returned and I said to him, "Sydney, much of what you said was true. We did have storms. We did have some terrible times. But now, we've been renewed. We're getting better. I see blue sky ahead." And Sydney looked at me with that dark, soulful expression and said, "I hate to be the bearer of bad tidings every time I'm with you, but this show is going off the air within forty-eight hours."

I winced. It couldn't be. This time even the great Sydney Omarr had to be wrong. Somehow we finished the show. Two days later, I got a call from Chet. He sounded down. "What is it, Chet?" I remember asking. "Did Henry Fonda drop out?" He was to be our star guest that night. Chet asked me to come over to the Beverly Hills Hotel as soon as possible. I rushed over there and was told we had been canceled. I was out. Westinghouse was going with Merv Griffin. That was that. Yes, indeed, Omarr had been right. It was a struggle to get through the show that night. My friend Tom Battista was in the audience. I didn't have a chance to talk to him before the show, but one look at my face, and he knew it was over for me.

And the rest of Sydney Omarr's predictions came true, too. Personally and professionally, I was in the dumper. In those days, talk shows were few and far between. Over the next few years, it was one crisis after another. My son Dan was born with complicated congenital anomalies and my failing marriage finally ended. And as for the earth moving under my feet? That happened, too. In February of 1968, it rained for two straight weeks in Los Angeles. Day and night, it was a heavy, unrelenting downpour. It wouldn't stop. I had a home on a hillside overlooking Universal City and, one rainy day, half of the backyard slid down the canyon. City officials rushed in, ordered the house evacuated and, when I couldn't pay the bills to shore up the property, I lost the house entirely. Well, I didn't exactly lose it. The city of Los Angeles paid me one dollar to get out for good.

But there's one more Sydney Omarr prediction I can tell you about. It happened on the final broadcast of *The Joey Bishop Show* in 1969. Joey had left the show a few weeks earlier and a variety of people pinch-hit for him as the remaining weeks wound down. They gave me the very last show to host, and guess who I asked for as a guest? Sydney Omarr. I wasn't through with him yet. Why not? What else could happen to me? As usual, I wanted to know about the future. I asked the question and braced myself. And Sydney said, "You will become a household name in America. Your name will be known everywhere. You will have great success." Well, this was more than I had hoped for. Now I really got excited. Sydney Omarr with good news? What could be more exciting? Naturally, my next question was when? "When, Sydney? When?" I begged. He said it wouldn't happen right away. It would take time. "That's okay," I said. "I can wait. But how long will it take? A year? Two?" And he looked right in my eyes and said, "It will take twenty years."

"*Twenty years!*" I screamed. Murderers get out of prison faster than that! Twenty years was forever! Twenty years would never come, I figured. "That's what I see," said Omarr. That was December of 1969. In September of 1988, our current show went national. And although we might not have been household names by 1989, Regis and Kathie Lee were on their way to making a twenty-year prediction come true.

Wednesday ☆ October 12

Burt Reynolds comes by to plug his new book. There probably couldn't be a worse time for him to be out on a media tour. He's currently embroiled in a messy divorce from Loni Anderson and the supermarket tabloids are feasting on him. All of the interviewers will want him to talk about the divorce, not about the book. But on our show Burt is warm and calm and very funny—the way we know him best. In fact, Joy and I have known Burt for almost as long as we've been married. We've seen all the changes in his life along the way. Years ago, we used to play tennis together at Dinah Shore's house, behind the Beverly Hills Hotel. We'd also spend a lot of time at Burt's house— the one with the big BR initials on the front gate—high above the Sunset Strip. We saw him become a box-office champ, starting with *Deliverance*. Because of our friendship, I interviewed Burt on his various movie locations over the years— among them, *Semi-Tough* (he tried and failed to tackle me on a muddy field), *Cannonball Run II*, and *The Man Who Loved Women*, in which he gave me a small part as a talk-show host. Acting! (Filming that part was the last thing I did in Los Angeles before we moved back to New York.) Late in the seventies, we had a wonderful dinner in London with Burt and Sally Field, his love at the time. And then came those parties at his home on Carolwood Drive in Bel Air and the romance with Loni and the wedding in the chapel he built on his Florida ranch. I remember when all of the fame and good fortune was just beginning for him. His close friend Bert Convy told me, "He's trying real hard to cope with all this. It's going to be tough." And it was tough.

Burt's an old jock. He's a competitor. And he's terribly sensitive. But Joy and I have always loved him. Warts and all, he's a friend. And today, he's feeling good. He's always been a great storyteller, always with self-deprecating wit. After his segment, I remind him not to let the reporters and their tough questions get him down. Just laugh it off, Burt. Laugh it off.

Twice a year, I meet with Dr. Jeffrey Borer for my semiannual checkup. Today it's my stress test. I don't mind that so much—it's the blood tests and those needles that drive me nuts. I hate them. But, so far, all is well. If anything, the visit always reminds me of what it was like living with those mysterious pains in my chest. They would come and go for a couple of months before they became so severe that I had to check myself into a hospital.

All through the final weeks of 1991, I remember complaining about the pains to Art Moore and Gelman at lunch. It never got much better and, by the end of January 1992, it finally caught up with me. I was on a Carnival Cruise ship, off the Florida coast, shooting a commercial with Kathie Lee. I would be making a brief cameo appearance at the end of the commercial, but we shot and reshot the scene. And the pains were hitting me hard. In fact, whenever I see that commercial I remember the extreme pain I was experiencing. Of course, I didn't tell anyone about it at the time. We had a commercial to do, discomfort or not. Anyway, it might have been the best acting I'll ever do, because I looked happy enough, although maybe a little green around the gills. But this time it wasn't Kathie Lee causing the pain—it was my circumflex artery, ninety-eight percent blocked.

That night, the pain swelled in my chest until I couldn't take it anymore. I went to the ship's sickbay, where the doctor got out of bed to give me an electrocardiogram and a checkup. Nothing turned up, but the doctor kept me overnight. In the morning, no one on the ship could find me. It was Frank Gifford who finally tracked me down in the sickbay. With Frank listening, the doctors urged me to have a complete check at Mt. Sinai Hospital in Miami Beach before flying home to New York. Within minutes, we would be docking in Miami Beach. So they packed me up, put me in a car, and drove me to the hospital where a whole team of doctors waited. Dr. Neil Schneider headed up my physical and, before I knew it, I was on a gurney being hustled down a hospital corridor to the angioplasty center. On the way, I remember kidding around with a pretty nurse saying, "Which one of these guys is yours?"

I was trying not to take this thing too seriously, maybe even avoid thinking about it altogether. Anyway, inside the surgery, they inserted a tiny camera in my arteries, ran it up to the pain area, and showed me what was causing the discomfort on a television monitor. It was fascinating. I could actually see the blockage. Well, they told me, I could have the angioplasty now or later. No time like the present, I figured. I was already on the gurney. Just go to it, I said.

As they prepped me, I began thinking, "This could be it. This could be the real thing. Anything could happen in an operating room." I remember experiencing a feeling of utter sadness, imagining that the unthinkable could happen. I would miss Joy and the kids and the show and all the laughs. Even all the little problems looked good at that moment. Another thought I had was, "And who would finish raising Gelman?"

Forty-five minutes later, it was over. The artery was

open, the pain was fading, the crisis had ended, and I would be okay. I had called Joy just before the operation, so she flew down immediately and spent the next two nights at a hotel, while they kept me for observation. Now you can just stay one night and walk out the next morning. They were a little extra cautious with me. But I felt great and relieved that the problem had been solved. They did warn me that the pain could come back within three to six months. (Just sixty percent of all angioplastys hold firm.) So I go back for a checkup every six months. Today, nothing is blocked. I will finish raising Gelman, after all.

Sunday ☆ October 16

Tom Battista and I go to the Jets-Patriots game at the Meadowlands. The New England Patriots are my pick to be this year's NFL surprise team and, because I made this prediction on the show, we've been invited by Patriots owner Bob Kraft to join him in his booth. Also in the booth is the entire Kraft family, all of whom watch the game very intensely. So much attention is paid to the players and the coaches that the owner has become the forgotten person in the pro football spectrum. He's the one who pays the bills. He's the one who lives and dies, emotionally and financially, with every game.

The main reason I picked the Patriots this year is their terrific coach, Bill Parcells. On the surface, he looks passive, but he's always ready to erupt at a moment's notice.

With the great young quarterback Drew Bledsoe under his direction, they could do it. Next year everybody will pick them. But I'm going with them now.

However, this is not their day. The Jets, unpredictable as ever, bottle up Bledsoe and win going away. I aim the binoculars across the field at Jets owner Leon Hess, white-haired and eighty and smiling. And here next to me in the booth is Bob Kraft, deep in mourning. Maybe I'm a year too early with this team.

Monday ☆ October 17

J oy is pinch-hitting for Kathie. That means an early wake-up call at the Philbin home. It's a great comfort for me to have a regular pinch-hitter on the show, and Joy has been the perfect solution since she began doing it in the seventies. She starting coming on *A.M. Los Angeles* when the girls were babies. She'd bring them out whenever our guest was the famous baby doctor, Lendon Smith. One day we needed a substitute host for Sarah Purcell, my regular co-host, and we asked Joy. She did the show and we had a great time together. The audience got to know her a little better and was fascinated to see how this husband and wife team got along on camera. Live television is not the best medium in the world for married couples, but it seemed to work for us. And I was grateful.

The co-host spot has become a wonderful sort of audition for other hosting jobs and I can't tell you how many people have sat in and then gone on to shows of their own. More importantly, a regular substitute gives our show a sense of continuity. The audience wants to see a familiar face, and Joy is always a welcome sight. But she has never desired to be the regular co-host on a permanent basis—probably in the best interest of our marriage.

So today we handle the situation as we always do: If we see a movie or attend an event the night before, we'll save our opinions or comments for the Host Chat. It's a little strange, I know, but it plays better the next morning. More spontaneous and real. It got dicey only once. That was the morning after we went to see *Schindler's List*. We never made it to the movie. We almost didn't make it through the night. She had been at a *Haven* rehearsal and suggested we go catch the movie. I scanned the listings to see where the movie was playing and we headed off in a cab. And that's when I realized that I'd mixed up the location of the theater and the starting times. Joy likes to accuse me of never knowing where I'm going and, on this night, she was right. And furious. Then I got mad that she was so mad at me. And we didn't speak. All night.

Next morning, Kathie Lee calls at seven to say she's snowbound in Connecticut and asks Joy to pinch-hit for her. But we still haven't spoken since last night. We get up and get out of the apartment without exchanging a word. And we're supposed to go on the air and make pleasant chat in front of America! Show starts and I'm very worried. How will we get through this? We start the Host Chat, but our conversation is obviously strained. Finally, I realize the best way out is to tell the audience the truth. That we stopped speaking at seven last night. So we both proceed to tell our side of the story. That not only breaks the ice, but makes for one of the best Host Chats ever. Naturally, the audience is on her side, but I'm used to that! And, in my heart of hearts, I couldn't have been more proud of her. I've watched Joy develop into a real broadcast pro. When I see her work alone on her *Haven* show, I realize just how good she's gotten. And when her fan mail pours in—particularly from men—I realize just how beautiful she still is.

☆　　☆　　☆

Tonight at Radu's fiftieth birthday party, however, she sustains a diss from Gelman. All of Radu's workout clients and friends were waiting to surprise him at Nino's Restaurant on the East Side. It was Gelman's job to lure Radu to the restaurant without tipping off the surprise. Finally, he brought Radu in. Radu was stunned. He couldn't believe it. It reminded me of a birthday party Joy threw for me in Los Angeles twenty years ago: Hottest night of the year in August, with a hundred people stuffed into our home. It was stifling. Don Rickles was broiling and kept groaning about it. Finally I arrived. I guess I don't handle surprises well, especially this one. What's worse, I had to make a speech after Rickles roasted me at the podium set up in the backyard. You try to follow Rickles while you're still in shock. I didn't talk to Joy for three days after that.

But Radu handles it well and eventually we move to a table for dinner. We sit with Gelman and Vinnie Rubino, my old associate producer. Gelman is next to Joy and they are deep in conversation when Cindy Crawford asks if she could join us. In mid-sentence, Gelman sizes up the situation and literally catapults himself over the table to sit next to Cindy. I don't think he ever finished his sentence, much less excused himself from Joy. "The man got up and climbed over the table!" I exclaim. I've never seen anything like it. Joy was snubbed for Cindy! Gelman had dissed Joy. And the redhead never forgets.

Tuesday ☆ October 18

For the past year, I've been watching the construction of a dazzling new building right across the street from our studio. It stands on the former site of the *All My Children* taping stages. I've been eyeing this building with a longing in my heart. It would be so convenient to live there and just tiptoe across the street every morning to work. Also, the building will have a fabulous gym, great restaurants, and ten movie theaters on the premises. I've been nudging Joy about this for months, but she loves the East Side and doesn't want to move to the West Side. This morning, however, she got a taste of what I've been complaining about—that traffic-snarled trip across town. It's usually okay until you hit West 67th Street. Then it's pure torture, as you inch up that final block to the station. Today, it's as horrendous as ever: limos side-by-side outside *Good Morning America*, a sanitation truck outside the Café Des Artistes, plus a school bus and an oil truck, all stationary, all immovable. And behind all of this, Joy and I sit trapped. I get such a kick out of her reaction. The Furies begin to build in her and then comes the eruption. She has a fit and this is only her second day on the job this week. I tell her to try it for eleven years. That doesn't help.

During the Host Chat, I recount this story and plead with her to consider living in the building across the street. "Wouldn't it be easier to live across the street," I say, "jump in here, do the show, and hop home for lunch?" And she says that's exactly why we're not going to live across the street: "I don't want you hopping home for lunch. I married you for better or for worse, but not for lunch!"

Speaking of which, we have lunch later at the Italian Bistro at the Trump Tower with Lawrence Krashes, an old friend who's an executive with jeweler Harry Winston. There's a magazine shop right next to the restaurant and who do you think I spy picking through the racks, but Donald Trump! He comes out with his reading material all rolled up, so I can't see what he's bought. Donald says, "How are you?" He's all smiles. One thing about Trump—he's always up. Even when the papers were beating his brains out with headlines about his divorce from Ivana for days on end, he kept his head up and his smile beaming. But I want to know what he just bought. "Okay, you got me," he says. And then he unrolls the *National Enquirer*, the *Star*, and *People* magazine. He may not like what they say about him, but as long as they're saying it, he wants to know what it is. He leaves with a smile. He also picked up the tab for lunch. So I leave with a smile, too.

Big stars aren't always big talkers. And few stars are as big or as tight-lipped as Warren Beatty. Warren is now a reformed playboy, having married and had children with actress Annette Bening. But he likes to have an air of mystery and, by never saying much, he keeps the mystery intact. No matter how hard I try to break him.

Today I try again, as he makes the rounds to promote his new movie *Love Affair*, the remake of *An Affair to Remember*. With Warren, you need every edge you can get. Years earlier, I interviewed him about his *Dick Tracy* film and I remember wearing a black silk shirt that he seemed to admire. Afterward, I bought him the same shirt from Beau Brummel and sent it to him. During the making of *Dick Tracy*, he had begun a relationship with his co-star, Madonna. And, a few months later, Madonna invited me to interview her before the release of her movie *Truth or Dare*. So I put on the black shirt again, thinking it would remind her of Warren and loosen her up. I think it did remind her of Warren, because she seemed a little shaken. Or maybe she was just chilly. All she wore was a flimsy nightie. Anyway, I guess it was over with her and Warren. Frankly, I think she found me more attractive. I remember she felt my muscles and swooned a little. Well, she actually just rolled her eyes— but it *seemed* like a swoon, if you didn't look too close.

I wore the black shirt again the last time I talked to Warren, around the time of *Bugsy*, the movie that brought Annette into his life. I came to his suite at the Plaza Hotel and started chipping away at him. But I don't think the shirt made a difference.

Today, at least, he actually comes to our studio, which is a first. But he's still nervous. I ask him if he is intimidated to take on the Cary Grant role in *Love Affair*. He isn't. What was it like working with his wife, who had the Deborah Kerr role? "Great," he says. I ask, Doesn't she have the greatest eyes in the business? "Yes," he says. Oh, well. It's never easy with Warren. Maybe next time I'll send him my pants.

Saturday ☆ October 22

I'm in Washington, D.C., to emcee the St. Mary's College Alumni Auction, which benefits the Aging Religious, many of whom are in dire straits after a lifetime of doing good for others. The organization is called SOAR and we hope to raise money by auctioning off trips, vacations, and various St. Mary's and Notre Dame memorabilia, plus tickets, footballs, etc. For me, the event is a natural, after surviving sixteen years of Catholic school education.

I spent my first eight years studying under the presentation nuns at Our Lady of Solace School in the Bronx. I never forgot those nuns. Even now I can recite every one of their names. And the one nobody could ever forget was Sister Mary Michael, my eighth-grade teacher. She was the toughest. But she had to be, I guess, just to get us ready for life out there. Everybody feared Sister Mary Michael. My seat was right in front of her desk, which presented me with an interesting opportunity. Every morning, as we knelt to say our morning prayers, I took a key from my pocket and worked on cutting my initials into her wooden desk. But I cut them at such an angle so that no one could see the R.P. except me. My desk obscured everyone else's view of the handiwork. I suppose it was my first attempt at seeking immortality. Or, at least, a little personal publicity. For six months, I kept chipping away, a few minutes a day, so as to engrave the letters perfectly. And, in the end, it was just gorgeous. You couldn't ask for a more beautiful defacement of school property.

Then, one bright May morning, Sister stands up and says, "This is Spring Cleaning day!" So she starts moving her desk back and tells the class to do the same. And I'm thinking, "Wait a minute! She's going to expose the initials! I'm a dead man!" And I was. There it was, for the whole class to see—a big beautiful R.P. Well, there was only one R.P. in the class, and did I pay for that! It should have said R.I.P. "Bend over!" said Sister Mary Michael. And out came the big thick ruler. To this day, I still can't sit correctly.

But I keep on paying back. For this auction, I bring down some of my Notre Dame mementoes and a glitzy dress from Kathie Lee's wardrobe. The event also gives me a chance to visit with my son Dan, who lives in Washington. We drive around D.C., have lunch and do some shopping, then go to a meeting with the St. Mary's ladies. Back in South Bend, St. Mary's is located across the Dixie Highway from Notre Dame. In the old days, Notre Dame was men only and St. Mary's was women only.

But many marriages between the student bodies eventually took place. Thus, the alumni from both schools combine forces for causes like this one.

Tonight's auction is held in the school auditorium at the Academy of the Holy Cross at Kensington, Maryland. I open the bidding and items are auctioned one by one. Just to pad out the list of prizes, I put on the block a package that includes tickets to our show, an introduction to Kathie Lee, a tug of Gelman's hair, and lunch with me. I'm amazed at how the bidding mounts for this prize. It goes so well, I raffle off four more with the same results. What a haul for the old nuns, brothers, and priests! And they've earned it. I guess it must have been Gelman's hair.

Sunday ☆ October 23

Back to New York. Pouring rain. I go directly to the Four Seasons Hotel for a scheduled interview with Robert De Niro. Bobby, my Bobby. My favorite actor. Such intensity. A few years ago, Joy and I had cameo roles in his movie *Night and the City*. Bobby played a down-at-the-heels, lowlife attorney and promoter named Harry Fabian. It was just a one-day shoot at Elaine's and a chance to work with De Niro. What a dream. In the scene, Joy and I are seated at a table, when Harry comes in for a drink, spots us, and can't resist coming over to try to get one of his clients booked on the show. The script was simple enough. All I was supposed to say was

"Thank you"—or something equally innocuous. Don't laugh, but I remember actually rehearsing the words *thank you* over and over and over again. After all, I would be working with Robert De Niro, probably the greatest actor of our time!

Joy was pinch-hitting for Kathie Lee that day, so we went right over to Elaine's after the show. There was the director, Irwin Winkler, and Bobby (only his friends call him Bobby—don't *you* dare!). And he couldn't have been more cordial. We posed for pictures. For months, I had been making a fuss over him on the show, saying we were close friends and that he called me every night. Yes, every night my phone would ring. I would answer. No one would be there. I always said it was him. I always knew it was. He's not known for being much of a conversationalist, but I said this was just his way of staying in touch. If he knew anything of this, he never let on. He just smiled a lot that day.

Working on a movie is exciting—in theory, anyway. But it's actually kind of a slow, tedious process—especially when you're used to the spontaneity of live TV. But this was a scene with Robert De Niro and I was getting very, very excited. Joy and I waited in our trailer on Second Avenue, outside the restaurant, while they set the scene. I practiced *thank you* ten different ways. I wanted to be ready for Bobby. Finally, we were called in. Joy and I sat at our table and pretended to be in conversation. Out of the corner of my eye, I saw him come in the front door, order a drink at the bar, casually glance in our direction, and recognize us. I saw him whisper to the bartender, "Is that Regis Philbin?" I could see him fighting with himself about coming over to bother us. Wow, I thought, this is great acting.

Now, here he comes. Pretend to be surprised. "Pardon me," he says, just like everyone else who has ever come up to me at a restaurant. "I know I shouldn't be doing this, but . . . " I looked right into those intense eyes a few inches away and realized I was smiling when I shouldn't be. In fact, he was so damn good, I broke out laughing. What a dope! I was so mesmerized by his acting that I forgot to say, "Thank you." We shot the scene again. And again. And again.

He was working in a tan overcoat which he never took off. I marveled at his patience and his stamina and his presence. And now he began ad-libbing the scene, tailoring his conversation to us as no scriptwriter could. He was talking directly to us. I was answering him. Suddenly, there was no script. I don't want to sound presumptuous, but, for Joy and me, it was just magic. What a thrill to be in sync with Robert De Niro. We were caught up in his rhythms. Forget about *thank you*. Forget about the script. This was a creepy guy wheedling to get his client on our show. Trying to ingratiate himself and failing and knowing it. As he left, he gave me his card and the scene was over. I glanced at the card. It said, "Harry Fabian, Attorney at Law," with a phone number and an address on West 22nd Street. De Niro—so deep into his character—actually had Harry Fabian cards made up when anybody's business card would have sufficed.

Joy and I were sky-high when the scene was over. There was just one more crowd scene to shoot with him outside the restaurant, peering inside. Then the picture would wrap. We stayed into the night while they shot some pickup scenes around Elaine's. And through it all, there was Bobby. Always in that overcoat. Always in motion. Always in character. Always working. What endurance. We spoke only briefly. I asked if he would take a rest after this was over. "No," he said, "I'm getting on a five-thirty A.M. flight to Vancouver for my next movie, *This Boy's Life*." At one forty-five that morning, it was over. We embraced, I thanked him and watched him head for his trailer. My God, I thought, what a life. From one movie to the next. I guessed he would start shooting *This Boy's Life* the next day. Months later, he told me otherwise. "Oh no," he said, "we didn't start shooting for a month. But I had to get out there to pick out my wardrobe for the movie." He didn't sleep just so that he could pick out clothes! This guy is heroic.

But today there's another movie to talk about. De Niro playing the monster in *Frankenstein*. He'd flown in from Las Vegas—where he's working on Martin Scorsese's *Casino* with Sharon Stone and Joe Pesci—to do publicity. My old friend Stan Rosenfield, who handles Bobby's personal P.R., brought him into the room at the Four Seasons. And he looks better than ever, despite working nonstop all these years. We have quite a reunion. He seems genuinely happy to see me. Or is he still acting? No, couldn't be. Could he? Usually, I see the star's movie before any interview. But they previewed this picture while I was in Washington, so I'm at a disadvantage. But Bobby and I have rapport! Who needs research!

As always, I begin the interview by reminding him of our epic scene together in *Night and the City*. But then we have to talk about *Frankenstein* and his daily eight-hour makeup job to look suitably monstrous. My only frame of reference are all of those Frankenstein movies I saw as a kid. The ones with Boris Karloff stomping around the moors with his arms outstretched. Bobby patiently explains this isn't the same Frankenstein. His head isn't even flat in this one. For a guy who hates to be interviewed, he's getting better and better. But I have to get back to more important matters. I say, "I thought after *Night and the City*, we should have worked together more frequently. After all, your best scene in years was with me! Didn't I bring out something special in you, Bobby. You know that! You've admitted it. Forget Joe Pesci! It should be me and you, Bobby! On and off the screen, we should always be together. Come on!" He laughs and promises to tell Joe when he gets back to Las Vegas. Hear that? *It's over for you, Joe!* But I guess it's over for me, too. Our interview is finished. A hug. Goodbye. And he's gone. Meanwhile, I'll be waiting for those late-night calls. One of these nights I know he'll say something.

Monday ☆ October 24

Let there be light! Flattering light, for a change. This is the day for our new lighting on the set. Believe it or not, this has become a major negotiating point in my new contract. Kathie Lee and I are sick and tired of being told we look so much better in person. Ten years of it. Every day. Every night. Everywhere we go. The lights haven't been changed in our studio since they built it who knows when. Not only that, but we don't even have a lighting director or a video operator who could smooth out our lighting flaws. Cap Cities is a bottom-line-oriented operation. I do love their efficiency, but we're the only show on television without lighting considerations. When I tell my friends in the business about this, they don't believe me. So my agent Jimmy Griffin and I have gone to the mat with WABC-TV general manager Walter Liss. And he agreed to some new lighting by an independent lighting man, Deke Hizirjian—but forget the video operator. Deke used to light my Lifetime cable show, which I thought looked very good. And he's appalled at the conditions in our studio. He goes to work though, but keeps reminding me there's only so much he can do without a video operator. He's been working all weekend and the change today is startling. In a good way, that is.

Kathie Lee and I dash off to B. Dalton on Fifth Avenue to sign copies of our new cookbook, *Entertaining with Regis and Kathie Lee*. Our first cookbook stayed on the *New York Times* best-seller list for months. Unheard of for a cookbook. So the inevitable follow-up—full of home-entertaining ideas—is ready for the shelves. Lines of people are already backed up onto the street outside B. Dalton. Kathie Lee is complaining that she should be home with the kids and not here. Yeah, sure. We sit behind a signing table and I get lucky for a change. She is the first one to greet the people, which means she has to do most of personalized inscriptions. All I have to do is sign my name. That's the way I like it.

Wednesday ☆ October 26

NBC's *Dateline* program is doing a piece on us. Kathie Lee and I meet Jane Pauley at the Pierre Hotel to do the interview. Scheduled time is twelve-thirty and I'm there at twelve twenty-five, just like a good broadcaster. At one, we're still waiting for Jane. She shows up at one-fifteen and, by this time, I'm out of gas. No more momentum. I don't have it anymore. Jane is apologetic and we begin the interview. I'm never comfortable being interviewed, but it's always a piece of cake for Kathie Lee. Ask her anything and she'll give you twenty minutes on how happy she is. Jane Pauley has a habit of eyeballing you in such a way when you talk that you feel your answers are inadequate, inarticulate, or just plain disappointing. Makes me very nervous. But she covers all the bases and it seems to go well, although they can still kill you in the editing.

Monday ☆ October 31

When I stopped in at Gelman's daily meeting last Thursday, they were talking about the Halloween show. Gelman said he and the staff had come up with an idea: What if the hosts trade identities and places. That is, how about me dressing up as and becoming Kathie Lee, and her becoming me? It sounded okay. I asked if they had anything else. No, as usual.

On Friday, I checked the outfit: the wig, the pearls, the earrings, pantyhose. There was a lot to consider here, which I quickly considered, then never gave it a second thought until this morning. Now all I have are second thoughts. I come in fifteen minutes early, around eight-fifteen, and go immediately into makeup. They dress me in the outfit, including the padded bra, which intrigues everyone. Arlette, the makeup lady, is the first to fondle my new breasts. I can't believe it. How dare she just help herself! Then two other female members of the staff also take advantage of me. Finally, Gelman comes in for a last look and he, too, helps himself. I'm shocked. People just coming up and groping me like I'm a piece of meat! I should have slapped them, but how do you hit a woman? Or Gelman, for that matter?

What surprises me most about the fashion drill is the feeling of being encumbered from every angle. The pantyhose itches. The medium-high heels give me an unsteady feeling. My bustier feels awkward and makes me an unwilling friskee. I feel an unaccustomed chill up my skirt. The wig looks too red and too weird. And this makeup! Well, I look more like Mrs. Doubtfire or Julia Child than Kathie Lee. It's only Halloween morning and already I'm scared! I don't see her at all until I reach the studio entrance. Ordinarily, we open the show from behind the table, but today we want to get the audience's reaction to us on camera. So with ten seconds left before airtime, I glimpse her—or is it him?—for the first time. This face pops out of the darkness. She looks like me with a brown wig and one of my jackets and a tie. And then, at a certain angle, she looks exactly like my cousin Chris Boscia. It's stunning. And terrifying. I remind myself that to make this thing work, I have to be her—and vice versa.

Julian cues us. The show starts and we walk out through clouds of thick fog. Gelman loves fog machines for things like this. And our prop guys love to pour it on. Fog is everywhere—so thick that I've completely lost sight of her and everything else. I can hear the audience but see nothing. The show has begun and, suddenly, all of the things I've been hearing from her for nine years are now spilling out of my mouth. I've been possessed! I open my locket to show a picture of the Love Machine. I talk about bathing with Cody and what Cassidy is wearing to her Halloween party. I flash a big gaudy ring which, I announce, I'll be donating to charity after the show.

I'm beginning to enjoy this! And she's keeping right up with me, delivering every word in a slightly annoyed tone, complaining, sounding put-upon. She's got it down cold. This is fun and very cathartic! But what's even better for me is that she has to keep the conversation moving when it slows, get to the trivia question, intro the guests, give Gelman the occasional shot, show the headlines, keep me in check while still giving me a chance to tell the latest Cody story and get herself some laughs at the same time. I know that after many years of seeing our openings, people take it for granted. But frankly, it's the only thing of its kind on television and it's not that easy to do.

I remember how it started on my first television show, back in San Diego, in 1961. I booked the guests, came up with all kinds of crazy, physical things to do on the show—but how to open the broadcast was a mystery to me. Then I thought of Jack Paar, who was still hosting the *Tonight Show*. I always loved the way Jack would walk out, sit on the front of his desk and seemingly just talk about what was going on in his life. Thirty years later, Jack would tell me that most all of his openings were written in advance by him and two writers. But he delivered it so effortlessly and spontaneously that I thought he was really just talking off the top of his head.

I had no writers, but for a once-a-week show, it was easy for me to store away the unusual things I had seen or heard during the week. The funny little episodes we all experienced—anything that could lead to a story with a punch line to conclude it. So I would open on a stool, talk about the week, and it caught on. Later, I would use the same techniques with Joey Bishop. After his jokes, he would call me out as his sidekick and I would introduce things I knew he would get a laugh with. Joey was a great counterpuncher. Bring up something, let him hit it. Just make sure it would lead to something. No dead ends. Some nights it was just magic. Dean Martin once told him that the show's opening was the funniest eight minutes on television.

After the Bishop show went off the air, I spent three years on KHJ-TV, a local Hollywood station. I worked on *Tempo*, a three-hour live talk show every morning, co-hosted by a variety of people including Ruta Lee and Stan Bohrman. At the time, the Vietnam War was raging, America was racked with doubt and dissension, and Bohrman was totally opposed to it. Politics wasn't my cup of tea, but Bohrman loved it. He ranted and raved about America's participation in the war. The phone began ringing off the hook. The station manager, Walt Baker, came to see me. "You've got to present the other side of the argument," he said. "It looks too one-sided."

And so every morning I had to do battle with The Bohrman, as I called him. They fired him three times and brought him back twice. I would cry out, "The Bohrman is back! And he is furious!" He was a great provocateur and had a gift for riling up people and scaring them to death. My own mother, watching from San Diego, would phone me to say, "Tell him to be a nice boy!" And I would say, "Mom, he doesn't want to be a nice boy."

Host Chat has been my signature ever since. And I've always made sure to crank up a little of that old Bohrman agitation whenever possible. Back in 1975, it took on the two-headed format that's prevailed to this day. I was hosting *A.M. Los Angeles* with Sarah Purcell, who'd also come from my old San Diego station, and I explained to her how the routine worked: First rule—no talking before the show. Whatever you want to bring to the table, do it right on the show. Keep it as fresh and as real as possible. Personal true stories always played best. It was the same back then as it is today—complete with a simple trivia question to include the folks at home.

And now, after all these years of Host Chats, I am wearing a dress, watching someone who looks like me go through all the motions. I simply sit there in my pearls and every once in a while blurt out, "Cassidy, I love you!" And I don't have to worry about intros, guests, or cues to the commercial breaks—and apparently neither does Kathie, because every segment runs long. In fact, the show runs halfway through *Oprah*. Finally, it's over. I peel off my clothes, slip out of my high heels, scrub off all that makeup, and am totally exhausted. Still, it's bound to be the most talked-about show we've ever done. Joy, always my most astute critic, says she loved it. Frank thought I had great legs. Hearing that, I've decided to keep my pantyhose, just as a little remembrance. If you don't mind. Besides, after a while, I kind of got used to them.

Wednesday ☆ *November 2*

Attention, Mr. and Mrs. North America! I'm reading the new book about Walter Winchell by Neal Gabler called *Winchell: Gossip, Power and the Culture of Celebrity*. I knew Winchell. And long before I knew him, I revered him. When I was a kid growing up in the Bronx, New York City was a rip-roaring newspaper town. Must have been twelve dailies battling it out every day, with the greatest columnists in newspaper history going head-to-head in each edition. But the most powerful, most feared, most dynamic columnist of them all was Winchell.

My uncle Mike Boscia was a CBS Radio press agent. He represented Arthur Godfrey and Edward R. Murrow. Before he was married, he lived with my parents and my grandmother and me at 1990 Cruger Avenue in the Bronx. Of all my relatives, I suppose I was closest to him. As a kid, he would take me to his office at 485 Madison Avenue, and then we would make the rounds of his shows, including *The Arthur Godfrey Talent Scout Show*, broadcast from Dave Letterman's home base on Broadway, the Ed Sullivan Theater, even before it became the Ed Sullivan Theater. Everytime I go through the side door on 53rd Street to do Dave's show, I remember this was the same door I would enter with Mike to see Arthur Godfrey.

One night in the theater, I met Nick Kenney, who, like Winchell, wrote a column for the *New York Daily Mirror*. I was impressed to meet him, figuring he and Winchell had to know each other. I asked him questions about Winchell and listened intently. Winchell was the king. His column crackled with the names of the famous: presidents, royalty, movie stars. It was a time when Broadway hummed. Sidewalks were packed to the wee hours of the morning. The city was at its peak. And Winchell owned every inch of it. Even had a number-one-rated radio show. "Good evening, Mr. and Mrs. North America, and all the ships at sea!" he would bellow over the air. "Let's go to press!" Terribly exciting stuff for a young kid who looked at far away Manhattan with awe, wanting to be part of that world but thought he never could.

Years later, on San Diego's KOGO-TV, where I finally landed my own Saturday night talk show, I would have the great Winchell as a guest. To this day, I'm most thrilled with the guests I grew up admiring. Nowadays, most of those people are gone. But back in the sixties, I had to pinch myself everytime I met one. Winchell was no exception. And he was coming. We plugged the show heavily that week and, on that Saturday night in 1963, he showed up in his trademark blue suit, powder blue shirt, dark blue tie, and gray fedora—and we went to work.

Of course, this wasn't difficult for me. I couldn't forget the old days in New York, and fed him a question every time he stopped talking, which wasn't too often. He'd known them all: President Roosevelt. Lepke, the gangster. Joe DiMaggio, the Yankee Clipper. He talked fast and furious. Stories poured out of him. I hung on his every word, because every word was simply dynamite. Here was a real live New York character, displaced in quiet, dreamy San Diego making the night come alive. We sat side by side in two chairs, and behind him I could see the doors to the studio. Suddenly, they swung open. I was amazed, startled. No one ever came in or out while a show was in progress. But now, a convoy of firemen in boots and helmets, carrying axes, were rushing in. I couldn't believe it. Winchell saw the strange look in my eye but never slowed down a bit. The fire chief stood just outside of camera range. The next instant Winchell drew a breath, I said, "Walter, we have company." I pointed over to the battalion and yelled, "What's going on, Chief?"

"We have a report of a bomb planted in your studio," the fireman told me. The audience gasped. I gulped. And Winchell, God bless him, just started telling another story. I said, "Walter, wait a second! Let's go to a commercial and start again from the top." We faded to black. The chief then announced to the audience what he was looking for. A bomb. Naturally, it got emotional. I invited the firemen to look around. Seconds were ticking away. Winchell and I approached the audience. He tried to calm everyone down: "We've got the marines here in San Diego. We've got the navy in the bay. We've got all the protection you need. Don't be afraid of the Ratzies and the Nazis. I won't let this bomb go off." A lady came out of the audience. Only one. She couldn't take it anymore. Winchell intercepted her. "Don't leave!" he pleaded. "Don't go." She said, "Walter, I love you. But I don't want to go to hell with you." And she was gone.

The commercials ended and we were back on the air.

Firemen were still all over the studio. Walter picked up his story again right at the top, as though nothing had happened. I was hanging in there, one eye on him and one eye on the firemen. Finally, they were done searching and filed out. We finished the show at about 1:20 in the morning. What a night. Winchell called the bomb scare just another prank. Someone who disagreed with his politics, he figured, was probably out to embarrass him. Then we made arrangements to drive—separately, thank you—to a downtown restaurant to talk about the show.

Over Chinese food, he continued talking. His stamina was incredible, his energy bursting out just like his staccato sentences. But I was fading fast. My head was spinning. Here I was, hanging around with Walter Winchell in the predawn hours. His hours. He was twice my age but in that moment I felt old. He stood at the table and did a soft-shoe. As a kid, he'd started dancing with George Jessel, and now after a lifetime of writing and talking, provoking and producing, he was asking me to go across the street to the *Union* office where he would crank out one more column. I've regretted this all of my life, but I begged off. I was so whipped I couldn't see straight. We stood on the sidewalk. It was after three A.M. We shook hands. He straightened his hat, turned, and walked jauntily across the street. I went home exhausted, but exhilarated. Walter Winchell had been my guest.

But another surprise was coming. A plug in a Winchell column. I was dazzled to see my name mixed into his parade of legendary three-dot items. There was one item about Aristotle Onassis, spotted at the Blue Sea Café with a ballerina. "But she is not The One!" wrote Winchell, who probably knew who The One would turn out to be. And how about this: "Have a wince: The Paul Newmans

. . . were allegedly turned down for a N.Y. apartment at a swank East Side co-op. Not because they are showfolks, but because Paul is non-Aryan. (Hisssssss!)" I guess nothing really changes much here in New York.

But sandwiched in between all of these famous names was this shocker: "Att'n network execs on both coasts: His name is Regis Philbin. No. One Rating-Getter in Southern Calif. Via Channel 10 (San Diego to Santa Barbara). He is showbiz from head to toenails. Plus style, class, dignity. The only late-show personality around, we believe, who matches Johnny Carson's way with a guest or a coast-to-coast crowd." I'd made the column. So had my toenails. And I was thrilled.

Tuesday ☆ November 8

Larry King comes on the show today. Enters wearing a dark blue suit, but quickly strips off his jacket to reveal matching tie and braces. Larry is very proud of this. I explain to Larry that I used to wear matching tie and a pocket hankie when I was a teenager. But I got over it! Larry isn't listening. He proudly tells me his suspender set is from Turnbull & Ascott in Great Britain. We talk about the elections and he makes his predictions. (Accurate except for one.) And then we talk about his new book on the art of conversation. Larry lists a number of rules including the most sacred one: "Be a good listener." Every time I hear that phrase, I think of my first meeting with Joey Bishop, and the amazing way it came to happen.

In 1966, I had two weekly shows—one Saturday night on KFMB-TV in San Diego, and another in Hollywood during the week on KTTV. I was part of an all-star line up in Hollywood, sharing the week with Tom Duggan, Louis Lomax, Melvin Belli, and Joe Pyne. I was like a babe in the woods with those guys. One night, I had as a guest one of those psychic healers from the Philippine Islands. He was called Dr. Tony and he could allegedly enter the human body with his own hands and pluck out the diseased part of the anatomy. In the sixties, the psychic healers were attracting a lot of attention, making them great TV guests. Dr. Tony made quite a convincing case for himself. He even showed some dramatic film footage of one of his nighttime fireside meetings with the afflicted, deep in the Philippine jungles. Very effective stuff.

There was enormous response to the Dr. Tony show. I even got a call from Joe Pyne. Old blood-and-guts Joe Pyne. The toughest interviewer of them all. An ex-marine with a wooden leg who gargled with razor blades. It turned out that he wanted to visit Dr. Tony in the Philippines and asked if I would arrange it. I struck a deal with him: I would set it up, if Joe came on my show afterward to talk about what happened. I wanted him to tell me before he could tell his own audience. He agreed. Pyne made the trip, then kept his end of the bargain and came on with his story. Joe was such an intimidating presence, nobody ever dared to interview him. But I couldn't wait. And he told his tale: He had flown halfway around the world, to the Philippines, picked up a guide in Manila, then made his way through the jungle to Dr. Tony, who was conducting his fireside miracles. There he found a cluster of American tourists, many of them seriously ill, watching Dr. Tony go through his routine. Pyne edged as close as he could to a clearing in the woods, where he got a good look at the doctor. Within minutes, he decided Dr. Tony was a phony.

"All that blood was coming from a contraption up his arm, just like a magician," Joe said. "He wasn't entering the body at all!" So he simply turned around and came home, without spending any time at all with the doctor. I was incredulous.

"You went all around the world and stood on the perimeter of this crowd and then left without even talking to him?" I said. "Without ever getting up close to him? Without ever letting him touch you? All around the world and you come home after thirty seconds?" I yelled, in my best Dana Carvey voice. Here I was, this young upstart, pushing the old fire-eater and everybody, Pyne included, was enjoying it. (Months later, I would learn why Pyne wanted so desperately to meet Dr. Tony. He was dying of cancer.)

After the show, I returned to my home in San Diego and, the next day, my agent Noel Rubuloff called me from Los Angeles. "Quite a show last night," he said. "People are talking about it and, what's more, I just got a call from Joey Bishop's agent over at William Morris. Joey is starting a late-night show to go up against Johnny and they're looking for an announcer-sidekick."

Of course, I had heard about this. Joey had been sensational, pinch-hitting for Johnny on *The Tonight Show*. Meanwhile, ABC was itching to do its own late-night show, so Joey was a natural choice. Only Noel and I knew that my show on KTTV would soon be going off, which meant the timing for this was perfect. But I was twice burned by Hollywood now. My current show was all but over, and my Westinghouse show lasted twenty painful weeks. I was in no mood for further disappointment. So I said to Noel, "No, forget it. Tell them thanks, but no thanks. I don't want to go through it again." He said, "Let me get this other call and I'll get right back to you."

I waited on the line and gave it some more thought. I already knew that every announcer, disc jockey, character actor, and comedian in town had auditioned for that job—and yet Joey hadn't made his decision. My mind began to race. I remembered that wonderful things had happened to Hugh Downs and Ed McMahon, the two *Tonight Show* announcers. Hugh Downs went on to host the prestigious game show *Concentration,* and Ed had all those commercial deals. Meanwhile, Joey was a member of Sinatra's legendary Rat Pack. And it would be a network show. Lots of national exposure. I thought, What, am I crazy passing on this? Why not do it? What else is there? Suddenly, I regretted telling Noel that I wasn't interested. Suddenly, I wanted that job. Only he wouldn't come back on the line. Maybe he was telling them to forget it over at William Morris. I began to panic. "Come back, Noel!" I begged. "Come back!" He came back, and before he could say anything, I said, "Tell them I'll be there at three this afternoon." Like that, he set the appointment, and I jumped in the car and raced up to Los Angeles.

I arrived right on time and was immediately ushered into Bishop's office. Joey was dressed casually, wearing an orange sweater, khaki pants, and his usual hangdog expression. Here was this official jester of the Sinatra Clan, the guy who kept Frank and Dean and Sammy laughing all those nights. I was intimidated, but he was very cordial and complimentary. He said, "I saw you with Joe Pyne last night and I enjoyed it. You have a talent."

A talent, he said. That made me think. When Steve Allen resigned from his nightly Westinghouse show two years earlier, I had been selected to take his place. Steve, of course, had been one of my favorites. He was intelligent, articulate, and a tough act to follow. I became very self-conscious. On my initial publicity tour of the Westinghouse stations, I found myself on the defensive. Back then, TV critics were crusty old types. Right away, they were deeply suspicious—even hostile—in their interviews with me. Just who was this kid out of San Diego with a local show once a week? Where does he come off filling the shoes of Steve Allen? It was in Cleveland where a sour-faced old critic finally zeroed in on me. He asked the fatal question which would haunt me for a long, long time. He said, "Steve Allen is a comedian. A genuine wit. He writes books. He writes songs. He plays the piano. So what's your talent?"

I absorbed that question like a ham-fisted blow to the solar plexus. *What's your talent?* His nose was almost touching mine. Well, what *was* my talent? I just stood there. I couldn't answer him. I didn't know what my talent was, much less if I had any talent. There I stood, paralyzed. Finally, I made a small joke and moved on. But that one moment froze in my memory and dogged me until the day I met Joey Bishop.

Now, on this late November afternoon, a knowledgeable show business veteran was telling me I had a talent. I'd waited years for this. Finally, I was going to find out exactly what that talent was. So I said to Joey, "What talent? What's my talent?" And Joey literally rose to the occasion. He was a pretty good judge of ability and loved to express his opinions. So he stood up behind his desk, outlined against the window and paused to get his thoughts straight. What could he possibly say? Behind Joey, I watched the branches of a tree outside shake in the wind. It was quite a moment. Long, dramatic pause. Finally, Bishop said, "*You* are a good listener."

A good listener? That was it? I listened good? I was slightly stunned. I'd been hoping for a good interviewer or a great sense of humor or a pleasant personality. But no, I was a good listener. I smiled meekly and, before I could say a word, Bishop said, "I like you. Why don't you go around the corner and have a cup of coffee at the drugstore and come back in an hour."

I took him up on his suggestion and walked around the block to the Beverly Wilshire Hotel's old-fashioned drugstore. I sat at the counter over a cup of coffee and thought about our meeting. Did I really want this job? It wouldn't be my own show, but then I really could never do my own show in Hollywood. Not like it was in San Diego. In Hollywood, everything was created by writers—jokes, punch lines—with no time for my stories on a stool. But this would be Joey's show. I would be the announcer. I walked back to Bishop's office, unsure of what to do, but curious about what would happen next.

When I returned, the office was filled with people. Joey's face was beet red. It looked like he had been in an argument and had done some yelling. Present in the room were his agent Norman Brokaw, his manager Ed Hookstratten, and his assistant Mel Bishop—all of whom were silent and not too friendly. I suspected the argument was about me. And I was right. This was a key decision for them and Joey's advisers were playing the old devil's advocate routine: This kid had his own show, they said.

Maybe he wouldn't be content with the announcer's role. Maybe he would try to upstage the star, make a name for himself and turn into another raving Hollywood pain in the ass.

Joey started right in on me now. There was no more cordiality. His staff had alarmed him. Suddenly, he wasn't so sure about me. He yelled out loud, "You had your own show! Now you're going to be the announcer! How do I know you're going to be content with that? How do I know you'll be able to sit there on the couch, night after night, without trying to butt in? How do I know you'll be able to keep your mouth shut?" he screamed.

I stood up immediately, totally unfazed, and repeated back to him, "How do you know all these things? How do you know this? I'll tell you how you know. Because . . . *I am a good listener!*"

Silence. He showed no recognition that I was reminding him of what my talent was. What *he decided* my talent was. He took it in as though it was the first time he'd heard it. But apparently he liked what he heard. I got the job.

Tuesday ☆ November 15

I'm a cab guy. Limousines just embarrass me. Like anybody else, when I see a limo on the street, I wonder who's riding in back. Whoever it is, I expect to be impressed. Whenever I've gotten talked into riding in a big sedan, I can't help but think I'm going to let people down by stepping out of it. They want Madonna to be in that car. Or Donald Trump. Or Kathie Lee! I don't want to be responsible for that kind of disappointment! So for eleven years now, I've taken cabs to and from work. From Park Avenue on the Upper East Side. Through Central Park. To the Upper West Side studios of WABC-TV, where the show originates. The fare is usually four dollars and twenty-five cents. With a seventy-five-cent tip, it's an even five bucks. With traffic problems— garbage trucks stuck behind school buses stuck behind oil trucks stuck behind a moving van stuck behind a delivery truck and on and on—the fare can run up to six-fifty.

Anyway, before leaving for work this morning, I check my wallet, like I do every morning. I find two one-hundred-dollar bills. I'm sure lots of people would like to find two C-notes in their wallets. But no New York City cabdriver wants to break a hundred-dollar bill at eight-fifteen in the morning. He'd rather break your neck. So I tiptoe into our bedroom where Joy is sleeping soundly and I look through her purse. I find five lovely one-dollar bills. I take them, leave a hundred in her purse, and quietly leave. Also, I find two quarters on my desk, so I'm all ready to take that trip across town. How I would dearly love to live on the West Side and avoid all of this counting. But what are you going to do?

No problem getting a cab downstairs. I give the driver the destination, call him by his first name (even though I know I'm mispronouncing it), and we take off. Right away, he is unable to make a left off Park Avenue at 83rd Street, in order to get over to the 79th Street transverse through the park. So we go all the way up to 85th Street for that transverse. This detour, of course, will add fifty cents on the meter. But that's okay—we'll make it. Traffic is light this morning. Funny that I worry so much about this little commute, but eleven years of cabs will do this to you. On Central Park West, we pass the Museum of Natural History, where my sainted mother took me to see all of its wonders when I was a small boy. Suddenly there's a cop car cruising alongside of us and the cop is motioning us to pull over. I can't believe it! This has never happened before.

The cop yells that the taillight is out on the cab. The fare is already three-fifty. I've got to be on the air in forty minutes. I've got five and a half bucks on me. And I'm tired of worrying about whether or not it'll to be enough for this trip. Stopping now will screw everything up. I jump out of the cab, hoping the cops will recognize me. Big smile. Hey, they do! I tell them, "Kathie Lee won't stand for this!" They laugh and tell me, "Oh, go ahead, Regis." Back in the cab. We're on our way. The meter is now four bucks. We continue down Central Park West right to 67th Street and make that right turn smack into the delivery truck, the moving van, the oil delivery, you name it. Gridlock. The meter hits four seventy-five. I'd wanted to give him a seventy-five-cent tip, which means I can ride no farther. So I hand over the five-fifty, get out, and walk that long block in a chilly drizzle, over to Columbus Avenue and into our studio. East Side, West Side, New York, New York. The moral here is live near where you work. And if you can't do that, just get the damned limo.

Part II

Where is she? How is she? What's she like? Her. Her! HER! All right, let's get this out of the way! In answer to the most asked questions of my life: She is irrepressible, indefatigable, unsinkable, ambitious, a whirlwind, and, frankly, she is the one who's really out of control. She's feisty and fearless, brash and loving, sentimental and shameless, generous and demanding. There's more than one woman here. Forget about Sybil—there's a whole platoon of Kathie Lees, and they never get tired. Never!

Today we tape our "Silver Bells" duet out on 67th Street for her CBS Christmas special. Terrible timing. I'm deep in laryngitis. Totally hoarse. Almost inaudible. I'm growling. I'm barking. And I'm supposed to sing? With her? The critics are going to kill me, but we have to shoot this now. The production schedule of a TV special waits for no man. Somehow we muddle through it. We stroll up the sidewalk and sing to a track playing in our ear. I look over and see that familiar light in her eye when she sings. She loves it. God, does she love to sing. And she sounds great. Singing. Smiling. She is in heaven. Until a dog in a first-floor apartment window begins to bark. Even that doesn't stop her. Nothing fazes her. We do it again. This time, the dog is quiet. Smart dog. Took me years to learn.

Once we finish, I do a quick interview with a *TV Guide* writer covering the special. Guess what her first question is? But there's more. She wants to know what is it that drives Kathie Lee so hard. This is her angle. She says, "Kathie Lee is a driven woman. What makes her run?" An interesting question, but I wonder if even Dr. Freud could answer it. I've only been with her every day for nearly ten years now—and I'm still unqualified to answer. What makes her run? I remember the first day I worked with her in 1985. She was running even then. She ran up 67th Street from *Good Morning America*, where she'd been pinch-hitting for Joan Lunden. She raced into our studio wearing her running shoes, flushed and panting, and that's how we began our co-hosting relationship. "My new co-host can't even get here on time!" I teased her. It took about one show before she called me a jerk on the air. Yes, she was off and running. And, frankly, she hasn't stop running since.

In my stage act, I do a bit about her business acumen. I tell the audience, "Now it's possible to keep your marriage together while you watch her infomercial, take a workout with her fitness video while you're listening to her new album in your new Kathie Lee dress, wearing your Timeless Essence perfume. You just read her book, you just came off a Carnival Cruise and, boy, do you need a Slimfast." She's selling more stuff than Bloomingdale's. She does TV specials. Has a lullaby album in the works. She's going to sing this month with the Detroit Symphony. And she's still looking around for more. And the reporter asks me, "Why?" Let's just say her work ethic is enormous. She's not afraid to work to attain the kind of lifestyle she enjoys. I've seen her go from a brownstone on the Upper West Side to a magnificent Mediterranean manse on her own peninsula, jutting out into the Long Island Sound. And listen carefully to me: She's not through yet.

Thursday ☆ November 17

It's impossible for me not to get excited about Perry Como. Perry does our show today and I'm beside myself. He's one of my heroes. I remember going to see his old Chesterfield television show while I was still in college. There he was—tanned and handsome with that smooth, beautiful voice. And many years later, I would find any reason to sneak onto the sets of his various NBC specials.

The first time we met was back in Los Angeles, where he was taping his Christmas special. The huge studio had been transformed into a white winter wonderland. Perry was rehearsing a song, dressed in a tan overcoat, strolling toward me, booming out in that glorious voice. I stood behind a young cameraman, who was in awe. "My God," the kid muttered to himself, "my mother told me this guy could sing, but I never thought he'd be this good." Made me feel old. But Perry couldn't have been nicer to me. Said he used to watch Joey and me every night.

After returning to New York, I had fun with my Como

obsession and, whenever he came through the area, I'd go out with a camera on safarilike quest to find him. I'd wander around the Westbury Music Fair grounds, crying out, "Where's Perry? Perry, are you there? Perry!" He always played along perfectly, popping up at the last minute, chuckling at my foolish hysterics. Another time, he surprised me by coming on our show—but did it in disguise. I was introducing a makeover contestant—a construction worker we pulled off a site outside—and in came Perry in a hard hat.

But I guess my most famous experience with Perry was the Florida boat-stalking episode. The ironic part is that I never found him. Kathie Lee was in the early stages of her relationship with Frank and she mentioned that his Florida place in Jupiter was fairly close to Perry's home. Frank lent us his place for a family vacation and also use of his boat. So I hatched a scheme to take the boat along the intracoastal canal in search of Perry's house. I arranged for a cameraman to ride along with Joy, the girls, and me. And I even got Perry on the phone and convinced him to come out and wave to us from his pier. He said he'd do it, but I shouldn't be late because he had to leave for an appointment.

Meanwhile, Frank was pinch-hitting for me back on the show and thought it would be funny to give out his Florida phone number, so fans could wish me well. Of course, the phone started ringing off the hook that morning. And I had to answer each call because I was waiting to hear from the cameraman who was running late. That slowed us down even further. So, by the time we cruised over to Perry's, he was long gone. But I kept yelling at the top of my lungs, *"Perry! It's me—Regis! Perry! Please come out! Please!"* But there was no Perry. Though it may not have showed, I was crestfallen. Really felt badly. I've played that tape on the show many times since and it's become a classic. And quite poignant, in its own pathetic way. Perry later told me he received mail from many angry viewers wondering how he could treat Regis like that. Poor Perry. He'd probably never gotten an unpleasant letter in his life and now this crazy fan with a TV camera made him look like the bad guy.

But today all is long forgiven. He comes out looking great at eighty-two years of age. You just want him to live forever. There's never been anybody as cool and as calm. We even get him to sing, sitting right next to me on his stool. His conductor Nick Perito is at the piano and Perry glides into "It Could Happen to You." He's effortless, yet deep into the song, phrasing like a champ. Every line goes smoothly; he is totally focused on the lyrics. I'm just inches away from him—and to witness that concentration up close is awesome. Even though it's just a simple morning show, he still puts his whole heart and soul into that song. These are the moments that I cherish.

Friday ☆ November 18

Gelman's big day. His brainchild, the "Giggles, Gags and Goofs" comedy special, takes to the airwaves. This is a compilation of funny moments that happened mostly by accident on our show. All through the week, the staff has picked, edited, and worried over their pieces. I kept reminding them that excerpts always need explanation when taken out of context. There should be a setup and then a punch line; without the setup, there can be no punch line. I'm still suffering from my virus, which has all but entirely closed me down vocally. Gelman insists that we be in formal attire because this is such a big deal. Meanwhile, he comes to work in a T-shirt.

We open with a goof-clip of the day a phone call interrupted our Host Chat. In all the years that phone has been sitting next to us, I've never heard it actually ring. We only use it call out. But there it was ringing. Somebody was actually calling us. I couldn't wait to see who it was, since absolutely no one has the number. I don't even have the number. Maybe it was the White House. Maybe Hollywood. Who could it be? "Hello?" I said, tentatively. And the voice of Letha, our station receptionist, said rather briskly, "Could you please send an audience coordinator to the lobby." I'd never heard of such a thing! Here we are, trying to do a live TV show, and someone is on the phone requesting an audience coordinator. Only on our show.

The special proceeds with the usual assortment of stunts and oddities, but the best of the bunch is David Letterman's surprise visit. He walked onto the show one day last spring with some wilted flowers for Kathie Lee. And he handed me a half-eaten sandwich he'd found in the backseat of his cab. I think it was tongue. Anyway, David has walked on twice now and, each time he does, he says, "*Where's Oprah?*" Then he turns to Kathie Lee and says, "How are the twins?" On this day, he also gave our first trivia caller the *answer*—not the question—and told her to enjoy the luggage. That was terrific, but midway through the rest of the special, Kathie Lee and I are not so sure the other clips are all that funny.

To the staff all week, I've been saying, "You want comedy? Go to Gelman." Now, during each commercial break, I'm repeating this to our audience. Maybe we're too close to the material. Is this funny? The only definitive source is Joy. All through my career, Joy has been the final arbiter. She knows when it's good. She knows when it's a bomb. She has exquisite taste, she's smart and, like Gelman, she knows comedy. I can't wait to call her after the show. "Was that funny?" I yell to her on the phone. And Joy, in her infinite wisdom, pauses and says, "Well, some of it was funny. And some of it was interesting." *Interesting*? Interesting is a good word for a *National Geographic Explorer* show on A&E. Interesting is a bad word for comedy. But she's right again. It was funny. And darn it, it was interesting, too.

Tuesday ☆ November 22

My oldest daughter, Amy, calls from California. She and her husband, Dan, are writing music for an audio walking tape I'll record next year. Something to listen to while out pounding pavement for cardiovascular improvement. They also wrote and performed the music for my exercise video, which sounded terrific. Amy's always been a fine singer. Music is all she ever really cared about. I remember standing on a San Diego street corner with her when she was about five. We were waiting for a red light to change. Suddenly, she burst into singing the National Anthem, which she had just heard for the first time the night before. But the song had lingered in her little head. Now, out of the blue, she just started belting. It startled me and the other pedestrians around us. But it was an indication of what was ahead for her.

Now I'm staring at a picture of her, taken years ago at *The Joey Bishop Show*. I used to occasionally take Amy to the show with me when it was taped earlier in the evening. She looked like a pretty little waif back then—and her eyes would widen as she listened to Johnny Mann lead the big orchestra. After Joy and I were married, she came to live with us for a while and later decided to go her own way. I always wished I could have done more for her. I still do.

Saturday, November 26

Sun and shows in the desert. We're off to Phoenix, flying via America West Airlines. All is quiet at the airport. Odd for a Thanksgiving weekend. We go with Gelman, Kathie Lee, Cassidy and her nanny, and Kathie's secretary, hairdresser, and makeup lady. We were expecting Cody and his nanny, but the little guy's come down with the chicken pox. I was hoping he'd come anyway, so I could frighten all of Arizona. I wanted to say, Cody's come out to spread infection and start a pox epidemic. But he's not here.

How to start trouble? Before boarding, I try to engage

Gelman in an argument with Bryant Renfro, Kathie Lee's hairdresser, over my wardrobe. For the last six years, Bryant has never uttered a word about my Beau Brummel wardrobe. But today he ventures a negative opinion and I leap on him saying, "Gelman loves my wardrobe! In fact, he picked out most of it!" But nobody bites and nothing happens. I get bored.

No Cody. No fun. I do miss the little fella. Can't let his mother know. Of course, Cassidy looks just like him with her blond hair and blue eyes. But there's one difference. She's a girl. If he were here, he'd be marching up and down the aisle, wrestling with his X-Men, and I would have some material to talk about at our concerts this weekend. But Cassidy mostly just sleeps. For fun, I grab her beloved rag doll, Fluffy. I snatch it right out of her hands and run to the lavatory. But even this goes largely unnoticed. I can't get a rise out of anyone. Now I'm really getting bored.

For the past two weeks, I've been battling a cough and laryngitis. Even now, with our stage show coming up tomorrow at the Sun Dome, I'm not sure I can make it. Nothing is worse than trying to perform with laryngitis in front of a crowd of six thousand people. Not even this flight, which drones on. Gelman tells me that Burt Reynolds's people called to say I've been awfully quiet since the Florida State game. Last January, Burt challenged me about this year's F.S.U.-N.D. game. "If Florida State loses, I will do whatever embarrassing thing you want me to do on the show," said Burt. "And the same goes for you if Notre Dame loses." I thought maybe he might have just forgotten about it—given all that's happened to him this year, divorce and custody battles and such. But no. He's called and he wants his revenge. I tell Gelman to go ahead and book him on an upcoming show. Let's just hope he has some charity left in his heart.

Sunday ☆ *November 27*

We appear in concert this afternoon at the Sun Dome, near Phoenix. About six thousand people have filled this beautiful auditorium, comprising what one reviewer calls "a surprisingly multi-generational audience." My Calendar Girls onstage range from college age to a seventy-nine-year-old woman from South Carolina with the implausible name of Peaches Walker. She's the last one up and, naturally, she's a riot and becomes our new Miss America. Kathie Lee does both of her medleys and falls down twice. Maybe she should rethink the footwear. Just trying to help here. Also, my voice goes out early in the show. Still, we can do no wrong. We're a smash at the Sun Dome.

Monday ☆ *November 28*

Pretape day for our remote broadcasts from Scottsdale. That means I have to go roving around. We always try to get some local color pieces taped ahead of time. Gives viewers a better sense of where we are. Gelman wants me to investigate the flora and fauna of the desert. How fascinating. We enlist the services of a Native American guide named Flint. Flint is terrific—good sense of humor, colorfully dressed, and desert-savvy. We bounce around in his Explorer wagon, looking for the flora and the fauna. All I see is lots of cactus. Cactus everywhere. Way too much cactus. Enough cactus already!

Gelman also wants us to climb a mountain ridge. He tells me we're going to climb a little-known range called Regis Peak. Like a dope I believe him. But there it is, looming formidably ahead. A sheer cliff. Flint scales it quickly, leaving me way behind and already exhausted. The sun is beating down. I try to take off my hat and it gets tangled up with my canteen strap. I am perilously close to falling off this cliff. Now Gelman tells me he made up the name Regis Peak. Very funny. So then what am I doing here? Not only can't I make this climb, but I'm certain I'll fall to my death any second. There's only one thing to do. Fire Gelman. And that's exactly what I do. I fire him right here on this stupid cliff that isn't even called Regis Peak. Gelman doesn't care.

Tuesday ☆ November 29

Live-show day in Scottsdale. The location is a golf course, forty-five minutes away from our hotel. To avoid a monumental traffic jam, Kathie and I take a seven-minute helicopter ride over. Five thousand fans are en route to the show—via a single one-lane road. Down below, we see a long line of headlights snaking through predawn darkness. It's still dark as we make our entrance onto a set we've never seen before. We get a big Arizona welcome.

Onstage now. I've asked Gelman for just two things that I need to run the show: a monitor so I can see what the cameras are shooting, and a clock so I can keep track of the time. Both are in place. And, of course, neither is working. I can't believe it. On the air, I actually walk over to the monitor and press the "on" button and still nothing. Later in the show, Julian, our stage manager, discovers that the set has been unplugged. And the clock? Somebody put it on the set at two minutes before airtime and the hands never moved again. Nobody does television remotes like we do. Nobody would dare.

Somehow, though, we get through both of them. The first show starts in the early morning darkness. And it's *cold,* which I can't stop mentioning. This doesn't please the local citizenry. I borrow a pair of mittens from one of the ladies in our audience. For the second show, we start taping around nine-fifteen. The sun is now shining brightly, as it does 333 days a year, according to the Scottsdale Chamber of Commerce. The golf course makes for a beautiful setting, surrounded by majestic mountain ranges. And everywhere you look, more cactus plants. The show goes reasonably well.

In the afternoon, Joy flies in. So do our Los Angeles pals, Barry and Susan Glazer, for another set of our epic tennis games. We're the best of friends—but very, very competitive on the court. Joy and I win the first two games, but suddenly the Glazers can't do anything wrong. I miss some easy shots. And then something unsettling happens. A lone spectator appears at the top of our court, staring down at us. She's just a fan, but she unnerves Barry, who whispers to me, "I hate people watching us."

It would be rude to ask her to leave, so we continue to play. But now it's not Barry who's rattled by her—it's me. And I didn't even notice her until he pointed her out! I feel her eyes on me. Suddenly, my serves won't go in. I can't do anything right. My temper escalates. I wish she would go away, but I can't ask her to.

I've broken lots of rackets over the years. Just last year, I broke my prized Weed racket. It was a big oversized racket made by a little company in Ohio, and they're thrilled every time I talk about it. They even sent me another racket to replace the one I broke. They said it was the last of its kind off the production line. Said they had saved it, in case my temper got the best of me. They even had a little inscription etched on it: "Relax, Regis. Breath deeply. Don't get upset." So now I'm breathing deeply. I'm fighting back the anger. But that woman keeps staring down at us and I keep making lousy shots.

Finally, I let the racket go. My Weed flies across the court and into an adobe wall. The impact is too much. My beautiful Weed is broken. It was bad enough to lose, but now I've busted my racket! What a dope. Why don't I just quit this game? Of course, Joy is mortified by my behavior and I feel badly as I walk off the court ahead of the others. And who's there to meet me? The lady who stared down and caused all of this. And what do you think she wants? She's coming to New York on Friday and wants two tickets to the show. I've got her name on a piece of paper and the damned tickets will be waiting for her next Friday. That is, of course, if I don't kill myself after my next tennis game.

Friday ☆ *December 2*

Our last day in Arizona. I've stayed on through the week for a little relaxation while Kathie Lee has gone back to New York to hold down the fort. Today I watch Dana Carvey pinch-hit for me, and it's good to see him again. Of course, he can't stop doing me. He's out of control! And getting the big laughs. She eggs him on beautifully, and he veers off in all directions.

I remember the first time I saw him impersonate me on *Saturday Night Live*. Joy and I were sitting in bed watching the show, dozing a little. Suddenly, we heard the *Live* theme song and there was Dana—playing me! Jan Hooks was Kathie Lee. And they were perched behind a coffee table, opening the show with the small, inane bits of conversation. According to the skit, I was outraged over the terrible seat I had gotten at a banquet, wedged behind a post, and she kept yelling, "Reege! Reege! Reege!" It was a riot. Then Dana said something that I had never said on the air—although it was soon to become my trademark. "*I'm out of control!*" he yelled. Ever since, wherever I would go—whether it was strolling Fifth Avenue or visiting Mishawaka, Indiana— somebody would holler out to me, "Hey Regis! I'm out of control!" Yeah? Good for you.

Meanwhile, Dana is tearing up the place this morning.

I remember when someone else substituted for me, nearly ten years ago. And somehow it was a turning point in his career. Shortly after arriving in New York and starting the show, I was hospitalized with a kidney stone that simply would not come out. For ten days, I lay there at Lenox Hill Hospital in terrible pain, waiting for this thing to move, and it just wouldn't.

Every morning, I would watch the show to see how they were doing without me. One of the subs was the always brilliant Billy Crystal. At the time, however, he was in one of those valleys that occasionally catches up with everybody in our business. On that morning, Billy did it all. The full range of impressions. He jumped up and ran behind the couch, hid from the audience, popped up again and had them screaming. I laid there enjoying it tremendously, even though the pain was killing me. After the show, one of our associate producers, Judy Jones, got a call from *Saturday Night Live*. They had seen Billy and wanted him as a regular on their show. The rest is history. Billy did a couple of years on *SNL*, resurrected his career, and went on to the movies. Billy, you're welcome.

As for that kidney stone—it stayed and stayed and nothing would shake it loose. Finally, the doctor scheduled surgery, which would have incapacitated me for another four weeks. The ABC brass were going crazy, but there was nothing they could do about it. The surgery was set for a Monday morning. I was dreading it. I was thoroughly disgusted and depressed. On Sunday, I thought of a previous guest on the show who might be able to help. Her name was Laura Norman and she specialized in foot massages. As a matter of fact, she wrote the definitive book on the subject of reflexology. And she believed she could dislodge that kidney stone by foot massage. So she came to the hospital that Sunday evening. We were both a little self-conscious about it. She sat at the end of my bed, placed her hands under the covers and started rubbing my feet in the area that would correspond with my kidneys. Over and over, for about ninety minutes, she worked until visiting hours ended.

I hated to see her go. But nothing had changed. When you're waiting for a kidney stone to pass, you're always given a cup with a strainer in which to urinate. It's the only sure way to know if you passed the bugger. The massage gave me a good night's sleep, although I did wake up a few times to go to the bathroom since I was filled with fluids. Next morning, the attendant came to my room with a wheelchair. Surgery awaited. He had that sad I-hate-to-take-you-down-there look in his eye. Dejected, I asked if I could go to the bathroom one more time. I went in there and gave another try. Picked up my cup and heard the sweetest sound in all the world. A slight rattling. Something was in the cup. I couldn't believe it. I shook it again. And there it was. A tiny particle, so small I couldn't believe that it was responsible for all that horrible pain. I literally jumped for joy. I bounded out of the bathroom, hugged that attendant and showed him the magic stone. When his face lit up, I knew my troubles were over. Somehow during the night, after all that massaging, the stone had shaken loose and finally escaped. Within minutes, I was dressed and heading for the street and a cab, thrilled to be free and not on my way into surgery. How close I had come! I even brought the stone onto the show and proudly displayed it. Maybe it was the microscopic size of the thing that elicited the same response from everybody: "*That's* it?" No sympathy!

I remember all of this, happily, as I take one last walk around the gorgeous property of the Scottsdale Princess. Joy and I pack our bags and head for the airport. On the plane, Joy is deep in her new book, *Disclosure*. The head winds that made it so tough to get out to Arizona now help get us to New York an hour faster. We wait at the baggage carousel for our luggage. Gelman, who has stayed on with us, grabs his two bags and makes a dash for his ride to the Hamptons. My two bags arrive. Then one of Joy's. And that's it. The carousel finally stops, and all the bags from our flight are picked up. Joy's second bag never shows up.

People think that dark cloud is permanently locked over my head. Not always. Sometimes it shows up over her head. Usually it's over both our heads. The airline people assure her the bag will be at our place by morning, and we finally leave.

Even after a trip to someplace as beautiful as Scottsdale, it's good to be home. Suddenly, the tempo of the city grabs me. I want to know what I've missed. I want to know what's going on. We always ask the driver to put on the all-news radio station, WINS, and out it comes. Fast and direct. More often than not, the news is overwhelming. No city produces as many tragic stories as New York. And among the most tragic are the bulletins of cop shootings, which is exactly what we hear now. Two cops foiled a robbery-in-progress at a Brooklyn bike shop. A fusillade of bullets were fired. One cop was shot, then rushed to a nearby hospital. Four suspects are finally arrested, among them three sixteen-year-olds.

We're on the Triborough Bridge, taking in that picture-postcard view of New York. The whole Manhattan skyline is luminous, with every light on in every window. An awesome sight. Somebody made a great city over there, and sometimes all you can do is look at it in wonder. Then the reporter comes back on the radio. He's at the hospital. And he's telling us that the cop is dead. Raymond Cannon is his name: He's been on the force four and a half years, married for two months. And now he's dead. Nothing sadder. Somebody made a great city, all right. And somebody else is always making it so tough to live here.

Sunday ☆ December 4

We drive back to the city from Connecticut earlier than usual to attend a screening of the new movie *Speechless*. A dinner party follows at Mortimer's. Sunday is an unusual night for a screening here. You never know who'll be in town. You wouldn't dare try this in the spring or the summer when the Hamptons are in full bloom. But in December an interesting crowd can show up. I think the movie is well done. Michael Keaton and Geena Davis star.

In New York, so much national publicity is generated with all of its TV and magazine and newspaper outlets. Even the parties following the screenings are thought to be quite crucial to a movie's success. And the problem of who will sit at the star's table becomes something only the U.N. should settle. Publicist Peggy Siegel, who is in charge of this party, decrees that Joy and I should sit with Michael Keaton at the head table. But suddenly there's a mix-up. After cocktails, 110 people begin to look for their seats at Mortimer's. No one knows where their table is so everybody just plops down into the closest seat.

Joy and I sit where we are told, with Michael Keaton's brother and niece, the movie's producer, and Judd Rose from ABC's *Prime Time Live*. (Judd has never missed a dinner party in his life.) But there's no Michael Keaton. Eventually, author Gay Talese sits down next to me. Talese tells me that one of the best magazine articles he's read in recent years happens to be the *Esquire* profile of me from last summer, written by Bill Zehme. And I say to Gay Talese, "Isn't that nice, because you wrote the definitive profile of Frank Sinatra thirty years ago in the same magazine—'Frank Sinatra Has a Cold.' " I ask him what he's working on now. Urology, he tells me. The older he gets, the more fascinated he is with urology. I think it's fascinating, too, and ask him if he knows why I now get up two or three times a night to go to the bathroom. He smiles knowingly and, as he's about to answer, we're informed of an embarrassing seat mix-up at our table. Michael Keaton should be sitting where Gay is. He understands and moves on. Michael, who proves to be a nice guy from Pittsburgh, sits down and I never get the answer to my urology question.

It's incredible how invigorated you feel after a vacation. Our show is only an hour long, but after a few months of the daily grind, it wears you down. But today, I feel strong, Don Pardo! Feel good. And we fly through the opening of the show. If only I could feel this free and uncluttered all the time. Later, I walk down the block to the *Good Morning America* set where Joan Lunden, my co-host for the Walt Disney World Very Merry Christmas Parade, and I tape some promos for stations carrying the parade.

Back in my office, the mail is stacked up a mile high. Sometimes I feel it's not worth it to leave for a week. I have a lunch date with some Notre Dame friends who are in town for the Hall of Fame dinner tomorrow night at the Waldorf. But I have underestimated the traffic outside Radio City Music Hall, where crowds are lined up for the Christmas show. My cab comes to a complete standstill. I get out near Seventh Avenue and start walking. The streets are jammed with holiday tourists. I'm okay until I reach the Music Hall, where suddenly I'm discovered. Somebody yells, "There's Regis!" Then: "Where's Kathie Lee?" Then: "I'm out of control!" I keep smiling, nodding, walking.

Tonight, Joy and I see the new Michael Douglas–Demi Moore movie about sexual harassment, *Disclosure*. While I'm watching this, I am concocting a similar scenario involving a television co-host team. The lady decides one day that she enjoys working alone, and tries to lure the man into a sexual relationship, even though he's happily married. Naturally, I'm thinking this would be a funny story to tell on tomorrow's Host Chat. People wonder where my material comes from. Well, from the time I say goodbye on the air, I'm looking for it and thinking about how I can use whatever I'm seeing or doing.

Tuesday ☆ December 6

This morning I lay out my version of *Disclosure* in the Host Chat. It flows well. One laugh after another. Finally, I look directly at Kathie Lee and tell her, "From now on, I'm watching you like a hawk!" Later, I make the mistake of saying, "I've got to leave in a hurry after the show." "Why?" she wants to know. I don't want to tell her. But she doesn't like that. She doesn't like the "no" word. In fact, she can't stand that word. But I'm firm. I won't tell her where I'm going. Naturally, this only intrigues her more, but I'm gone.

Where I go is to a satellite studio in Rockefeller Center. I'm here to talk to some TV stations about the glories of Grants Farms Essential White Bread. An advertising agency in Dallas had introduced me to this bread— enriched with all the fiber of wheat bread. For years, white bread has been losing ground to wheat bread, mainly because of the lower fiber content. Once, on the show, I said that I still preferred white bread and the sandwiches I'd eaten as a kid. The agency heard this, called me and proposed that I talk to some media in cities where this white bread was being introduced. And that's what I'm doing. But do you think for a minute I was going to tell her where I'd gone? First of all, she'd never let me get through that story. And then she would slowly beat it to death: "Regis Philbin eats white bread and talks to America about it!" No, thanks.

Wednesday ☆ December 7

I was hoping she'd forget. But no. The first thing out of her mouth this morning is, "Okay, where were you yesterday?" I'm even more determined not to tell her, but the woman is relentless. "Where? Where? Where?" She has to know. "No!" I think. I'm not going to tell her about my white bread. She'll never understand. I tell her she'll have to read about it in the book I'm writing. "It's in the book," I say. I remind her of actor Charles Grodin, who always used that line to great comic effect when he was writing one of his books. He'd say it as though it would be the final word on any subject. Then he'd add, "Now don't bother me!"

Tonight at dinner, with Marvin and Terry Hamlisch, four people come over to interrupt us and ask, "Well, where were you yesterday afternoon?" So she won after all. To each of them, I reply, "It's in the book!" And now it is.

Thursday ☆ December 8

Premiere of *Nell* tonight at the Ziegfeld Theatre. This movie may be one of the year's leading Oscar contenders, especially for actors Jodie Foster and Liam Neeson. Claudia Cohen is covering the premiere, interviewing the picture's stars and other celebs in attendance. After the movie, we head for the party a block away at the Museum of Modern Art. Claudia cannot find her driver. He's always right there. Always. But tonight he's not, and she's furious. We walk into the museum entrance on 53rd Street only to find the party entrance is on the 54th Street side. And still no driver. Claudia is not taking this well. But we do have a few laughs about it and walk around the block.

The museum hosts many of these parties and there are a number of rooms in which to have dinner. Claudia selects one and we make our way through the buffet line and take a table. It's the deadest room at the party. We should never have let Claudia make this decision, not with the luck she's having. All the action is elsewhere. And at this point, we're not even sure her driver is outside. I say a small prayer that he is.

Peggy Siegel, publicist for the event, has discovered Jodie Foster and Liam Neeson in another room. I go with her to wish them well. I remember interviewing Jodie when she was in high school. Even then, she was sharp and articulate and on her way to Yale. Now in her thirties, she's beautiful and the winner of two Academy

Awards. She probably comes as close to Bette Davis in this era as anyone. And big Liam has turned it around. He's become a real movie star, with *Schindler's List* and now *Nell*. He's on the cover of *Vanity Fair*. He's made it. Five years ago, he came on our show, brooding and introspective and I wondered if he would have the patience to put up with Hollywood. I wondered if he would give himself time to crack through. And now he has.

Finally, the party's over. We head outside, where the street is cluttered with cars and limo drivers. Where is he? Where's the driver? Claudia is silent. I'm getting nervous. Suddenly, there he is. Frank is an ex-cop with a big, friendly Irish face, but he's no one to fool with. Still, even he knows what's ahead. I step between the two of them, trying to avert any problem, and talk nonstop about the movie until we are all safely inside the car. We drop off Claudia first. Another crisis alleviated.

Saturday ☆ December 10

I'm aboard a Continental Airlines jet heading for Fort Lauderdale and the annual Winter Fest Boat Parade up the intracoastal canal. For the second year in a row, I'm the grand marshal, thanks to Charlie Folds, the peripatetic promotion manager of WSVN, Channel 7. Years ago, practically every television station had a Charlie Folds. A guy who tirelessly promoted his station, its personalities, and the city itself. He made things happen. He got press. Got people excited. And that's what Charlie has done for this parade, station, and city. He's pressured me relentlessly until finally I find myself on this plane flying directly into his clutches. Gelman is already there. Said he's come to give me support, but he's really there to see his family and newborn nephew Andrew. Uncle Gelman. He's warming up to the idea of children. Getting closer to the inevitable.

But so am I. I am now filled with dread. Charlie will probably have his usual airport greeting. Motorcycle police escort. A big limousine. A noisy reception at the gate. All I want to do is sneak off the plane and grab a cab. But I don't think so. The flight takes two hours and nineteen minutes. Quick and easy and you're there. I deplane and find no one in the terminal to greet me. Could I really be this lucky? Then some spectators break into what sounds like rehearsed applause and Charlie and Gelman make an appearance from behind a counter, smiling proudly. A TV camera gets in front of me. There are pretty girls carrying banners behind me. En masse, we walk through the terminal. People yell, "Where's Kathie Lee?" Outside, there's the limo. A super-stretch limo. And there are the cops and the motorcycles. Charlie has struck again. I wish I could crawl in a hole.

How to dress for this boat parade? It's a problem. Gelman, who knows everything from comedy to weather, last year insisted I bring a lightweight summer jacket as opposed to a heavy coat. And I froze. The temperature dropped into the low forties. A chill wind whipped the boats and my teeth chattered endlessly. It was brutal. This year, I brought an assortment of heavy, light, and medium clothing. And as it turns out, the temperature remains at seventy-two degrees, day and night. All I need is a T-shirt. As usual, I blame Gelman for not foreseeing this.

The parade, meanwhile, is spectacular. Boats of all sizes, draped in full array of Christmas lights and decorations, cruise up the canal in single file. They're flanked by hundreds of small boats moored on either side, and hundreds of thousands of people waving and shouting from gorgeous waterfront homes, restaurants, high-rise condos, and parks. Parties going on everywhere. And there on the bow of the lead boat are Regis and Gelman and a sea character named Trident, in a white flowing beard and wig, who looks and sounds suspiciously like Jerry Stiller. It's a four-hour boat ride and we end up hoarse from shouting hellos. My back is killing me. And I couldn't be happier. Perfect night, except for my back.

Sunday ☆ December 11

It's windy and bleak when I wake up at the Guest Quarters Hotel in Fort Lauderdale. The flight home goes even faster. Tonight, Joy and I are going to Jack Paar's annual Christmas party. But my back is aching from the air travel and standing all through last night's cocktail party and boat parade. I have a degenerate disk which gets compressed after too much standing. Same thing, I remember, happened last year after the boat parade. I came home stooped over. Even Gelman, at his tender age, has a bad back. We both had to sit for part of the parade. What's happening to me?

At Jack's party I'm captured by Mike Dann, the programming genius behind CBS's great reign of the sixties. He launches into stories about how the old network stars were serviced back then. Judy Garland had to have a lavish, fully-equipped mobile home near her studio. When Danny Kaye found out, he had to have a three-bedroom, three-bath bungalow built outside his studio. This is all great inside stuff, but my back is killing me. I have to sit down. Mike Dann doesn't care whether he's sitting or standing when telling a story. He just keeps going. And I'm his audience. We sit at the same table for dinner and I'm still his audience. My back is still aching. Jack Paar comes over. He thinks I'm down. He likes me to be up and yelling and now he's worried that I'm not having a good time. Nothing worse than letting your host down. But I've got Mike Dann who has now worked his way into network tales from the seventies. And there's no end in sight.

Finally, the conversation switches to the O.J. Simpson trial and no one at my table—myself included—thinks O.J. will be convicted. As with all dinner parties at the Paar home, guests are seated at two separate tables. Jack presides at the head of his table. But if he hears too many laughs at the other table, he's up like a shot, flying across the room to see who is getting the laughs and why. I've had the pleasure of driving him crazy in this way on several occasions. "What? What?" Jack will ask, nervously. He hates to miss anything. And he never does. Being around him is always great fun. Even with a backache.

Monday ☆ December 12

Joy and I buy our Christmas tree today at Dimitri's on 2nd Avenue. The trees are displayed behind a cyclone fence, topped by a double strand of curled, barbed wire. Not a pretty holiday scene at all. But that's Christmas in New York. Tonight, Joy and I watch a tape of last Friday's NBC *Dateline* Regis and Kathie Lee segment. Jane Pauley and her staff did a terrific job of sifting through our shows and constructing an entertaining report. Even I have to laugh a few times. The segment won't make any headlines. It won't even be remembered very long. In fact, it was almost like our own show. We thoroughly enjoy it.

Tuesday ☆ December 13

Kathie Lee seems edgy this morning. She informs me that she is going to call me on things. Anything I say that she doesn't agree with, she'll pounce. And I can see she means it. I tell her that I'll do the same. Then I predict: "Ninety-five is going to be a rocky year around here—so hang on to your seats, everybody." I'm just kidding, but now I'm thinking that maybe something is bothering her. For nearly ten years, it's been give-and-take in the Host Chat. And as I have said many times, we've never had an argument. Not even a harsh word. We both know that the opening is the heart and soul of our show. It's a tightrope to get across every day and, so far, we've done it. Now this. Yes, something is definitely off.

Wednesday ☆ December 21

Off to Disney World. Time to co-host another Christmas parade. Weather in Orlando is the opposite of New York—rainy and cold. Perfect. I check into the Grand Floridian Hotel and go immediately into a taping session heralding Disney's newest attraction, Alien Encounter. Over the years, I've done features about so many park attractions while they were still on the drawing board or under construction. Once I sat in a huge mud hole to announce the construction of Typhoon Lagoon. Climbed a rickety ladder to the top of a five-story pile of steel and wood that eventually became the Grand Floridian. Wandered the swampy landscape on which the Disney-MGM Studios would be built. I've seen all of the nonstop expansion up close and personal. I'm exhausted just thinking of it.

Joy and the girls won't be joining me down here. J.J. isn't even back from school yet. We're all scheduled to meet Christmas night in Aspen for a family holiday. Meanwhile, my son Dan will be joining me here in Florida. And I'm looking forward to seeing him tomorrow.

Thursday ☆ *December 22*

Danny arrives, looking good and in great spirits. His girlfriend is joining us tomorrow. It's been a long road for both of us to be together this Christmas at Disney World. It wasn't easy. It was never easy. But we're here. If they ever ask me who my number one hero in life is—it's him.

I will always remember the day he was born in Los Angeles at the old Cedars of Lebanon Hospital. I had just lost my Westinghouse show. It wasn't a good time. I was in the waiting room with some other expectant fathers, anxious for the news. They all seemed so nervous to me. Lots of pacing around. Finally, my wife's doctor entered the room looking older and grayer than I remembered. He wasn't smiling. He congratulated me on the birth of my son. And then he hesitated. Nothing in my life has ever surprised me more than what he told me next. There was a problem with my son's legs. They were bent and stiff, couldn't move. He said there didn't seem to be any muscles in them at all. He'd never seen another case like it. All of this news was slowly washing over me, staggering me. I was totally unprepared to hear what he was telling me. I couldn't focus. Couldn't grasp what he was saying. I interrupted him when I heard him mention the muscles. I said something like, "We can fix that with weight training, can't we?" And he stopped me and said, "No, you don't understand. There *are* no muscles. And he doesn't have a sacrum or a sacrum bone or the last three vertebrae, either. He will never walk."

How can I explain how I felt? My wife and I could barely fathom it. This little boy would never run or walk or play ball or do all the things little boys have always done. My knees buckled. A wrench dug deep into my heart and it has stayed there ever since. It's hard to recall what happened after that. I remember going around to anyone I could think of who knew anything about muscles. I even went to Jack La Lanne, who, like the doctor, had never heard of such a thing. In the next few years, birth defects would become big news—an area for specialists. But now it was truly a phenomenon.

I continued to search for help. I was desperate to try anything. There was a faith healer in the San Fernando Valley who saw us. One night I held Danny in my arms in this man's living room, which was filled with mostly older, sick people. One by one, each of us approached him. He laid his hands on Danny's legs while I held my breath. But nothing changed. There was another doctor in La Jolla who specialized in leg problems, but he just pulled on Danny's legs and put them in casts. It was terribly depressing to look at this baby, so tiny and helpless. He had no idea what his life would be like. I felt profoundly sorry and frustrated and angry.

Word of his condition had gotten around. Friends and fans alike wanted to know about the prognosis. What did the doctors say? People assured me, "They're working miracles these days in medicine." Twelve, twenty times a day they would ask after him. And I would have to go through the whole story over and over again, until finally I couldn't talk about it anymore. I suppose I should have handled it better. Kept a stiff upper lip and smiled my way through the pain, like some people can. But I couldn't.

So the years went by—with operation after operation. About sixty-five surgeries in all. He endured month after month in hospital recovery rooms. Long periods of pain. Once, a doctor mistakenly nipped an artery in one leg and gangrene set in. The leg had to be removed up to the knee. A few years later, Dan decided to have the other leg taken off at the same place. We tried artificial legs, with no success. Long after his mother and I divorced, he stayed at the Crippled Children's Clinic in Desert Hot Springs, where he underwent daily therapy. How well I remember driving to the desert, where the mountain clinic was located, and feeling overcome with sadness about what he was going through. But he was so good about it, so patient, that he actually gave me strength.

Somehow Dan was able to continue his education and become a top political science student. I mean, he really knew his politics and, after my job brought me back to New York, I flew him to Washington for his first visit. He loved it. The Capitol inspired him. One summer we got him an internship at Congressman Bob Dornan's office. And he mastered the art of navigating Washington, wheeling himself to the nearest Metro line and then on to the Capitol building and to work. He took on every challenge and conquered them all. This was where he wanted to be. He graduated from college and continued graduate school in Washington. Now he's about six months away from his graduate degree in political science. He holds a permanent and responsible job at a government agency in Washington, where he is respected and admired. And, frankly, I couldn't be more proud. He did it. He made it. When I think of how he got there—the odds he had to overcome, the pain he has endured—I want to stand up and cheer. He's one hell of a son.

Friday ☆ *December 23*

Run-through. We do the rehearsal parade in the morning at Disney World. Two hours of jam-packed happiness and joy on Main Street. This parade comes on like a tornado, unleashing all the trademark characters ever created by Disney. From Mickey Mouse to the Lion King, they're all there. Even my own boyhood favorite, Donald Duck. I always thought Donald was trapped in Mickey's happy shadow and never got his due. And I loved the way the duck talked, especially when he got agitated. (Reminds me of somebody—I can't think who.) Today's only problem is the weather—it's cold and windy. Florida isn't supposed to look like this. But we tape the parade as though it's the real thing, because the weather could turn even worse on Christmas Day.

Afterward, I meet Danny's girlfriend. She's attractive and sweet and shares his strong sense of humor. Her name is Lila. She seems deeply devoted to him. I have wondered all of his life what she would be like—or if there would be anyone at all. Like him, she's a graduate student. She's prelaw. They met at his agency where she interned during the summer. I'm happy that she's a part of his life.

Sun comes out just in time. Bright and warm. It's Florida again. What a morning for the Christmas parade. People are streaming into the Magic Kingdom. By eight-thirty, Main Street is full. The parade is a rousing success. Tom Elrod, the president of marketing and entertainment, and boss of bosses here, is pleased. Elrod used to be a weatherman on local TV in Indianapolis. (There were two weather guys at his station; the other one was David Letterman.) So Elrod loves us to give the temperature during the two-hour parade. We begin at sixty-one degrees and end at sixty-eight. I'm not sure it's accurate, but it sounds great and makes Tom happy.

Afterward, I take Danny and Lila to England for lunch, at EPCOT Center. Over fish and chips comes the bombshell: Danny and Lila tell me they are actually talking about marriage! Nothing definite, but they're talking about it. This is turning into some Christmas.

There have been other memorable Christmases along the way. Two of the most memorable took place, back to back, in Los Angeles. Joy and I had purchased a home in the Hancock Park area formerly owned by comedian Harvey Korman. Of course, in Los Angeles, you're nobody unless you live in the former home of a famous person. So, one Christmas Day, at about three o'clock in the afternoon, we sat down to holiday dinner. Joy's mother was there. My mother was there. The kids, of course. And the doorbell rang. We weren't expecting anybody else. I opened the door and there was Harvey Korman with his son and daughter. Harvey said, "Do you mind if we come in and just look around?" He had been in the neighborhood, having dinner with his cousins, and he must have felt a flood of memories. What else could I do but invite him in? I figured it would take a quick five minutes to walk him through his old house. A little holiday nostalgia. I understood.

But Harvey lingered in each room, becoming more and more nostalgic. And bittersweet. His eyes grew misty. Upstairs, his kids explored their old bedrooms. In the master bedroom, I saw a couple of tears well up in Harvey's eyes. Then his kids turned to him and said, "Why did you move? Why did you take us away from here?" Suddenly, they were engaged in a heart-wrenching family caucus. Here it was Christmas and my mood was plummeting. Finally, the Kormans left and the Philbins ate a somber meal.

One Christmas later, it happened all over again. As we're sitting down to dinner, the doorbell rang. I looked at Joy and said, "Naw, it couldn't be." But it was. There on the doorstep was Harvey and his two kids. "Gee," he said, tentatively, "can we come in and look around?" Of course. I welcomed them in and let them wander through the house. Again, he shared memories with us, recounting golden days of his years on the premises. And again, his kids got upset. "Why did we move!" they asked him. "You changed our lives!" It was like watching a Sally Jessy Raphael show explode before your eyes. Finally, they left. And, once again, our family fell into a gloomy funk. Nobody felt like talking. We ate in grim silence.

The next Christmas, we went out to dinner.

☆   ☆   ☆

Time to leave Florida: I leave for the airport, with the help of Tim Wolters, my loyal Disney guide for the past six years. Tim is as efficient a human being as I have ever met. He shepherds me every minute, from arrival to departure, smoothing out each detail along the way. Airport check-in goes well. The flight to Denver will be uncrowded. Joy and the girls are meeting me in Aspen. Gelman is already there, tearing up the slopes. As I have said on the show, I'm not really looking forward to this trip. I've been on skis three times in my life—without much success. I know that people who ski can't tell you enough about how wonderful it is. For them, it is. All I know is that nothing in the world seems more agonizing than getting to the top of a mountain from a ski lodge. Nothing. It's an ordeal from beginning to end. And I hate it.

On the plane, I take my seat, relieved that the parade is behind me. Now I can relax, read a little, maybe even do some writing. I reach for my glasses. They're not in my pockets. Not in my jacket. Oh, God. I've done it again. I've lost my stupid glasses! Can't read, can't write. What a long trip this is going to be. I probably left them in the car, which Tim is now driving back to Disney World. I get that old familiar sinking feeling. This is why Joy hounds me about things. Just when I'm resigned to my misery, the flight attendant comes around the corner with my glasses. Tim found them and ran them all the way back to the gate for me. That's my Timmy.

Suddenly, a woman rushes aboard, looking very harried. Don't tell me she's my seatmate! But, of course, she's my seatmate. She throws two bags over me and climbs to the window seat. She doesn't recognize me at first, which is fine, but begins telling me about the problems of traveling to Colorado to ski with her two daughters and one of their boyfriends. I casually mention that I'm heading there, too. Now she recognizes my voice and starts unloading all of her troubles. The boyfriend, she says, crashed her station wagon three weeks ago, and today he left his airline ticket at home and the trip hasn't even started yet. Oh, and ironically, this woman's name is Felicity.

Felicity orders a scotch and water and tells me she's a forty-five-year-old flight attendant, married for eighteen years to a pilot, and she's a rabid Miami Dolphins fan. I tell her about my New England Patriots pick this year and she reminisces about all the chartered pro-football flights she's worked, season after season. "All those big, rugged football players. Wonderful guys," she sighs, "just wonderful." The Patriots were regular passengers on her planes. "Whose flights were the best?" I ask. "San Francisco Forty-niners, no doubt about it," she says, dreamily. Now the good times spill out of Felicity. The carefree old days. The parties. What laughs. Joe Namath was on a flight. "What a guy," she says. I begin to get nervous. I don't know if I should hear much more. "Yes," I say, "he was a great quarterback." And then I quickly change the subject.

No more skiing. Never again. After four days, I am finished for good. I am now happily watching those mountains disappear from view. Joy and I are on a United Airlines jet heading for LaGuardia. Don't ask me how this holiday went. It began badly and got worse. On Monday, we started taping various segments around Aspen to use next week on the show. One hour into the first piece on the first day, I fell off my skis. Landed on my side. Cracked three ribs. They say kidney stones, child-birth, and rib injuries cause the most pain. I'm two for three. Every breath, every cough, every turn in bed is a killer. The pain is so intense, so piercing, that it forces you to cry out. I've been doing a lot of crying out. So don't ask how my holiday went.

Aside from the skiing, Aspen was nice: quaint and charming and filled with the beautiful people. Everybody is up and smiling. The staff at the Ritz Carlton Hotel is relentlessly happy and genuinely interested in your skiing adventures. That means ten times a day, as you walk through the lobby or sit in a restaurant, you have to answer the question, "How's the skiing?" I couldn't repeat my rib story one more time, so I lied a lot. Just gritted my teeth and smiled and said "Great." Joy and J.J. are the skiers in the family, and even Joanna got interested this trip in snowboarding, which is quite the current rage. So they had a ball, while I plowed through Gelman's heavy taping schedule, cracked ribs and all.

But I always feel guilty if I quit because of illness. Reminds me of last year when we had scheduled a shoot at the Cirque Du Soleil, a sensational Canadian circus that features amazing acrobatics. I'd had my angioplasty the January before, and they'd told me that the chest pains might come back. On this particular day in May, I had been feeling minor discomfort, but thought nothing of it. Then, an hour before the Du Soleil shoot, I was on the treadmill at Radu's gym, and there it was again. Unmistakable, intense—and I knew it was time to go to New York Hospital. But I couldn't stop myself from first going down to Battery Park, entering the big circus tent, climbing the trapeze ropes and twirling around like an idiot. Afterward, I agreed to go to the hospital, where Gelman actually took a picture of the two of us together before I checked in. That unnerved me because Gelman is always optimistic and it occurred to me he wanted maybe one last picture to remember me by.

A few hours later, I had an arthrectomy procedure on my blocked artery, a little Roto-Rooter job that took care of the problem. At least, so far. But that thin air in Aspen made me wonder all over again. I particularly noticed this on Tuesday when we shot the paragliding segment, in which I had to fly off of a mountaintop. We took the gondola up Ajax Mountain, which is a thrill-ride in itself, and then walked ten minutes to a sheer cliff. You're supposed to run up to the edge, then throw yourself off and, with luck, drift down to earth under a parachute. We waited forty-five minutes for the correct wind currents, which provided too much time to contemplate the big drop—and therefore question why I was doing this in the first place. But the ribs ached so much that I figured death couldn't be much worse. Plus, Gelman was also taking the jump, which meant he'd face the same odds. That made me feel slightly better.

Actually, the instructor, Dick Jackson, who founded the paragliding school in Aspen, inspired so much confidence, it wasn't as much of a challenge as you'd guess. With a small video camera, Gelman shot our descent from his parachute, and the footage should be as spectacular as the sensation of floating down into that valley below.

Tuesday night we dined in the gorgeous Snowmass home of Disney chairman Michael Eisner and his wife, Jane. Michael faxed us explicit directions, but Gelman still managed to get us lost on the way. The design of the house is based on a rustic Adirondack mountain lodge, complete with a birch-bark canoe hanging from the living room ceiling. Another dinner guest was Chevy Chase, who managed to lock himself out of the house during the meal. He'd gotten up to go get something from his car, and discovered that the front door had locked behind him. I noticed his chair at the dinner table remained vacant next to Joy's and wondered where he could be. Meanwhile, he was outside freezing on the front step, ringing the doorbell that nobody heard. Finally, he began jumping up and down outside the door. Someone saw his hands in the window above the door and let him back in. It was like a scene from one of his *National Lampoon Vacation* movies. And I thought these things only happened to me.

I knew Michael Eisner long before he became chairman of Disney. In the seventies, when he was the program director for the ABC Television Network, we lived in the same neighborhood on Sunset Plaza Drive above the Strip in Los Angeles. We attended the same neighborhood parties. He was always a devoted family man and, twenty years later, he still is. His home was filled with his kids, his friends, his mother—a warm holiday mix. Eisner, who is probably as tough as they come in this shark-infested business, showed us around his home like a funny uncle who can't do enough for his guests. He watches our show most mornings, as he and Jane work out, and he's not above picking up the phone and saying thanks for a Disney mention.

Wednesday was snowboarding day, with the two young whiz kids of the sport, Christopher Masarro and Jayson Onley. Why is it that all these guys in Aspen are great-looking, athletic, and uniformly under the age of twenty? Even Gelman looked a little long of tooth here, so I could only imagine what these guys thought of me. Anyway, Gelman concocted a dream sequence in which I'm filmed snowboarding with this kid, leaping off cliffs and racing downhill at blinding speeds—except we'd use a double for me. At the end of the piece, you see me wake up wondering if I'd really performed these feats or if it was just my imagination. Of course, gimmicks like this have been used since the dawn of Hollywood, but Gelman carried on as though he'd revolutionized television.

Since my ribs were aching, I gladly took the easy way out and sat out the actual snowboarding scenes. Finally, it was over. Back at the hotel, crippled with pain, I walked in and the doorman cheerily asked, "Well, how was skiing today?" "Great," I answered. "Just great." And it hurt even to say that. At this point, the only thing that can make me happy is a Notre Dame win over Colorado at the Fiesta Bowl next week. But I won't hold my breath. Even that hurts too much.

Readjusting to life in New York again. Out on the streets, it's cold and ugly. I thoroughly depress myself by going to a supermarket. Grocery-shopping was one of the biggest transitional problems we found after moving here from Los Angeles, where supermarket aisles are wide and spacious and filled with music. Here, the aisles are narrow and usually blocked with boxes or carts or people who just stand and stare. It drives me nuts. The checkout lines are long and slow until finally you're back out in the gray streets, dodging dog dirt. After Disney World and Aspen, this is a definite comedown. Maybe it's just my ribs. Who knows? Later, Joy calls from a shopping excursion, and I meet her at a store on Madison Avenue to exchange a Christmas gift. People are looking at me and nudging their friends and whispering. I'm feeling like some of the merchandise. I can't wait to get out of there. On the way home, Joy and I walk down Madison Avenue. She's cooking tonight and needs a head of lettuce, which I forgot to pick up earlier.

Buying a head of lettuce on Madison Avenue is ridiculous, but neither one of us wants to go over to Lexington Avenue to the dreaded supermarket. So she darts into one of the Korean grocery stores. I opt to stand outside rather than go through the identity drill inside and I look at her through the window. I watch her picking through the lettuce and she looks great. Then a tall good-looking guy, obviously a bachelor shopping for his dinner, ambles toward her, where he inspects the artichokes. The romaine is three bucks a head, which she questions with the proprietor. The good-looking guy says, "If you think the lettuce is high, wait until you see the artichokes." They laugh and then comes more conversation, which I can't hear or make out.

Now my ribs begin hurting even more. This is some picture. I'm standing on this windswept corner of Madison Avenue, watching Joy and this guy have giggles and laughs inside. Now they're at the checkout counter and the conversation continues. This guy is in full pursuit, while Regis Philbin, nervous husband, watches from the window. When she comes out, I remind her that Phase Three of her life can offically begin once I'm ten feet under. She laughs and says that I'm crazy. But I mean it.

Saturday ☆ December 31

New Year's Eve. We're on our way to dinner at the American Renaissance Restaurant down in Tribeca with the Battistas. I don't know what's worse—skiing with these cracked ribs or riding over New York City potholes. I talked about this restaurant on the air after our first visit a few months ago. I raved that besides having fabulous decor, a great chef, and terrific food, this place had the best men's room I'd ever been in. Of course, Kathie Lee wanted to know in explicit detail what made it so great. So I described the marble floors, the gold fixtures, and the two TVs mounted behind glass over the urinals, which gives you something to look at while you stand there.

Immediately afterward, the restaurant was bombarded with media attention and curious patrons dying to see such a fancy bathroom. Tourists streamed in. *Newsweek* came with a photographer. Nippon Television wanted to film footage of it. So here's one of New York's top chefs, Eric Blauberg, proud of his wonderful new menu—and all anybody wants to talk about was his bathroom. If only Kathie Lee hadn't asked. Naturally, he's thrilled to see me show up again. I try to contain my enthusiasm this time, but, frankly, there's no bathroom on earth I'd rather use.

After dinner, we go to the Regency Hotel to see Lainie Kazan sing. This is one of the last great hotel showrooms in town, and Lainie is in terrific form. An elderly gentleman stops at our table and says he remembers when I worked with Les Crane, which I never did. "No," I said, "Les Crane worked alone with a shotgun microphone. I worked with Joey Bishop." The man says no, it was Les Crane. But Les Crane did his old late-night talk show all by himself. I see there is no way to change his mind. So I tell him, on second thought, that he's right. Yes, indeed, Les Crane and me, weren't those the days! What laughs we had. I give up. The elderly man walks away, feeling triumphant. Happy New Year.

Sunday ☆ January 1, 1995

The new year starts quietly. In fact, it's down-right boring. Nothing duller than being in New York over a winter holiday weekend. It's gotten cold. The wind is howling and I'm beginning to remember how and why I hate the next two months.

Monday ☆ January 2

J.J. leaves for London and her semester abroad in the student exchange program. She's not with her classmates from Notre Dame. In fact, she isn't even enrolled in the Notre Dame exchange program in London. I guess she didn't apply soon enough, so she's taking a Butler University program. But now she realizes she'll be all alone in a city of strangers. At least, that's how it feels at the moment. It's always loneliest in the beginning. How does she get into situations like this? She'll be living with an English family for a weekend before settling in at Birkbeck College. I tell her to be careful of the eccentric, weird uncle all those English families have. But that frightens her more than amuses her. I was only kidding, of course, but when I think about it, I get frightened, too. I've got to stop that stuff.

To compound my gloom, Notre Dame is getting decisively whipped in the Fiesta Bowl. It's not even close. But they do get some momentum going in the third quarter, score one touchdown, and are driving for another when a Colorado linebacker intercepts Ron Powlus and that's that. I keep thinking Lou is a year away from a national championship. But maybe it will take two or three.

J.J.'s boyfriend takes her to the airport, waits there with her, and, finally, has to push her on board the plane to London. Later, we go to sleep thinking about her and missing her. She really is a terrific kid.

Tuesday ☆ January 3

Family wake-up call. Joy is pinch-hitting for Kathie Lee for the rest of this week and Joanna is temporarily filling in for my assistant. As a result, the three of us getting out of the house together in the morning is reminiscent of a Marx Brothers stateroom scene. It's always tough getting back to work after a vacation, and this break has been unusually long. After Florida, Aspen, and New Year's, it seems like two years since we did a show. But the audience is responsive and I get a little sympathy for my ribs. Although not much. Joy says they're just bruised, not broken. I prefer to think of them as broken. What's the difference? They still hurt.

Richard Simmons is a guest. We want to kid him about his appearance on Dave Letterman's show on Friday night. The two of them did a segment wandering around a New Jersey town in the rain, with David zinging him at every turn. It was a scream. But Richard doesn't want to play along today. He's all business, plugging his latest video, his upcoming appearance at Wal-Mart, his new no-fat cookies, and his work with one overweight fan. I love Richard dearly. After all, I'm the one who introduced him to television back in the early seventies. It was Joy who actually discovered him in an aerobics class at his West Hollywood exercise salon, Anatomy Asylum. But I wish we could have some fun with him once in a while.

We also play the first segment of our Aspen adventure: skiing the slopes. As the segment progresses, we carefully work in a skiing instructor dressed like me, leaping over moguls and careening downhill at blinding speeds. It's so well done, the audience thinks it's actually me. And I say nothing. Let them think what they want. It's a free country, isn't it?

Tonight, the phone rings. It's J.J., of course. Alone and upset and suffering with insomnia in London. Calls like this are every parent's nightmare. You wish you could do something to make it easier. I can just see her lying awake in that strange bed so far away. Joy and I have a hard time getting to sleep ourselves after we hang up.

Wednesday ☆ January 4

Ratings for yesterday's show went through the roof. Almost made up for the sore ribs. Today we play the snowboarding segment, which Joanna especially enjoys—since one of the instructors is very, very cute and spent a lot of time with her. After some sensational editing, the piece looks fabulous. Again, we substitute a double and now the audience seems to be catching on to me, but I don't say a word.

Tonight, J.J. calls again. Still hasn't slept. Even under perfect conditions, J.J. has trouble sleeping, so I believe her. It's after two A.M. London time and she's wide awake. When do you stop worrying about your kids? Never, I guess.

Thursday ☆ January 5

Ratings continue to be spectacular. We had a nine rating with a thirty-one share in the New York overnights yesterday. Getting a nine at nine o'clock in the morning is extremely rare because of the limited number of sets in use—so we are thrilled. Each morning, Gelman brings me the numbers and, if they are good, he does a slow build worthy of any press agent in show business. This time it was worth waiting through his routine.

I heard that Oprah was on with Larry King last night and somebody called in to gauge her opinion of the competition, namely Ricki Lake. Ricki's been getting a lot of attention in the press lately, but what isn't being said is that her show is run twice a day in many markets. Today, for instance, she got a four rating in New York's early afternoon period, and then a five in the late afternoon slot. That gives her a nine, which is terrific. When you do that in enough cities, the national ratings jump dramatically. It's impressive enough to make me wonder whether we could do the same thing. We air only once a day per city, which used to be enough. But it's war out there. Anyway, Oprah's answer to the Ricki Lake question was that she considers her competition to be Regis and Kathie Lee, not young Ricki. Oprah knows who her competition is! Maybe the rest of the world will eventually catch on. But who am I kidding? Frankly, there's Oprah and then there's everybody else.

Monday ☆ *January 9*

Danny calls tonight with stunning news. He and his girlfriend, Lila, are talking about wedding dates. This is getting serious. They are thinking about next November. I do point out, though, that she won't graduate from law school until the following May and delicately suggest they wait until then. What's the sense of getting married if you can't start out together? I don't want to come on too strong, but this is marriage. I should know. I was in my early twenties when I married my first wife, Kay. We did it hastily. The truth is, we probably didn't know each other well enough. That marriage was painful for both of us, even though it lasted eleven years and produced two terrific kids—a lovely daughter, Amy, who now works in the music industry in California. And Dan, of course, who's planning to marry a lovely young lady—after overcoming so many obstacles. I'm very happy for him.

Claudia Cohen has a new love and is smiling again. Claudia was divorced last year from Ronald Perelman, who runs Revlon. That split was hurtful to her and to all of her friends. Joy and I had so many great times with them over the years. We hated to see it happen. But Claudia kept a remarkably stiff upper lip. Despite her social standing, Claudia was never afraid to work and work hard. She was a columnist for both the *Daily News* and the *New York Post* years ago, and I remember hearing stories about how she'd return to the office in the wee hours of the morning after covering a late-night event, bang out the story, then sleep on the floor. In her fur coat, of course.

For our show, she's still out at all the major premieres with her camera crew, in the midst of the wild paparazzi scene, getting those interviews and bringing back the story for the next morning. She doesn't have to do it, believe me. But she loves it and we love her. But now there is someone in her life and Claudia is smiling. We are all sworn to secrecy about it. This is so private, I can't even write his name here. Yet. But it's good to see her happy again.

Wednesday ☆ January 11

I bump into David Halberstam today. He lives down the street from our studio. David is the Pulitzer Prize–winning author who writes about wars and politics and, once in a while, even baseball. He writes so eloquently and poignantly about baseball and the players I followed as a kid—DiMaggio, Ted Williams, Stan Musial. Could life really have been so wonderfully simple back then, or does everything just mellow in retrospect? Will we remember this era of players on strike half as fondly? I doubt it. The game is no longer a game. It's big business. Now I'm getting depressed.

Anyway, Joanna has been working with me at the show for the last couple of weeks before returning for her final semester at Brown University. She's very bright and energetic at the office. She spent last summer interning at the Letterman show, where life is very, very intense. She often came home from that job exhausted and beaten. She hadn't imagined it would be so much work. But a late-night show is brutal. Always has been. I don't want her to think every television show operates with such frenzy and high stakes. So she's getting a taste of how we do things here. After the show, Gelman conducts a casual meeting with the staff, then there's lunch, more booking of guests in the afternoon, and, by nightfall, the next day's show is set. A packet of information about the guests is assembled and sent over to my apartment. Gelman calls me to check in before bed. And, usually *in bed,*

I bone up on the guests and awaken ready to interview all comers. Don't get me wrong—some days it's a struggle to pull it all together, but nothing like the combat zone she saw over at David's show. Internships are designed to prepare you for career pursuit, but Joanna still isn't sure if TV is for her. Nothing is easy.

Thursday ☆ January 12

At lunch today, somebody asked me if I knew what John Severino was doing these days. Then he smiled. Ah, Severino, the man who brought me back to New York, the reason I'm here today. Of course, I knew that Sev had aligned himself with a German television broadcasting group and was doing fabulous things in Europe. And then I smiled back. Severino is the kind of guy who makes other guys smile. Particularly if you worked for him.

Our paths first crossed in Boston, October 1964. Remember that Westinghouse show and how I'd been hired to follow Steve Allen in the late-night spot? I was out on a promotional tour—first stop, Boston. On the ride into downtown Boston that Sunday afternoon, I saw groups of WBZ-TV workers standing at various sites along the route as my limo sped by. They were trying to create some hoopla for me, as though I was a big star—when in fact most of them had never heard of me. Nevertheless, the station insisted all its personnel take part in this press event. So there they stood with their "Welcome Regis!"

placards waving on high as I zoomed past. After passing one cluster of them, I looked back through the rear window by chance and, to my horror, saw one of them giving me the finger. I was shocked. One of the execs riding with me saw it, too. "Who's that?" I asked. "Oh, that's Sev. John Severino. He's starting a new job at ABC Chicago tomorrow, but we made him come out here today."

Fast forward ten years. 1974. Chicago. I've been out of work and now it's my first day at WLS-TV. I'm filling in during the summer as host of *A.M. Chicago*, whose regular host had moved on to *Good Morning America*, then suddenly died. I introduce myself to the Chicago audience and give the city and the powerhouse station a genuine plug. I'm thrilled to be here. Severino is still the general manager here, but this is his last day. He's on his way to Hollywood to head up KABC-TV. Before leaving, he told the station manager, Chris Duffy, that he appreciated the comments I'd made on my first day. I didn't get that job in Chicago and was really down in the dumps that November when he called me in Hollywood. We set a meeting and, when I arrived late in the afternoon, he was lying on the couch, crushed with a hangover. He got right down to business. "Could you do movie reviews for the station?" At that time, television newscasts were starting their own movie reviews. David Sheehan over at KCBS was already flying high with his reviews. And that's how my return to Los Angeles broadcasting started.

Every night at eleven I did a review or an entertainment feature or a celebrity interview. My years on *The Joey Bishop Show* paid off. All those stars I'd met back then remembered me and made themselves available for interviews. As a result of all that starpower, the news ratings began to climb. Sev wanted more. He put me on the six P.M. news, too. But those reports had to be different from the eleven o'clock reports. It was hard work, but I loved it.

Then the host job of *A.M. Los Angeles* opened up. I went to Sev and reminded him this was what I really did best. Sev gave me that job, too. Only he said I had to continue doing my bit on both newscasts. *A.M. Los Angeles* was ninety minutes long, so I reinstated my San Diego format. Some Host Chat for laughs, and then the guests. Some days the morning show would leave me exhausted. But I would still have to drive from our Hollywood station to Westwood, screen a movie, come back to the station, edit the film clip, write the review, and deliver it on the six o'clock news. Then I'd go find something else to do at eleven. It was a killer schedule, but my stuff was clicking with viewers. And Sev was watching the ratings go up everywhere and wouldn't think of letting me cut back. Finally, after more than a year of working around the clock, I gave up. I couldn't do it anymore. Reluctantly, he took me off the news at eleven.

From the start, Sev and I had a unique relationship. He was a dynamic general manager, full of machismo. At the station, it was always lots of good times and laughs and barbecues on the front lawn outside Sev's office. I would visit him every afternoon around five, open his refrigerator, pull out a Diet Coke and some cheese, and we'd talk and laugh. He was a fierce and savvy competitor who could chew out someone like you'd never heard before. But he was very supportive of me.

My only recurring problem was breaking in my next producer. They kept getting promoted. I remember when Frank Kelly, now at Paramount in charge of TV programming, left our show to become KABC's program director. They brought in Ron Ziskin, from San Francisco, who's now one of the most prolific television producers in Hollywood with his Five Point production company. Ziskin had never seen an opening like ours where the hosts just casually talked. He wanted to tighten it up and shorten it. So a problem developed. One day Sev appeared in the hallway where Ron and I were discussing the opening. Without even saying hello, he pinched Ziskin's cheek and, with his inimitable Italian swagger, whispered to him, "Do it his way, *kapeesh*?" And then he was gone. Ziskin said, "I fear him. And, incidently, what does *kapeesh* mean?" I knew from the Italian side of my family, it meant "You understand?" But I told him it meant "Or you die." The blood drained out of Ziskin's face and, from then on, we did it my way.

Sev had a masterful way of doing business. He got our station into high gear. Ratings were soaring. By this time, Cyndy Garvey had joined me as morning co-host after Sarah Purcell went off to other pursuits. I remember how Sev made that decision, too. Cyndy had come on once as a guest with her then-husband, Dodger great Steve Garvey. Sev thought she'd make a terrific co-host. I told him, "Sev, Cyndy's never done this before. Isn't the co-host job a bit much for her?" He said, "You're going to be the major co-host, and she's going to be the minor co-host." The only problem was he never told her. The show continued to fly anyway, getting unheard-of fifty percent shares on many days. Twice they brought in Phil Donahue to go up against us in syndication. And twice he was sent packing. *A.M. Los Angeles* had such a stronghold, even Donahue could not make a dent in our numbers. (We became part of Hollywood's daily rituals. Telly

Savalas wouldn't report to the set of *Kojak* until he'd seen our Host Chat.)

But despite our warm friendship and professional success together, Sev was all business during my contract renegotiations. He was both cunning and cute. I didn't have an agent then, so I had to face him alone. And I was absolutely no match for him. "Here's how we're going to do this," he would say in the quiet of his office. "You write down four numbers for four years of salary and I'll do the same. Four years, four numbers. And we'll see how they compare." Naturally, I would never write down what I thought I deserved, always opting for a fairly modest figure. I'd hand him my numbers. He'd hand me his numbers, which were slightly higher than mine. And he'd say, "Tell you what. You're doing a terrific job. Let's take my numbers." We took his because mine were so low, naturally I'd be very grateful for my raise.

After that four-year stint, changes were in the wind. Syndicators began noting our local show's big ratings and were checking us out. But they never understood the simple magic of that opening segment—two people just talking. National audiences would never accept it, they said. But I was getting eager to try. After nearly eight years at KABC—every morning at nine, every evening at six—I was itchy. The ABC network recognized our station's ratings prowess by promoting Sev to president of the network and taking him back to the New York headquarters.

Meanwhile, my contract was running out. And either Sev had forgotten or was too busy preparing for his big move east to be concerned with my situation. There were lots of farewell parties for him and, at the final one, he thanked me and popular anchorman Jerry Dunphy for making all this possible. I hated to see him go. The station would never be the same, I thought. And it never was. But, more importantly, my contract was up. I wanted to try my hand nationally. And still, no one said a word to me about my future.

By now it was summer, 1981, the year the great Grant Tinker took over as president of NBC. A longtime fan of the morning show, he called me and suggested we try it on the NBC network. Getting a call from Grant Tinker was like getting a call from God. Earl Greenberg, his West Coast program director, swung into action. And I was very flattered.

Once Sev got wind of this in New York, he was furious. I guess he might have been embarrassed about not locking me into a new deal before he left, but he now turned it into a matter of loyalty: Who gave me the big break back in 1974 when I was on the beach without a job? And what about all those Thanksgiving Days when I would call to thank him for that break? He made the decision difficult. Change is never easy for me. But after all those years of working local, here was my chance to go national. Tinker was changing NBC. He was highly regarded in the business and had built the powerful MTM production company from scratch. Why not go with him and make it happen nationally, once and for all? So I said yes to NBC.

What I hadn't considered was David Letterman's futile attempt to do a successful nine A.M. show on the NBC network. Dave wasn't morning. He was night. But the affiliates were burned by his morning show, which had just gone down in flames, and didn't want another one. So only about fifty-nine percent of the NBC stations agreed to broadcast my show. And then came word that the show would be a quick half-hour long. Worse yet, it would be taped the day before. This, they said, was the only way to beam the show back to the East Coast for nine A.M. broadcast—short of working in the dead of night. Suddenly, I was back on tape-delay (my Westinghouse downfall) with a mere half-hour to play with. My openings always ran about fifteen minutes. It just wouldn't be the same show.

Cyndy Garvey had moved to New York and I chose Mary Hart to be my NBC co-host. I had seen Mary work locally on *PM Magazine*, where her face lit up the screen. Meanwhile, my phone would ring late at night and it would be Severino calling from New York, making me suffer. My Irish Catholic guilt would spill all over the place and he knew it. So he would begin a scary litany of what I had done to him—a betrayal, a dishonor. Over and over and over again. It was a spiel worthy of any godfather, until I was dripping with perspiration and clenched with remorse. He told me that the new show would never make it under those conditions. Moreover, he said, he would order an all out promotional blitz for *A.M. Los Angeles* to bury me alive. And he did. He predicted that NBC would pull the plug on my show in April. And they did. Sixteen years after the Westinghouse fiasco, I had failed again nationally. How could I have let them put me on tape, cut me to a half-hour, and destroy me all over again?

Now it was 1982, and I was out of work again. I was older but apparently no wiser. One nice thing happened as I left the NBC studio after my last broadcast. Ron Ziskin, my old producer, waited after the show and told me about a new network starting up called the Cable Health Network, which became Lifetime. They were looking for shows. I would be able to package my own show, make my own decisions, and that sounded great. Joy and I went to work together everyday, and—with Bonnie Burns as producer—we set up production offices in Hollywood.

The cable show, *Regis Philbin's Health Styles*, was a nice enough experience, but I was losing heart all over again. The network was in its infancy, which meant their money was tight. We taped thirteen weeks of shows and waited for a renewal, which took forever to get. In the interim, months rolled by with nothing to do. The loneliest feeling in the world. J.J. was obsessed with playing Pac Man video games at the time and, after she went to school, I would take my place at the machine and try to beat my previous high score. I became addicted to Pac Man. In fact, it may have helped me survive a very tough year. I had been the king of Los Angeles mornings for so long— and suddenly I was now in hiding in my own home, getting better every day at Pac Man.

One night, deep in my doldrums, Joy and I attended a party for Duke Vincent, second-in-command for Aaron Spelling's organization and a former Blue Angel pilot. It was a big tented affair in the Bel Air backyard of Duke's girlfriend, Carol Moss. On this beautiful summer night, I suddenly spotted Elton Rule, the big boss at ABC, along with Fred Pierce, his programming chief. And next to them was Severino. He nodded across the lawn at me. Later, we bumped into each other at the buffet table. He said he wanted to talk to me. We hadn't talked for months and months. Of course, all of my friends were aware of the big feud between us. So they watched closely as Sev and I strolled to a secluded spot where we could talk. One of my pals, Mike Srednick, crept up behind Sev and smiled, as if to say, "Thank God you two are finally making up—maybe now he'll offer you a job." I, too, was hopeful. Sev looked at me very seriously—and just picked up where he'd left off on those late-night guilt-inducing phone calls. He began repeating what I had done to hurt him. Over and over and over again. How ironic, I thought, looking over Sev's shoulder at Srednick's hopeful face, listening to a rant Srednick could not hear.

That was the end of the party for me. For another six months, I lingered in Pac Man hell, wondering what would happen next. What happened next was a January phone call from a New York–based William Morris agent named Jimmy Griffin. I had never met him before. He said he was aware of a longtime problem in the ABC morning schedule there. The local nine A.M. slot had become a death valley since departure of veteran host Stanley Siegel. Nothing worked. It was an embarrassment for the whole network. Jimmy knew this. He also knew how Sev felt about me. But he took the shot, anyway. "If you think with your head and not with your heart," he told Sev, "you know he's the one who could make it happen for you here."

Sure enough, it worked. I was told to call Severino and talk to him. As I was dialing, I thought, "My God, what if he lapses into all of that what-you-did-to-me stuff. I'll shoot myself." But he didn't. He wasn't very friendly. He was all business. He hated New York and warned me, "It's cold and it's dark and ugly here. I just want you to know that." I knew that, but I didn't care. I had checked with my astrologer friend, Howard Sheldon. (We now use Howard on the show every Labor Day to prognosticate the upcoming year.) Howard checked my horoscope and said, "You must go to New York. There will be a tremendous success there."

Joy and I decided to go back and take a look around the city. Bill Fyffe, my old news director at KABC-TV, was now general manager of WABC-TV. He put us up at the ABC suite on the top floor of the Plaza Hotel. As a kid, I had always marveled at the Plaza from the sidewalk below. Now we would be staying there in that gorgeous suite. Joy and I were very excited, but wondered if we could actually bring Joanna and J.J. and make a real life in the city? Every horror story I'd ever heard about New York came to mind. All that crime. All that corruption. It wouldn't be easy.

We flew in on a Saturday night, George Washington's birthday, 1983. A limo met us at JFK Airport. This was the big time, all right. It was a thrill stepping out in front of the Plaza, having the doorman usher us in. We passed a sign outside the revolving door which said, "If it's important, it's happening at the Plaza." "That's us," I said to Joy. And we laughed. We went to check in at the big marble reception desk I've seen a thousand times since that night. "The room for Mr. and Mrs. Regis Philbin, please," I said. The clerk looked and looked and finally said, "How do you spell it?" That didn't help. There was no reservation. It was Saturday night, on a holiday weekend, in New York City, and we had no room. It was embarrassing. I couldn't believe it. I didn't have anybody's phone number to call. We might as well have been starring in Neil Simon's *The Out-of-Towners*. Joy was beginning to look at me as though it was my fault again. Finally, somebody recognized my name from *The Joey Bishop Show* and let us have our suite. From the windows, we could look across 58th Street into an office building. It was deserted. The lights were still on. It looked like a thousand desks, all lined up and ready for business. "This is going to be a big change for us if it happens," I thought.

The next day, accompanied by Beth Forcelledo from the ABC station group (another of my former producers who had shot through the ranks), we looked at apartments. The rents were staggering. The rooms were small. I wondered how we could ever move from that big comfortable house in Hancock Park to this city. It was biting cold. Piles of dirty snow were packed on the edges of sidewalks and the winter wind never stopped blowing. Just like Sev said, it was cold and dark and ugly. That night, Bill Fyffe took us to dinner at the Ritz Carlton Hotel, got us tickets to the Broadway shows *Dream Girls* and *Cats*—that "Memories" song stuck in my heart as I thought about the changes I was about to inflict on my family. I did love the fact that I would be working live again, that the ratings were so low there was no place to go but up. And it was strangely exhilarating to be back in New York City again.

In the morning, still in bed, I looked at the building across the street, at that office, now filled with working people, talking on the phone, doing business, making things happen. It wasn't even nine o'clock, yet they were all at their desks—a far cry from the Los Angeles malaise. We had a big decision to make. Joy could go either way. In fact, she was favoring New York. She thought it might be exciting. I wasn't so sure. Finally, we decided we couldn't do it. The move would be too much. We'd just never make it. I went to the station to tell Bill Fyffe. He was disappointed, but said I should tell Severino myself.

I didn't like that idea. They had flown us first class, given us the Plaza suite, bought us dinners and Broadway shows—but I had to tell him no. It would be the first time I'd actually seen him since that backyard party and my guilt was rising. Back then, ABC headquarters were on Sixth Avenue and the offices were quite imposing. Sev's was big and spacious. And sitting there with him was one of his lieutenants, Mark Mandela. Obviously, Fyffe had called and told him of my decision, but Sev let me tell him myself. I stumbled through it. Gave him all the reasons—the kids, the schools, the real estate, the apartments. And he began looking at me like I had let him down again. Suddenly, Mandela said to Sev that he thought I could be a big star here. "Hey, didn't you hear him?" Sev said. "He don't want to come here!" Thus began the good cop–bad cop routine played to perfection by these two Italian masters of the game. They spoke to each other like I wasn't even in the room. "He could do commercials and make lots of money," Mandela said. "How many times do I have to tell you, he don't want to come here!" Sev would answer. I just sat at the conference table between them and watched and listened. They put on a great show. Finally, Mandela said, "Hey, we're going to make an unprecedented offer to you." Sev shouted, "Don't waste your time!" "No," Mandela said, "I want him to hear this." Well, by this time, I wanted to hear it myself.

"We're going to make you an offer we've never offered anyone before," Mandela told me. "We're going to offer you a one-year deal with—and listen to me very carefully—a *special clause*. And we're going to call this clause a *misery clause*. One year from the day you start, you come to us and you say 'Hey, I'm miserable!' Then you can leave." I had to think quickly. Usually, I was stuck with four-year deals with no escape hatch. Here was a chance to try it for a year and, if we didn't like it, we could leave.

I asked Mandela to meet me in an hour at Trader Vic's downstairs at the Plaza, where Joy and I would give him a decision. I said goodbye to Sev, thanked him again, avoided his evil-eye, and rushed back to the hotel where Joy was packing.

But I came in and said, "Wait. There's a new development." I let Mark Mandela do the rest at lunch. They would fly me home every other weekend through the summer; in September, Joy and the kids would move here. I said, "Gee, my mother hasn't been to New York in years." Mandela slapped the table and said, "Hey! Here's a ticket for Mama, too!" All that Italian charm. Who could resist? One year? We could do anything for a year. We could make it for a year. We would treat it like a vacation. It'd be a great experience for the kids. We would somehow find the right apartment, the right school, and I'd be working again. I'd be live. Live in New York. We were on our way. Ready for the change of a lifetime. Which means that whenever I think of Sev, I can only smile.

Friday ☆ January 13

Friday the 13th. But we get through the show anyway. Everybody's talking about the weather in New York. It's the mildest winter in years. And this will be one of the warmest days in January history, with a high of sixty-one degrees. I hurry home after lunch to change into my walking clothes and head for Central Park. I've been doing that treadmill three days a week at Radu's, and it's fine—but a walk in Central Park in January is golden.

Apparently, everybody has the same idea. The park is filled with joggers and walkers and sitters and people with their dogs who haven't been out in the park for months. Everyone seems slightly stunned with the balmy temperatures. I keep a brisk pace and head for Belvedere Castle overlooking the large pond. And out there on the pond I spy a TV set, sitting all alone on the ice, which is slowly melting around the edges. It's a pretty silver TV set. You wonder how it got there. You see things in New York you just don't see anywhere else. This TV set. Who put it there? Why did they put it there? Will it survive the warm weather?

It's a great walk and, on the way home, I pass P.S. 6, where the girls attended elementary school when we first came here. Outside the playground gates on 82nd Street a large cluster of parents wait. That was us just a few years ago, it seems. Now it's their turn. I remember those days well. And I remember it all the more vividly because of what I wrote here yesterday. Funny how you relive emotions when you write them down. We came here and found an apartment on the Upper East Side so the kids could go to that school whose red doors you might remember seeing in the movie *Kramer versus Kramer*. We took a two-bedroom apartment. Foolishly, I thought the kids could share one room during this year of the Misery Clause. Not a chance. It was too close for comfort. Every night was fight night for them. Many nights they'd leave notes on our pillows, begging us to take them home to California. It was heartbreaking.

But the months went by and my year was finally up.

The ratings had started at hash marks in April 1983, but had grown noticeably. And ABC seemed pleased. But I knew we all were desperately missing California. There was only one thing to do. Go see Sev and tell him, "Hey, I'm miserable." And I was. It would be the only time in my career that I'd have this kind of leverage. I walked into his office and yelled it so loudly, there would be no mistaking it. "*Hey, I'm MISERABLE!*" Sev knew what I was saying. "Sit down," he said. And I knew what he was doing. He structured another four-year deal with my agent Jimmy Griffin, making our lives a little easier in the big city. But not before I had the satisfaction of saying, "I'm miserable."

Sunday ☆ January 15

NFL playoff day. Usually the best football games of the year. I position myself on the couch and let the games begin. But I'm sleepy. During the second half of the Pittsburgh Steelers–San Diego Chargers game, my eyes get weary. Pittsburgh is ahead, well in command of the game. It looks like a lock. But I lose consciousness and, when I awake, the Chargers are jumping up and down in the stadium that is strangely silent. Don't tell me they won? Yes, indeed, they did. And I missed it.

I decide to wake myself up with a walk. I head over to Central Park to see if the TV set on the ice has survived the warm weather. Not a chance. The pond is all water again. The set is probably on the bottom.

For the second game, the Forty-niners dominate, but the Cowboys fight back hard but unsuccessfully. Tomorrow's point spread for the Super Bowl will be tremendous—seventeen and a half points.

Monday ☆ January 16

Our opening is a little rocky this morning. Usually when the other person is launching into a story, the procedure is to lay back and let them finish the story. But not today. Today she won't let me get any rhythm going. I can't get started. I want to talk about a guy I met the other day, Bob Hurwitz, the president of Home Place, at his Las Vegas store. He told me he bought a lovely home for his mother, Pearl, in Florida a few years ago. He told her to call him whenever she got lonely. "Anytime!" he said. "Please, Mom!" She called him once, got the phone bill, was horrified at the cost, and never called him again.

Sounds just like my mother. For eight years, Pearl never called him. He always had to call her. Then one day last week, she called. He was totally surprised. This hadn't happened in eight years. He picked up the phone feeling a little apprehensive. Was she all right? "Hello, Mom," he said. "Bob," she said, "I just heard Regis Philbin is coming to your store to make an appearance." He couldn't get over the fact she called him about that—about me! Well, it's a cute story, but I couldn't get it out. Kathie kept interrupting: "Why didn't she make the call collect?" "Why didn't he call her more often?" Why, why, why? I keep saying, "Let me finish, please!" These rough edges are the charm of our show, I guess, but some mornings are tougher than others. I'm sure that once in awhile she feels the same way.

After the show, I fulfill a promise I made to some nuns who come to our show every so often. Sister Kevin is a major fan and you never know when she'll show up. One day I asked what she did and she told me she worked at a home that took in incurable cancer patients who could not pay for their treatment. I told her I'd come see her and her patients one day. Today is the day. It's St. Rose's Home on the Lower East Side, run for years by the Dominican nuns, founded by the daughter of Nathaniel Hawthorne, the famous author. I arrange to take a tape crew with me. I thought it would make for a great feature for the WABC-TV Saturday night magazine show. The nuns were very excited when we turned up. We took a tour of the place, visited with some of the patients, all of whom unfortunately knew their fate. One man had spent twenty-five years there. That's how good the care is there. The nuns are filled with love and dedication, and those men and women couldn't be in better hands. And all of this funded simply by donations. Too bad government health care can't accomplish anything comparable.

Late this afternoon Joy calls to say her purse has been stolen. I always worry about her out on the town, but I guess it could have been worse. She asks me to leave five dollars with the doorman to pay for her cabfare home. She was in Bloomingdale's looking at purses, ironically enough. She set her purse down and, just like that, it was gone. Ten years ago, somebody lifted her wallet out of her purse at Radio City Music Hall. This time they took the whole purse. She's on the phone right now canceling the credit cards. And she's not too happy. So I guess these things don't only happen to me.

Friday ☆ January 20

I try to help solve a murder case. Kathie Lee and I have been asked by the *Bill Cosby Mysteries* people to do a cameo on their show—by interviewing a murder suspect on our show. We'll film this right after today's broadcast, but before we can begin, I receive a phone call from Washington, D.C. It's Danny, who tells me that he's checked himself into the hospital with severe kidney pains. Could be either a kidney infection or a kidney stone. He's had both over the years and each condition is very, very painful. I feel that familiar pang in my heart. How I wish he could be free of pain for a long, long stretch of time. But it keeps coming back. He assures me he's okay and probably will be out of the hospital in a couple of days.

I go back to our studio to shoot the scene with Cosby and Kathie Lee. I can't help but notice Cosby is a hands-on producer for this series. He busies himself calling the shots before we do the scene. By now, the three of us have been friends for many years. Kathie Lee spent three years as Bill's opening act all over the country. And I remember his very first television appearance, on Jack Paar's Friday night show in the early sixties. It was his breakthrough debut appearance. I remember switching on the TV set in my San Diego newsroom, preparing the eleven o'clock newscast, and hearing Jack introduce the tall and youthful Cosby. I had just booked Cosby on my next Saturday night show and realized this was the same guy. I had never seen him. He had just released a clever comedy album in which he re-created a conversation between God and an incredulous Noah, who was told to quickly build an ark and gather pairs of animals.

My show would be Cosby's second television appearance and, through the years, we have reminded each other of that night. He followed hypnotist Michael Dean on the show who had put his subjects to sleep on camera. So Cosby came out and kept falling asleep during our interview. I'd ask him a question, then he'd slump down in his chair and pretend to doze. It was great fun. Of course now, thirty years later, he is fabulously successful and wealthy, a kingpin in the business. And Jack Paar, with whom I'll dine later tonight, is happily retired and living comfortably in Connecticut. Meanwhile, I'm still hanging on by my fingertips!

Tonight's dinner conversation between the Paars and the Philbins focuses on America's newest talk-show host, Charles Grodin. Jack first met Chuck at a New Year's Day brunch at our house last year and the two became fast friends. Chuck has authored three books and Jack was immediately impressed with his writing ability. A few weeks ago, Chuck replaced Tom Snyder as the nightly host of his own show on CNBC. Apparently, Jack has been extremely supportive, calling Chuck to encourage him and also calling various critics, urging them to pay attention.

Near the end of his first week on the air, Grodin called me. We chatted a bit, then he finally got to the reason for the call. Jack had been checking in with him frequently during the week preceding the show's debut. But since his first show, there had been no calls from Jack and it was driving Grodin crazy. Now it was Friday, and still no call. So Grodin called me to see if I would find out whether there's a problem. What does Jack think? Is he disappointed? Softly, I mention this to Jack at dinner and I'm relieved to hear that Jack thinks Grodin is truly terrific. He just hasn't gotten around to calling him. But he will, and Chuck will be able to sleep again. I could be turning into the Henry Kissinger of talk-show hosts.

Monday ☆ January 23

We fly into the talk-show battlefield. The annual NATPE convention is being held in Las Vegas. NATPE is where all of television's syndicators unveil their new shows—and make hoopla over successful long-running programs like ours—to station programmers from every market in the country. On the plane, Joy and I run into Suzanne Sommers and her husband, Alan Hamel. Suzanne had a talk show that didn't make it this year, but her syndicated primetime sitcom continues to flourish. The death of her talk show was a painful experience for her, however, and she doesn't mind talking about it. Reminds me of my own past failures and how lucky I am right now.

Besides attending the convention, we'll tape two TV shows from Bally's Jubilee Theatre and also appear two nights in concert at Bally's Celebrity Theatre. I saw Dean Martin perform in the same showroom back when Bally's was the MGM Grand. Never in a million years did I dream that I would one day do an act of my own on the same stage. Incidentally, my fellow Dean Martin fan, Bill Zehme, has reported to me that Dean's favorite restaurant, La Famiglia, has closed. Dean ate there practically every night for years. Dean has moved on to a new joint in Beverly Hills. Same time, same routine, same Dean Martin records playing softly in the background. And Zehme tells me Dean is looking better than ever. I'm happy about this.

Meanwhile, Danny Philbin is still in that Washington hospital, going through tests that have been complicated by the barium necessary for taking an upper GI series. Too much barium has clouded his upper body, thus making it impossible to pinpoint Danny's problem. That's the way it was in the old days, too. Always a complication. Always he would be hospitalized for much longer than expected. And always, it seemed, he would get much worse before he got well enough to get out. Then and now, I find it heartbreaking. But I know he'll see it through and conquer this problem, too.

Tuesday ☆ January 24

The NATPE convention is the usual circus. The booths seem bigger than ever and new talk shows are being unveiled in abundance. I remember attending our first NATPE convention seven years ago in Houston. Every reporter, station manager, and hotel bellhop all wanted to know what would make our show different. Ironically, in 1995—after an avalanche of daytime talk shows—ours is the only one that really is different. A darker style of talk has overtaken the airwaves. It started with Phil Donahue running through his audience in Ohio, then later in Chicago. Oprah took the concept to new, astounding heights, also in Chicago. This year's convention, meanwhile, is buzzing about Ricki Lake. And waiting in the wings are a dozen Ricki Lake types, ready for broadcast battle in September. The emphasis here is on youth. Next year, anyone over twelve can have a talk show. Cody should be ready soon.

Frankly, the concept behind all of these shows is simple: You get guests who are at odds with one another, real or presumed. Have your staff explain to them that they are there to argue. To get hostile. To get in each other's face, call each other names, make each other cry, and do everything but threaten to punch each other out. The crowd in the studio will react. They will play their role. Loudly. And if you are the host, all you've got to do is listen closely to that wire in your ear and repeat the questions the producers are feeding you from the booth. Then go get some press. Keep that hype flying. Try to get your show broadcast twice a day, so the ratings will seemingly grow overnight. Don't worry about media reporters catching on to these tricks. They will either be too lazy or too dumb to find out where the bigger ratings are coming from. So they'll join the pack and make another new star.

And so it goes, day after day: The most ludicrously salacious topics, brought to life by the poor suckers who wait in line for their fifteen minutes of fame, coached to unload their venom on wives, husbands, relatives, sons, daughters, boyfriends, girlfriends, and anyone else within striking distance. And, in turn, they willingly agree to be battered and abused by a hostile studio audience instructed to insult and humiliate all comers. It's a free-for-all, a circus freak show. The human race exploited right before your eyes. And the funniest part of this charade? All of it is produced, sold, and bartered, for the most part, by God-fearing, wholesome broadcast executives who drive to their TV stations and production offices from their leafy suburban homes, and whose kids are safely tucked away in private schools. These are the upstanding people who converge at NATPE and who vie to continue this daily pollution of America. That's the way it is, here in talk-show land, as of 1995.

But this NATPE has yet another twist in store for me. Funny, but true: Joy and I are appearing in different, competing booths. She will hold court at the Group W booth, representing her own red-hot decorating show, *Haven*. And, as always, Kathie Lee and I are working the Buena Vista/Disney booth, on behalf of *Live*. Gelman gets a camera crew and we make a tour of the convention floor in search of Joy. We roam the vast expanse, going from booth to booth, in hot pursuit. Never once do we find her. Or her booth. But we do find everybody else. Big stars, tomorrow's stars, no-chance stars, even my wrestling heroes from the World Wrestling Federation. We see Helen Hunt and Paul Reiser, whose *Mad About You* series is entering syndication. We see Vendela, the *Sports Illustrated* swimsuit covergirl, promoting a special for the magazine. I tell her she looks good, even with her clothes on. We see Jack Hannah's animals from the zoo in Columbus, Ohio. (Once he brought a flying squirrel on our show and the damned thing flew down my shirt and into my pants. Ever have a squirrel in your pants? It's no fun.) I approach actress Tori Spelling and ask, "How are things going on *Melrose Place*?" And, of course, she's not on *Melrose Place*; she's a veteran cast member on *Beverly Hills 90210*, which is the other big show produced by her father, Aaron Spelling. But, come on! These are Fox shows—how am I supposed to keep them straight? Tori just looks at me like I had kicked her dog or committed some other terrible faux pas. I'm sorry, Tori, *all* right!

Anyway, we cannot find Joy. We return to the Buena Vista booth, and Gelman sends the camera back out to locate her and bring her back to us. But, by now, she's wandering the floor looking for me—and having no luck, either. Later, we'll intercut all of this futile searching for a funny segment on the show. But for now, it gets frustrating. After we hook up at last, I visit the Group W booth, where Joy is flanked by homemaking icon Martha Stewart and bearded house-builder Bob Vila. All three of their shows are being sold as a home-oriented weekend viewing package—ninety minutes of practical how-to stuff. Joy is getting a big charge out of all the hoopla, and she loves doing her own show. I think it's got a good shot, especially with that Group W power-push behind it. Funny that Joy should be aligned with Group W, the company formerly known as Westinghouse, which thirty-one years earlier gave me my first national shot. Of course, that was a disaster. Joy can only benefit from all they've learned since.

Outside, on Bally's giant marquee, Kathie Lee and I can see our names lighting up the strip, which is a thrill. And beneath our names are those two magic words: SOLD OUT! Whenever I'm asked what I do in concert, I always respond, "What do I do? I sell out!" I know it's brash and abrasive, but I can't resist. Anyway, our Bally's shows go very well, with the second performance clicking especially well. In fact, it's one of the best shows we've ever done.

One highlight for me came during my Calendar Girl number, in which I invite audience members to audition for a co-host job. I tell them, "You think those nineteen minutes are so easy to do. You think you could do it. Well, you can. All you've got to do is make it fun. Make it interesting. Tell me funny stories from your lives. Don't come up here and stare at me. Keep talking." The last woman who comes up tells me a story about her first Turkish bath. "First of all," she says, "this handsome Turkish guy takes hold of you, eases you down onto a towel, and he proceeds to give you a very stimulating massage." She explains the massage in excruciating detail. And I'm saying, "Lady, please, you're getting me crazy!" The Turk has those sensitive hands, those soulful eyes. Finally, she describes how he began to massage her breasts. The audience is howling. But I've had enough. And I yell, "Bingo! That's it! You win! You got the job!"

Lots of talk around town about the Super Bowl this

weekend. Kathie, of course, will sing the National Anthem, but she's not showing any jitters. Since I'm in Las Vegas and nobody knows more about sports than me, I decide to place a bet. Why not make a few bucks at Bally's sports book? I simply cannot resist the twenty-point spread—so I take the Chargers and twenty, plus a parlay bet. I wager that the total points in the first quarter will be over thirteen, the total points in the third quarter will be under thirteen, and there will be under five quarterback sacks in the entire game. I'm feeling very confident. Until the bookie flashes me a knowing smile that leaves me unnerved. We'll see.

Thursday ☆ January 26

Dead tired. After two concerts, two broadcasts, and the NATPE madness, Joy and I pack up, check out of Bally's, and head for Los Angeles. As always, she's brought too many clothes, so packing is an ordeal. Finally, we get down to the car and out to the airport. The bags are checked curbside, but I always find there's more carry-on luggage than the stuff we just checked. I can barely close the overhead bins, so there's no chance any of our contents will be shifting. Later, at the Universal City Hilton, the lobby is jammed with conventioneers of another kind. My heart sinks. This one is for people in the business of public storage, mini-warehouses, and such. Why in the world would they need a convention? Apparently, they do. So there are more lines and more waiting. Maybe we should have gone back to New York.

But here I am at the same hotel where I started writing these daily accounts last June. This is where the *Larry Sanders* people put me up, where I can look out of the window across the freeway and see where my backyard slipped down the hill and forced me to lose my house, where the O.J. Simpson case continues to be the most celebrated murder story possibly of all time. Seems like it's been years since I was last here, but it's only been seven months.

Every time we return to L.A., there's a hot new restaurant that you simply must go to. Right now it's Eclipse, where we join our pals Barry and Susan Glazer for dinner. Eclipse opened at the former site of Morton's restaurant, the show business power room, which has now moved across the street to a bigger space, which formerly housed Trumps restaurant. Who can keep track of all these restaurants? But Eclipse has the usual contingency of celebrity owners, including Steven Seagal and O.J.'s attorney Robert Shapiro. As we enter the restaurant's waiting area we see Tony Curtis, dressed in his somewhat mysterious Nehru outfit. He rises to say hello and introduces us to his tall, blond, bosomy girlfriend who's wearing a glitzy, low-cut, red dress. No wonder Tony is behaving so charmingly.

Inside the restaurant, we can't resist celebrity-watching. Morgan Fairchild holds court in a booth with three men. Milton Berle and his young wife are dining just behind our table. Jackie Collins saunters in and takes the center table. And look who's joining her—yes! Tony Curtis and his lovely friend. The great theatrical producer Cameron MacIntosh is also here celebrating the Los Angeles opening of his show *Miss Saigon*. A waiter comes over to me and says, "Cameron would like to say hello."

So I go over to wish him well. "The newspaper reviews are coming out tomorrow," he tells me, anxiously. "I don't think they matter," I tell him. The show is still running in London after more than five years and is now in its fifth year on Broadway. So I think *Miss Saigon* will be safe in L.A. for its six-month run. Still, nothing is as charming as a successful guy who gets nervous about his hit show.

Friday ☆ *January 27*

Just like old times in California, Joy and I are having dinner again with Peter and Alice Lassally, at Mortons. The Lassallys uprooted from Los Angeles a few years ago and came to New York, where Peter has been David Letterman's executive producer. Now he's back on the West Coast to oversee Tom Snyder's *Late, Late Show*, also a production of Letterman's Worldwide Pants company. Fortunately, Peter and Alice are relishing their time back in California. They never warmed to New York life. Too hard and too cold, after too long in Los Angeles. I would tease Peter, saying, "Is this any way for you to go through your golden years in the business? Amid the chaos of New York and the frenzy of the Letterman show?" He'd just shake his head and smile. For twenty-two years, he had been producer for Johnny Carson's *Tonight Show*, running an elegant institution from behind the scenes, always with his unflappable air. Every day he'd pull on a sweater, drive from his Beverly Hills home to Burbank, and turn out another Carson show. He had that good life down pat. Back in the mid-seventies, Peter made it possible for me to tape a memorable interview with Johnny—one of the handful of television interviews he ever did. But there were certain restrictions. Johnny had said, "Well, if he meets me outside the studio as I'm parking my car, I'll be happy to spend a few minutes with him." It wasn't much of a commitment, but for Johnny you go along with anything.

So I waited one day outside the NBC soundstage in Burbank with a camera crew and my associate producer Tom Chasik. At around two in the afternoon, Johnny pulled up in his little Corvette (with RG license plates that stood for Regular Guy). He climbed out of the car, carrying only the small leather pouch in which he kept his keys and wallet. (Johnny travels light.) We talked for a moment, then I suggested, "Let's go inside and see what your first ten minutes at the office are like." We walked down the hallway toward his studio. First stop was the wardrobe room where every day he picked out the suit he'd wear that night. He let me pick it out that day. I went for a puce jacket, but then I reconsidered. "No, Johnny," I said, "I don't want you in puce." So I picked something else for him.

Then I said, "Come on, show me the set." So we walked onto the *Tonight Show* set, which was deserted. There was Doc's bandstand to the left. And there was homebase—the famous desk and, behind it, the background window overlooking the twinkling lights of Los Angeles. And then I said to him, "Show me what you do before you walk out onstage every night." So we stood behind the curtain for a moment, where there was a long mirror in which he took one last glance at himself before

Baby Regis. To the right, the
Bronxdale swimming pool.
Both of us all new and shiny
and just starting out.

Well, it's not Cody, but I did
have nice legs.

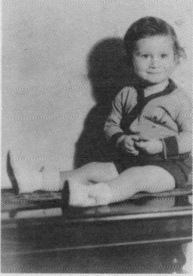

My father and me.

The first Power
Ranger, with a
homemade bow
and arrow and a
canteen, ready
to explore Bronx
Park.

My first true
love—Skipper.

Yeah, that's right; a pair of knickers.
You got a problem with that?

My mother, Florence, at home
in the Bronx in the 40s.

Boxing lessons from my father,
who once fought Barney Ross.

Working at Mac's candy store—our hangout in the Bronx opposite my school, Our Lady of Solace.

Graduation Day: Mom, Dad, Notre Dame stadium in the background. Ready to set the world on fire.

The ROTC ball at Notre Dame with my girlfriend, Mari Farmer. Do I look old enough to defend this country?

But first, two years in the Navy.

First on-camera job in San Diego doing "Feature Desk" on the KFMB-TV news.

My first talk show on KOGO-TV. Throwing passes and catching them from Jack Kemp, San Diego Chargers' quarterback.

KFMB-TV

KOGO-Radio

Everyone did our show Saturday night in San Diego. Richard Nixon, running for governor in California, watches while I sell Coca-Cola.

Ronald Reagan, before his political career began. I knew even then that he had a future in Sacramento and Washington.

Photography House

Regis Philbin Collection

An enormous thrill for me to interview the legendary Notre Dame football coach, Frank Leahy.

Bob Hope flying into San Diego via PSA. The first of many interviews with him.

New York columnist Walter Winchell showing off his column. He knew them all.

Bill Cosby—following hypnotist Dr. Michael Dean on our show, who had a certain effect on Bill.

Cosby and me 30 years later, still on stools, and this time I'm putting him to sleep.

Billy Graham in 1964.

My all-time favorite wrestler, Freddie Blassie.
You can see—he's afraid of me.

Every night doing seven minutes with Joey Bishop in his monologue. What an education!

Every day we'd walk Vine Street in Hollywood. Laughs at the old Ranch Market.

all of America saw him. I asked, "Do you still get nervous?" He said, "Oh, yeah. Oh, yeah." I said, "Really? After all these years?" He said, "Yeah, yeah. It helps to be a little nervous." And then we walked out through the curtain and over to the star on the floor, the spot where he delivered every one of his monologues. I stood right on his star, looking up at all those empty seats. I felt like I was standing in a Greek forum with the whole world staring down at me. Then I followed him behind the desk, sat in his chair, and made believe I was him. I don't think he was crazy about that. In fact, he kicked away one of the chair legs, so that I almost teetered and fell off. "Don't get too comfortable," he said. And nobody ever did. But what a thrill.

The day Johnny retired, I reran that interview, which reflected such a classy time for talk shows, a time never to be seen again. After Carson's final show, Peter moved back east, where he helped guide Dave Letterman to CBS and the top. But those late-night wars do take their toll. Each day is a new ordeal. And now Dave has sent Peter out to nurture the Snyder show. As a consolation, at least, he's back where he's happiest. And although Joy and I see a lot of Peter and Alice in New York, we've missed our wonderful times with them in California. The last time I saw them out here was at dinner with—of all people—Johnny and Alex Carson. Joy wasn't with me. I was alone. All alone. It happened last April, and I still get nervous thinking about it.

Call it *My Dinner With Johnny*. I call it painful. That was my fault. And it had all begun so pleasantly. Peter and I visited Johnny one afternoon at his Santa Monica offices. It's as impressive a place as I had imagined it would be. Johnny presides, very casually, in a beautifully decorated suite overlooking the ocean, with a staff of three. I found him calm, relaxed, and funny as ever. We talked about what it would take to bring him back to television. I suggested the Academy Awards, but Johnny said no. In fact, he had no idea what would lure him. I got the feeling he wouldn't be back at all. After ending his long reign with such class and fanfare, maybe there's no way to return. We all wandered out to lunch and had lots of laughs. I was telling Johnny about Peter's misspent golden years in New York and Johnny was enjoying it. So much so, in fact, that we all decided to have dinner together a few nights later at Granita, Wolfgang Puck's place in Malibu. The time was set for eight o'clock.

I remember leaving the Century Plaza Tower a few minutes later than I'd wanted that night. I took Olympic Boulevard, hoping to find an on-ramp to the San Diego Freeway. But there's no ramp from Olympic Boulevard. So I took a street that runs parallel to the freeway for a long time before I finally found a ramp. I got on and realized I'd overshot the turnoff to the Santa Monica Freeway, which leads to the beach. I had traveled so far to get on the freeway, I found myself completely off track. Suddenly, I was heading for Los Angeles International Airport. I felt ridiculous. I would probably never have another chance to dine with Johnny again. And now I was going to be late.

Streets that I had passed for years were flying by. I knew I had to get off on one of them and turn around. Of all places, I pulled off on Slauson, where I quickly learned there was no entrance to get back on the freeway in the opposite direction. So here I was, trapped on Slauson. Yes, the famous Slauson Cut-Off! How many times had I watched Johnny doing his Art Fern daytime-movie-host routine, giving directions to a car dealership located off the complicated Los Angeles freeway system! Always he'd tell viewers to find the Slauson Cut-Off, then recommend we get out of our cars and cut off our Slausons. And he'd whack his pointer against that map with a resounding bang. It was great stuff.

But now it was after eight o'clock and I was still driving around the airport neighborhood. Granita is at least thirty-five minutes away, which meant I was going to be *very* late. Totally inexcusable. I reached for the car phone. Believe it or not, this was the first time I'd ever dialed one of those things. I amazed myself by actually calling information to get the Granita number. Then I called the restaurant and explained to Peter that I'd gotten lost. He couldn't believe it, but stressed that I get there as soon as possible. I hit the pedal and raced to Malibu, but didn't arrive until eight-forty-five. And Johnny wasn't smiling, even as I babbled my explanation and apology. The Slauson coincidence didn't even amuse him. Forty-five minutes late. For Johnny. I kept Johnny waiting. And he was never the same with me. I'm still wincing. How could I get lost on the freeway! When will these things stop happening to me?

Sunday ☆ *January 29*

Got to get back to New York in time for the Super Bowl and, of course, the National Anthem. I take an eight A.M. flight, leaving Joy behind in Los Angeles for a family reunion with her mother and sisters. But I'm wondering about Kathie Lee. How are her nerves? Billions of viewers around the world will be watching her belt out Francis Scott Key tonight. Of course, I know she'll be great, but she might be feeling the pressure. Still, I've never seen her not rise to the occasion, especially when singing. I've been with her at concerts when she swore she couldn't possibly go on, that she didn't have it that night, that her voice was shot, or whatever excuse, and she goes out and knocks them dead. So I'm convinced the anthem is in good hands. And I'm also convinced that the San Diego Chargers might have a chance to become champions before the day is over. At least, that's how I bet.

The flight is uneventful. I'm home in plenty of time. So it's just me and the cats and the Super Bowl. But first, the National Anthem. And there she is. And there's Heather Whitestone, Miss America, who accompanies her with a sign language version. As Kathie begins, the camera zeroes in with an extremely tight close-up of her face. And I mean *tight*! Also on the screen, superimposed behind her face, are images of Heather Whitestone, of the rippling American flag, of jet squadrons rocketing through the skies. All very stirring. And, of course, she sounds terrific, singing the song the way it was meant to be sung—with a rousing arrangement by her conductor Paul Mann. But that close-up! When she sings, boy, she opens that mouth wide. I think I can even detect a little cavity on the third molar on the upper right side. She should really have that looked at as soon as possible. For her benefit, I'll tell her about it tomorrow. Oh, and about the game? Forget it. The 49ers easily prevail. No wonder the sports book guy in Vegas was smiling at me when I laid down my hundred bucks.

<hr>

Tuesday ☆ *January 31*

A fund-raiser tonight at an art gallery in Soho. Proceeds will benefit my alma mater, Cardinal Hayes High School in the South Bronx. The school looks exactly the same as it did when I was there, although the surroundings have deteriorated somewhat. At Hayes, I was a mediocre student and did absolutely nothing that would point me toward the career I eventually found. The closest I came, I guess, was tormenting my classmates to get some laughs. You've got to start somewhere. Martin Scorsese and George Carlin attended Hayes as well, and some of my own classmates went on to great accomplishments—Dennis Murphy, a triumphant marine general; John Chambers, a priest who spent twenty-five years working in a Filipino leper colony; even Mario Arunco, the astronaut. Whereas all I have to do is show up every morning and do battle with Kathie Lee.

Unlike so many Catholic schools that have closed over the years, Hayes keeps hanging on. When I returned to New York in the early eighties, it was teetering on the brink of insolvency, after surviving more than a decade of urban blight and the exodus of local businesses from the South Bronx. Now the entire student body is comprised of minorities, seventy percent of them live with single parents, and most can afford only part of their tuition. But these kids are just as driven and polite and proud of their school as I like to think we were. Does my heart good to see that hasn't changed.

The current principal, Father John Graham, is battling and winning ongoing financial crises. He's the kind of priest who could head up any corporation in the country and turn it around. He spearheads so many drives, calling upon Hayes alumni to start endowment funds to offset the deficit. And that's what we're doing tonight in this art gallery. This event was put together by Dick Reilly, who heads the K-III Communications group, which publishes *New York* magazine, among other concerns. Dick never attended Hayes, but nevertheless has cajoled his corporate friends into making donations that have kept the school afloat. In fact, he's largely responsible for installing what may be one of the finest computer classrooms in any high school. I smile when I think about how lucky kids are today, mastering their computers, these mysterious mechanical monsters. I'm still struggling with mine, but I can see it's the future. I do feel better when Reilly tells me that he's just as inept at it as I am.

I wander over to a corner of the art gallery, where two young women dressed in black are sipping cocktails. I strike up a conversation and thank them for supporting my old high school. They have no idea what I'm talking about. They say they were just out gallery-hopping in Soho, saw this crowd, thought it might be a hot gallery, and came inside. They do tell me that they feel good vibes from this crowd. Always happy to share my vibes, all right?

Wednesday ☆ February 1

I go back to the Central Park South studios of photographer Neil Barr to pose for yet another picture for the cover of this book. If the dust-jacket shows me in midair with a stupid grin on my face, you'll know the Hyperion people had their way. They're very high on calling this *I'm Out of Control!*, based on that Dana Carvey line from *Saturday Night Live*. Pretending to be me, he kept shouting, "I'm out of control! I'm out of control!" It was funny, but I never said it. I've been resisting it as a title, but, frankly, I can't think of anything better. So, for the jacket photo, they want me out of control, bounding off the ground, hands and arms extended like a lunatic. I'm resisting that, too. I'm opting to keep my feet on the ground and my arms only slightly open—a compromise. These are the things you don't think about when you write a book.

Thursday ☆ February 2

She can't get enough of me. Kathie Lee wants to have a Regis at home now. She'll settle for a dog, though. A dog named Regis. On this morning's show, she will adopt her canine Regis, which she plans to give to Frank. The Giffords live near the water and Frank wants a dog that can swim, retrieve a floating stick, and bring it back to shore. Frank enjoys the simple pleasures. Anyway, Warren Eckstein, our dog expert, comes with three adorable puppies from which she will make her choice. For the selection process, Gelman mounts a version of *The Dating Game*. It's *The Puppy Game*. Three dogs are hidden behind a partition, while Kathie Lee asks pertinent questions and Warren answers them. I play game-show host. On *The Dating Game*, Jim Lange got to preside over beautiful women contestants. I get dogs. Naturally. So Kathie Lee fires the questions at Warren, but her mind was made up from the start. She wants a light-colored male Labrador and that's what she gets.

He's a blond little Lab who, not unlike his namesake, couldn't be cuter. I think he makes a perfect Regis. And he's one lucky dog to go from a New Jersey pound to live with them. He's going to have a terrific life. To prepare him, we run a montage of clips featuring his predecessors, Chardonnay and Chablis, who Kathie acquired years ago to satisfy her maternal urges. Back then, Frank was still stalling for time. She wanted a baby and Frank said, "How about a puppy?" She got the puppy, but a year later said again, "I want a baby." She got another puppy. Until Cody came along, Chardonnay and Chablis were her only babies. Now they're just dogs again. And this morning they come out to meet little Regis for the first time. But they don't seem too enthused about him. They're a little indifferent, in fact. Just get used to it, Regis. It's not easy being us.

_____

Back to Atlantic City for two nights of shows at Resorts. The weather forecast has our attention. The winter's first major snowstorm is approaching and the weather people are jumping up and down with glee. All winter long, they've had nothing to talk about, waiting for the snow that never came. Now, in February, they're doing their war dance: "The big one is coming!" We rehearse in the late afternoon and I begin watching the Weather Channel as showtime approaches. Snow would have an affect on the audience turnout. But other than a quick flurry, the snow doesn't materialize in Atlantic City. We get a big crowd and give them a good show.

Afterward, in my hotel room, I sit on the bed watching the Letterman show. And, magically, I'm on it. Actually, I turn up in a taped segment, done weeks earlier, that happened so quickly I forgot to mention it in these pages. It was a bit in which Dave drives around town and sends his neighborhood deli man, Rupert Jee, out to make trouble. Rupert is rigged with a tiny camera in his baseball cap, an earpiece, and a hidden microphone. Dave watches him from the van and tells Rupert what to say to whomever he approaches. Usually, he's instructed to say ridiculous things and cause confusion. Their plan on this day was to have Rupert descend on our station, talk his way past the guards, and come upstairs to bother me. Dave's producers told me to be prepared, but not to let anyone in the reception area know anything, especially that they were going to be filmed. "Just let him come," they instructed. So I didn't tell the guards.

Rupert arrived and immediately alarmed them with his bizarre behavior. He asked to see me, so they buzzed my office, and I said, "Send him up." But they must have been worried, because they detained him for a while. So Dave tells Rupert, "All right, lie down on the floor." And he does it. Then he tells him, "Go kiss the picture of Oprah in the lobby." And he gets up and does it. By now, the guards think they've got a certified wacko on their hands. Finally, he comes up to my office and says to me, "Can I have a kiss on the forehead?" I said, "How about an autograph?" He said, "No, I want a kiss on the forehead." I said, "How about an autographed picture?" He said, "No, no, I've got to have a kiss." And so I kissed his forehead, which looks strange through the secret camera-in-the-cap. Then the producers asked me to do it again, but more quickly. So I did. And then I did it once more. Suddenly, I'm getting deeply involved with a deli man! And once Rupert left, Dave came up to say hello. He didn't ask for a kiss, though. He never does. Dave doesn't like to be touched.

Saturday ☆ February 4

The snow came during the night. Big time. Sixteen inches in Princeton, New Jersey. Twelve inches in Philadelphia. Nine in New York. The Weather Channel is on fire. Reporters are breathless. "It's here! It's here!" I look out of my Resorts window at the boardwalk below and there's nothing. Not a flake. The local Philadelphia newscasts are filled with the usual snow scenes—cars stalled, trees down, snowplows chugging. Scary stuff, but tonight all of the seats are full again and the audience is receptive. We thank them all for coming out in the middle of the blizzard of '95, such as it is. Then I look at Kathie Lee onstage and say, "You know, it's kind of romantic being here at this hotel, snowed in by this big blizzard. Frank's not here, Joy's not here, and I know what you're thinking. But the answer is still no."

Monday ☆ February 6

Letterman wants me again. He stops by after our show today to tape a funny feature in our studio. The segment will play like this: One more time I'm supposed to be running down his aisles, firing up his audience. But I stop midway and point out to Dave that I'm always running down his aisles and he never does the same at our show. He says, "Okay, let's go." We run out of his studio, run the fifteen blocks up to our studio, then he careens up and down our aisles. This morning we hold the audience so he can tape the part where he works his way through the crowd. I don't know where David finds the energy for these tapings. He tells me they're exhausting and, at this moment, I can tell he's not in a great mood. So we begin immediately. I lead him running into the studio and up the aisles, where the audience goes crazy. There's handshaking, hugging, yelling. He fights his way through the mob and the place keeps going nuts. Finally, he plants a goodbye kiss on Kathie Lee, gives me a wave, and he's gone. I'll do the rest of the bit with him on another day. Or another night. Running through the streets of New York with Dave. Let's see if he can keep up.

Wednesday ☆ February 8

Time for an identity crisis. This morning I get into a cab with a driver named Angel Rodriguez. He's listening to radio station WPLJ, whose on-air team is doing the usual outrageous things. Angel tells me he hears me on with them all the time. Practically every morning, he says, I call in on that program. Actually, it's Scott Shannon and somebody pretending to be me, but rather than destroy the illusion for him, I don't tell Angel. So we listen as we drive through Central Park. Suddenly, the deejays take a phone call and I'm thinking, "I hope it's not me! Angel won't understand." Sure enough, it's me. It's Regis on the line! The caller is doing his best out-of-control Regis stuff, yelling about Gelman, complaining about Kathie Lee. I don't think he sounds like me, but Angel does. In fact, only now does it begin to dawn on Angel that I couldn't be on the radio and in his cab at the same time. And so now Angel is wondering why I hadn't been altogether truthful in the first place. If he enjoys the gag, let him think it's me, I figured. But no, they had to do their bit while I was in the cab. Not five minutes before I got in or five minutes after I get out. No, they have to ruin my morning. Embarrassed, I confess the truth to Angel Rodriguez, my freshly disillusioned fan. I know he'll never feel the same about me. Sorry, Angel.

Monday ☆ February 13

Sure hands. That's what I've got. Today I demonstrate once again. Super Bowl MVP Steve Young, quarterback for the triumphant 49ers, comes on to test my mettle. He will fire off a long pass to me down Columbus Avenue and the hands will be waiting. This challenge has become a tradition on the show: Over the years, we've had such great quarterbacks as Joe Namath, Boomer Esiason, Warren Moon, Troy Aikman, and many others firing passes at me. And, so far, I've managed to catch them all.

I realize that all sports streaks must come to an end, but not today. Not with the Super Bowl MVP throwing to me. And he seems like a great guy. Good-looking, outgoing, easy to talk to, and happy to be here. But this pass will be difficult, because Columbus Avenue is currently torn up with construction. So I chart a new route. I will run across the street at the corner of 67th, then cut to my left on the sidewalk and let him heave it to me, directly over the construction site. We wait for the green light and then I go: dashing across the street, cut to the sidewalk, turn left, keep running, as he throws it. This could be tough—it's almost too high, it's in front of me, my hands are cold, here it comes, I stretch, get my hands on it, but bobble it. Then I pull the ball back in, tuck it into my arms, and yell, "Touchdown—Notre Dame!"

Steve seems to be very impressed and I know why. It really wasn't a great pass. As a matter of fact, it was way off. Too high, too wide, but, as usual, I save my guest. Only kidding. Anyway, the hands are sure as ever. And my streak remains intact. Later, Steve calls the Gifford house to crow about the catch. I think he wants me on the squad next year. I'm not sure if Lou Holtz saw it. But he knows I'm always ready.

Tuesday ☆ February 14

Our annual Wedding Week officially begins. Viewers seem to love Wedding Week, but I confess that it throws off my rhythm. Any kind of change in the show's format is always a big strain on all of us. This is almost a complete departure from our regular show, except for the opening. And today we find out that even the opening will be different. By attempting to shoot the wedding at a better angle, Gelman has moved our homebase set to the other end of the studio. So we're instantly disoriented.

Not only that, but he plants us directly in front of some stained-glass windows that will serve as the backdrop for the ceremony. Nothing like trying to get laughs in church. Worse yet, there is hardly any audience. Apparently, a flock of friends and relatives were expected to be on hand for the wedding couple, so our regular audience was considered unnecessary. But now it seems like there are only thirty people scattered in the white chairs in front of us. And they just stare at us with hushed reverence. They think they're in church! You can hear crickets! So we die a horrible death in the opening. We drown in a sea of empty chairs and blank faces—with stained-glass windows behind us. It's like Custer's last stand, except he got a better crowd turnout. This could be the worst opening we've ever done. And just when I was beginning to believe that Gelman really does know everything! Things will be back to normal tomorrow, I promise you. Fortunately, the wedding itself goes well: Two hard-working single parents with children, starting out all over again with each other. You can't help but root for them. I just wish they'd brought more friends.

Wednesday ☆ February 15

Wedding number two: They were childhood sweethearts. They were in a car accident, which left him paralyzed, confined to a wheelchair. She stuck with him. Today they marry. One thing Gelman does right are the weddings themselves. Everything is taken care of—from the tuxedos and bridal gowns to an exotic honeymoon. This couple is in a state of shock over the whole treatment. It's a joy for us to see how happy we've made them.

After the wedding, I go out to shoot some footage with groom number four, who'll be married on Friday's show. We tour the famous sites of New York City, culminating in a trip to the top of the Empire State Building. This groom is interested in architecture, so he gets a bird's-eye view from the observation deck. What you would never guess is that he's had four brain tumor operations and the prognosis is not good. Being with him on top of the great skyscraper, you can't help but imagine how he feels staring off into the horizon, knowing his time couldn't be more precious. But his spirit is incredible. So positive and appreciative.

The Empire State Building is still a great tourist attraction, of course, drawing three million visitors a year, according to our tour guide. It's still one of the wonders of the world, immortalized in the movies *An Affair to Remember* and *Sleepless in Seattle*. Whenever I'm up on top, I still look around for Cary Grant and Deborah Kerr or Tom Hanks and Meg Ryan. Then I look down at the city racing in every direction far below. Our groom loves it. I tell everyone how I used to work as a messenger on the 59th floor at the Martin Travel Bureau during the summer after high school, just before Notre Dame. I would pick up and deliver tickets at the airlines and steamship offices up and down Fifth Avenue. I never forgot that summer, or the hustle and bustle of Manhattan of that era or the thrill of being a part of the Empire State Building. It all comes back to me as we gaze out at the city. I mention this to some of our staff members who are accompanying us, but no one is really interested. So I just remember it all to myself.

Meanwhile, part two of the Letterman shoot is scheduled for tonight. We'll now tape the middle part of the bit—getting Dave to our studio. We'll run rampant through the streets, with me leading him uptown. A light rain is falling, which I thought might cancel their plan, but no. We will run. I arrive at the Ed Sullivan Theatre Office Building at around 7:30 P.M. and go up to the fourteenth floor. Three of Dave's writers sit in a conference room eating take-out, preparing to watch their favorite show, *The Simpsons*. Dave enters, wearing the same suit he wore while running around our studio last week. I'm also wearing the same plaid suit I'd worn. We're ready and so is his director, Hal Gurney, and crew. We all charge out of the Ed Sullivan Theatre and begin a night of running in the rain. We peel around the corner, then tear up and down the side streets. It's a liberating feeling, running crazily like this. We stop and run and stop again, then move to another street. Between setups, he makes a little small talk with me, never too personal. "So how do you like living in Connecticut?" he asks. "Well, Dave," I say, "we've talked about this for six years now." Then we run again. I decide to take a big lead and sprint several paces ahead of Dave, shouting, "Come on! Hurry up, Dave! Run, Dave!" Dave is panting, "I'm coming! I'm coming!" Then he wildly overshoots his turns rounding every corner, like Buster Keaton. I could only imagine what the startled pedestrians were thinking as we flew past them. Was it another hold-up? Another chase? Another catastrophe? No, it's just David Letterman and Regis Philbin running through the streets with a camera in close pursuit. And finally, we're done. Dave disappears onto an elevator, heading back upstairs to work, and I go home with my legs aching.

Wedding number three is about the renewal of vows. Gelman had asked Joy and me to do it, but we'd done it before, years ago on my short-lived NBC morning show. No way we'll do it again. That time it happened on our twelfth wedding anniversary, for no other reason than to draw ratings. We were "married" by Merlin Olson, the former football player, who was then starring as TV's *Father Murphy*. (Nothing like a fictional holy man presiding over your vows.) My best man was Ed McMahon, who was to Johnny Carson what I was to Joey Bishop, which somehow explained his participation in the nuptials. Mary Hart was maid of honor. Joanna and J.J. were flowergirls. And Joy was mortified. She still shudders when she remembers it. It was totally embarrassing. Then they sent us off on a second honeymoon to the Bel Air Sands Hotel, perched above the freeway traffic! Never again, Gelman! Forget it.

Even Kathie Lee and Frank declined to renew their vows for this show. So we have a couple from Utah, married now for forty-seven years. He wrote a letter to the show, sharing the ups and downs of a long life together, including how hard his wife had worked all those years. It really knocked me out to hear what this woman had been through—how the family relied on her and how she never let anyone down. It was an unforgettable letter and life. We're happy to have them with us.

Final wedding today, at the Rainbow Room atop the G.E. building in Rockefeller Center. As I arrive at 30 Rock, I gaze across 49th Street at the crowd gathered outside the windows of the *Today Show* studio. Just last year, the *Today* gang moved to this ground-level studio so crowds could watch from the sidewalk the way they did when Dave Garroway was host. I decide to surprise Bryant and Katie in my tuxedo, so I go over and pick my way through the mob, only to find they've drawn their blinds. Just great. Millions of dollars to build a new studio so the public can look in, and they draw the blinds.

Wedding number four goes well in the gorgeous Rainbow Room. The groom is the calm center in this room full of tears. Like the Rock of Gibraltar. He is pure courage. After we leave the air, the place is transformed into a reception for all four of the week's couples and their friends. It's quite a blast. (The whole event costs about $200,000, but who's counting?) Gelman and stage manager Julian Abio and associate producer David Mullen and I dance with all four brides, changing partners, twirling each one around the floor. And that's when I'm called to the phone. It's the Letterman show. I have a sinking feeling they want me tonight for the final piece in the "run through my audience" feature. I answer the phone by saying, "No, not tonight. Not at the beginning of President's Weekend!"

But, of course, that's exactly what they want: Give up

my Friday night. Get into that plaid suit one more time. Get over to Dave's theater, where we'll set up the bit on tonight's show. And here's how it goes: The writers have Dave open the CBS mailbag. First letter is a request that some night he throw Ping-Pong balls around the stage. Dave says, "Hey, how about tonight?" The backdoors fly open and here comes Regis with a basket full of Ping-Pong balls. At least it's not my exercise video again. I trot down the aisle, throwing the balls, inciting the crowd. I get up onstage, throw more balls, run back down the other aisle, and fight my way out of the theater. Dave closes the mailbag, but before he can proceed, I come back down the aisle with a request of my own. I say, "Dave, I've been running up and down your aisles for a year and a half now—and you've *never, ever* run up and down my studio aisles!" He says, "Well, I'll buy you some breakfast sometime." "No," I said, "I don't want any stinking breakfast. I want you in my studio." And the crowd cheers. Reluctantly, he agrees.

We run out of the studio together. Then they roll tape of our last two excursions. There we are running through the rainy streets to our WABC-TV studios. And there we are blasting onto our show—Kathie Lee looking on, stunned, as Dave works our audience. It's all beautifully edited and very funny. I watch all of this on a monitor with Dave behind the theater doors. "Geez, this looks pretty good!" I tell him. "Yeah!" he says. And even Dave seems happy with the result. When it's over, we burst back into the theater. I see a little light flicker in his eyes, as he scoops up some Ping-Pong balls off the floor and starts whipping them at me. I'd kept some in my pants and I hurl them back at him. Suddenly, we're caught up in a big Ping-Pong ball fight before I finally leave. The whole bit feels like we've made a mini-series, and it lasted just two and a half minutes.

Saturday ☆ *February 18*

Joy and I have dinner with Alyssa and Chuck Grodin in Greenwich, Connecticut. Chuck, who lives in neighboring Westport, is about a month and a half into his new CNBC talk show, and I'm looking forward to his report. I know there will be one. Chuck is a marvelous storyteller and getting his own talk show started should provide him with plenty of material. Usually the act of bringing these shows to life is a horror story, like creating Frankenstein's monster. I've been relatively lucky with mine because I know exactly what it should be. The only times I faltered was when I had to tape in advance. That never worked for me. But I know producing even a relatively simple live show like Chuck's can lead to problems. And I'm not wrong. He unleashes a string of anecdotes— the personality clashes, the conflicts, the misunderstandings, the trauma of it all. He's spellbinding, remembering every detail, every slight, every hurt. And when he finishes, we sit in silence for a moment and then Joy asks him, "How do you feel about doing a talk show now?" And he said, "I've never been happier in my life."

Still in Connecticut. I've been thinking about Chuck Grodin and his start-up horrors. God knows I understand the trauma. Bizarre things happen at the outset of all shows. And I guess the most bizarre moment of my entire career happened early in the Bishop years. I don't talk about it much. For a few days there, I became a sort of footnote in talk-show history. You might say I slipped on my second-banana peel. The incident made headlines. Then it was over. In fact, it happened so quickly, the whole uproar still seems like a blur. But people remember. And they ask me about it. And I avoid telling the whole story. Because it's a very long and strange story. But, for the record, here are the facts: I did it on a Monday night, July 8, 1968. And that was the night millions of Americans watched me walk off the show. I've never seen a tape of it myself. I'm not sure I ever want to.

First, understand this much: Late-night talk-show wars are nothing new. Long before Leno and Letterman, there was Johnny and Joey and Merv. Even I tried it for a minute, with Westinghouse's syndicated *That Regis Philbin Show*. Johnny killed me. It wasn't even a fair fight. But I've already told that story. I wandered away from the fray. Then Joey Bishop brought me back. He wanted me as his sidekick, his announcer, his Ed McMahon. ABC put Joey on the air in April 1967, sent him into battle against Johnny. At the time, we pretended that it wasn't war, that there was plenty of room for two network late-night shows. But none of us really believed it. We wanted to fight and win. The same way that Jay and Dave want to topple each other. That's television. That's life. Each night I introduced him at the top of the show, exclaiming, "Ladies and gentlemen . . . *it's time for Joey!*" And that's what we all believed—that it was Joey's time to take his shot. And that meant all of the pressure was on Joey. I knew the feeling. It's murder.

Back then, as always, Johnny Carson was colossal— already on the job for five years, he was an institution. His *Tonight Show* was still based in New York and carried across the NBC network on 210 stations. Joey started with only 144 ABC stations, which meant he couldn't win anyway. But how we tried. After all, the Bishop show would be different: First of all, Joey wasn't Johnny. Johnny was shy, reclusive, reserved, and not a showbiz party-guy. Joey, on the other hand, was pure showbiz. He made all the rounds. A nightclub comic of the old school, he was even a member of Sinatra's legendary Clan, later called the Rat Pack. Moreover, his show would be broadcast directly from Hollywood, where big stars were plentiful and booking them was a breeze. We had a beautiful, spacious facility at 1313 North Vine Street—the old Vine Street Theater—that could easily house the most lavish production numbers. The focus would be on big entertainment and every night we'd hit the air with a bang. And setting that mood was partly my job.

Joey had wanted me to ignite him. His comic pose was world-weary, put-upon, sly. He began each show with a short monologue, never more than three or four jokes. Then it would be my turn. He'd call me over to where he stood and I would do what I think I've always done best—just kibitz and lead him through an ad-lib conversation. (Think of it as a stand-up version of the Host Chat, played with big energy, mostly mine.) He demanded that I be revved up and that I rev him up about his guest lineup. So I'd come on strong, like a one-man pep rally, saying, "Okay, Joey! We're gonna get them tonight!" And our banter would fill up another ten minutes: me leading and Joey counterpunching. It was a fresh approach and considered to be one of the best elements of the show. Which is how Joey wanted it. He used to tell reporters, "I figured that if the worst thing happened and all the guests failed to show up, Regis and I could do the whole show together, and it would probably be our best show."

But we got guests and they were heavyweights, thanks in part to Joey's good standing with Sinatra, which translated to royalty status in show business. Oddly enough, Frank never did come on the show, which I know bothered Joey. (And you couldn't really question Frank's whims or motives—nobody ever did.) But Sammy Davis, Jr., was a regular headliner for us, doing all kinds of musical numbers and impressions. (He and Joey would engage in wonderful impressionist duels: Sammy liked to play Edward G. Robinson to Joey's Bogart.) Even Dean Martin dropped by during the making of *Airport* and remained a devoted fan of the show. Then there was Jimmy Durante, who'd come on and play piano and bust things up. And also John Wayne and Bing Crosby and everyone else you can think of. We did one show with Barbra Streisand at the Hollywood movie premiere of *Funny Girl*. Before airtime, I remember watching Joey and Barbra get into a long discussion of who would stand where. They both thought they looked better when viewed from one side—I forget which. Joey said, "But that's where I always stand!" Barbra said, "But that's my best side!" Joey said, "But it's also my best side!" So I popped up and said, "Waitaminute! What about *my best side!*" Everybody laughed and the tension was eased for awhile. But that was my role—never taking myself too seriously, providing quick comic relief, unafraid to look a little foolish if it could help Joey. It was our version of the oldest dynamic in comedy—the lovable grump and his playful straightman.

I guess that was a vulnerable position in which to place myself. And it earned me some knocks from the press. To them, I may have looked like Joey's little cheerleader, his overeager foil. I remember on our very first show the guests included Governor Ronald Reagan, Danny Thomas, and Debbie Reynolds, who began telling Joey about growing up as a tomboy. Debbie said, "Yeah, I can still mess with the boys!" So Joey turned to me and said, "Regis, why don't you just run across the stage." I knew I was in for trouble. But I got up and ran and she started running after me. Then she tackled me to the floor. So it looked like this woman overpowered Regis and knocked him down! Which she did, of course. But, as a result, I may have come across as some kind of a lightweight. What a great impression to make on opening night. And it was a harbinger of things to come.

But Joey was always appreciative and very loyal to me. From the beginning, he'd tell me, "As long as I'm doing this show, you'll be with me." He liked to say that I was like a son to him, even though he was only about fifteen years older than me. Joey was a complex guy, always interesting to be around, and he had a pretty hot temper. It was important to keep him loose. One day, during the early-going, our producer Paul Orr came to me and said, "Joey's restless. Why don't you take him outside and go for a walk?" I said, "Are you sure?" He said, "Absolutely." So I went to Joey and said, "Joey, why don't we go for a walk today." He shot me a glare. "What?" he said. "I've got a lot of things on my mind! I can't be worrying about taking a walk! Forget it!" So I went back to my desk in the office I shared with a writer named Trustin Howard, a very funny guy. Five minutes later, Joey walked into our office wearing a windbreaker and said, "Let's walk." And that's the way our daily ritual got started.

From that day forward, at the stroke of three in the afternoon, we walked together. We would walk from 1313 North Vine Street all the way up to Hollywood Boulevard, all the way over to Cahuenga, all the way back down again. It took about fifty minutes, just long enough for Joey to clear his mind. And for me, it was a genuine pleasure, walking and talking with one of the masters, day after day, soaking up his knowledge. He told great show-business stories. And, more importantly, he taught me a hell of a lot about the science of telling a funny story—how to set it up, how to pay it off. Every day I learned something new, including how to treat fans and viewers. No matter how terrible a mood Joey was in, he'd be very gracious and cordial to everyone on the street. I've tried to establish the same attitude wherever I've worked and, to this day, I'm proud to say our staff reflects that kind of friendliness.

Anyway, fifteen months had passed since the show started, but the ratings never really took off. Johnny kept winning. Joey kept losing. Instead of accepting reality— that we weren't being aired on enough stations to actually compete—the network was looking for a scapegoat. More and more, I'd been hearing that maybe I was to blame. I found out that one ABC executive had been going to Joey for months, urging him to fire me. Joey never budged. He saw me as an asset and made that clear. (In fact, Joey never told me about the network being on his back to get rid of me. I had to learn this through the grapevine.)

By that first week in July, I had heard it all and heard enough. I began to think that maybe I was wrong for the show, after all. Maybe I *was* holding our ratings down. From the start, I got beat up more than Joey in the reviews. It was one thing to be the butt of Joey's jokes, but more painful to endure it from critics. I felt badly stung. I never volunteered to be a sidekick in the first place. Joey had sought me out for the job. And I knew I could deliver what he wanted and still make an impression. But now rumors were rampant that I should or would be getting fired.

Early that week, during our afternoon walk, I brought up all of these rumors. "Do you think it's me?" I asked Joey. "Should I quit? If you think I'm hurting the show, I'll go." I reminded Joey that he had stuck his neck out for me and told him the last thing I wanted to be was a noose around that neck. Joey gave me a surprised look. "No, I don't think it's you," he said evenly. But I saw a little light go off in his eyes. Coincidence or not, we both knew that the following week Johnny Carson would be bringing the *Tonight Show* out to NBC's facilities in Burbank, our own backyard. Whenever Carson came west, it was a big event and his ratings soared. Joey, for his part, hated network politics and didn't much like his ABC bosses, especially the ones who wanted my blood. So he said to me, "I'll tell you a way to get back at them. Why don't you—only if you feel like it—walk off one night? Walk off right on the air, like Jack Paar used to do. You'll show them." Then he said, "Just know that if you walk, I'll make sure you come back."

Honestly, I didn't know what to make of this. You never know in this business—with all of its intrigues and behind-the-scenes shenanigans—what the real truth is. I thought it was possible that Joey wanted me off, but didn't want to fire me, because he'd somehow look bad. Then again, maybe the network had a gun to his head and he was giving me a way to embarrass them. Or maybe I was simply being set up to eliminate myself. But I think, more than anything, Joey was envisioning the publicity value of a televised resignation. After all, Carson was coming west, and we were sitting ducks for a ratings massacre. "You could make things interesting," he told me with a little smile.

My head was spinning. I kicked the whole idea around for a few minutes, weighing both sides of it. I thought, if they really want me to walk, I could walk. Even if I didn't come back, it might be the best thing in the world for me. My real ambitions never included being a second-banana, anyway. Joey knew that when he hired me. In fact, that was his biggest concern when he gave me the job. Whether or not I came back wouldn't really hurt my career, I figured. Not for very long, anyway. So I took a deep breath and gave him my gut-feeling. "What the hell," I said. "I'll go for it."

On Johnny's first night in town, I did it. Before the show, I was a nervous wreck. I also felt a touch of sadness. There was a good chance that I wouldn't return. Nobody likes change. I happen to hate it. But I also hated the idea that I was dead-weight on the show. My emotions were all over the map and my legs felt like rubber. But I did it. After Joey's monologue, I walked over to him, as usual. Except I didn't give him the usual pep talk. Instead, I started slowly. "I have something to say to you," I told him. "I've wanted to say it all day. I'm leaving this show." Joey looked stunned, like I'd hit him with a plank. I turned to the audience and said, "Joey hired me against everybody's better judgment—including the network's. Today I overhead something that disturbed me. I heard that for fifteen months they've been on his back because of me. So I'm quitting."

Joey struggled to make a joke: "Don't leave me," he said, "because they'll find out that it was me hurting the show instead of you!" By now, I guess I was shaking pretty good. But I went on: "Maybe I'm wrong for the show, maybe I'm holding you back, maybe we could do better without me here. They all could be right. So I tell you what—I'm going to go. I'm leaving." With that, I shook his hand and walked off the stage. The whole thing took up about eight minutes of airtime, but it felt like forever. All at once, I realized I was kind of choked up and also strangely relieved. And, as I walked behind the curtain, I saw our first guest waiting in the wings. Vic Damone. As I walked by, he said softly, "You're kidding, aren't you?" And I said, "No, I'm not coming back." And I kept walking. And Vic went ashen. Must have been a thrill for him to follow this weepy melodrama onstage.

Funny thing was, I suddenly felt okay. I didn't see Joey again that night. In fact, I went right out with the writer Trustin Howard. We had a couple of drinks and speculated about what would happen next. I watched the next shows go on without me, watched our bandleader

Johnny Mann do the announcing and kibitzing with Joey. And I saw Joey making comments about me—asking if anyone had seen or heard from me. Of course, they hadn't. I was lying low.

Meanwhile, the press was pouncing all over the story. Joey stoked the fervor by telling Kay Gardella of the *New York Daily News* that he heard me sobbing in my dressing room after the walk-off. Never mind that I'd left immediately. But he was playing it perfectly and for all it was worth. A tear-stained Regis leaves! He said he'd initially thought I was pulling a gag on him, but now worried that his show was turning into the nighttime version of *Peyton Place*. As for me, I kept quiet. I still wasn't sure whether I'd return. I was overwhelmed with all kinds of feelings, not the least of which being that I'd done the right thing, that I shouldn't go back. In a public relations panic, ABC issued a disclaimer about the whole mess, expressing surprise over what I'd said on the air: "We feel that Regis Philbin's statements were unwarranted and had no basis in fact."

That's because, overnight, the network had been bombarded with letters, telegrams, and phone calls. The fans were outraged and wanted me back. Hearing that, of course, made me feel much better. After a few days, the top brass went to Joey and demanded, "Enough! We've got to get him back." So over the weekend Joey called me and said, "It's time to come back." I must have hedged a little, since I was still shaken up by the fact that rumors had circulated in the first place. Joey said, "If you don't come back, you'll be hurting no one but me. I need you." And I could tell he meant it. My only hope was that some kind of on-air apology would come when I returned.

That day was Monday, the following Monday. I'd been

gone only four days, but the suspense had built up. People were curious and had been tuning in to keep tabs on the situation. That night, Johnny Mann did the announcing again, as I waited backstage. Joey did his monologue, then I listened for him to make an apology on behalf of the network. I had wanted a little satisfaction, after having sweated out the past days of anguish. After all, I didn't leave for any of the usual reasons, like wanting more money or better billing. All I wanted was to help the show. Or not hurt it. But all Joey said was, "Ladies and gentlemen . . . all's well that ends well! Here's Regis!" *All's well that ends well?* That's it? I couldn't believe it. I was surprised. There was no network apology, no explanation, no resolution. Just "all's well that ends well!" I was left hanging there. I came out anyway, and had a few laughs with Joey. I said something like, "I'm back now. Everything is going to be okay." And Joey said, "For a nice Catholic kid from Notre Dame, you're a real troublemaker!" And the show went on, like nothing had ever happened. Frankly, I'm not even sure whether we made any kind of a dent in Carson's ratings. So much for all's well that ends well!

But there was one funny postscript: Not much more than a year later, it was Joey's turn to quit on the air. He had gotten into a beef with ABC and decided he had had enough. He was through, but he loved those dramatic endings. So that night, after his monologue, he looked at the audience and said, "I've got an announcement to make. I've had a good run here, it's been a lot of fun, and I've enjoyed it—but it's over. I'm going to go home and have dinner with my wife, and Regis is going to finish the show for me." And so he walked off and never did come back. But as he walked off, who do you think he passed backstage, waiting to come out as the first guest? That's right. Vic Damone. Again. And Vic didn't think it was funny at all. Two times on the show—and two times before a walk-off. Just a coincidence, Vic. Nothing personal.

Monday ☆ February 20

President's Day, which means a day off for us. Before leaving Connecticut, I get a chance to watch the other daytime talk shows. It's the only time I can tune them in. Our show repeats the Halloween special when Kathie Lee became Regis and vice versa. And I still look like Mrs. Doubtfire. That's bad enough, but not as bad as what I see next. It's fascinating to witness how low this medium has stooped. And how society has followed. Rolanda has some big-busted blonde on and the bad taste jokes are flying. Jerry Springer has yet another angry racist on his show. Geraldo is spotlighting a bunch of strung-out kids with rings in their noses and ears. Phil has a restaurateur whose lifestyle keeps him out all night, but as long as he phones his wife at seven in the morning, she's happy. Richard Bey has a young divorced couple talking about why he refuses to pay child support for his baby. At one point, the woman produces a Federal Express envelope that he had sent her. Inside was twelve dollars in cash. The Fed Ex delivery itself cost fifteen dollars. All of it is insanity and garbage. And all that it's doing is convincing viewers that this is normal behavior. The whole thing sickens me.

The stock market is closing in on four thousand this week. The market happens to be my major vice. At all times, I keep the television in my office set to CNBC, where I soundlessly watch the ups and downs of American industries. I'm endlessly fascinated by this stuff—and especially love the gambling aspect of it all. What really appeals to me about the market is the fact that you never lose until you sell. That may sound naive, but it's true. You could buy a stock and watch that sucker go down, down, down—but you haven't lost until you sell it. If only I could remember all of the horror stories I've experienced playing the market. Luckily, I've blocked most of them from memory. Otherwise, I might weep every day.

Back in the seventies, I purchased some shares of MGM Grand—the biggest, newest, hottest hotel in Las Vegas at the time. A few days later, I was sitting at my desk in the KABC-TV newsroom, writing up a movie review, when I noticed all of the monitors were focused on a major fire consuming what looked like a very large building. "Where is that?" I yelled. "Las Vegas!" the newswriters yelled back. I watched more intently. A few moments later, ABC anchorman Max Robinson was announcing the MGM Grand was going up in flames, which meant my stock was going down in flames. Earlier, when I rejoined ABC in Hollywood, ABC stock was selling at twelve. I thought, maybe I should get in at that price, but no—I resisted. If I'd bought, I could have been accumulating and waiting for the day Cap Cities acquired the network for 144—and then watched it go to seven hundred before splitting. By now, I could own Trump Tower and several boroughs. But no. The mistakes haunt me forever. But I keep reading the *Wall Street Journal* every day, hoping for the best.

Thursday ☆ February 23

What a day of mishaps: Jerry Rice, the greatest receiver in NFL history, is our lead-off guest. He'd seen my spectacular catch of Steve Young's pass last week and asked to be on the show. Maybe he wants to look at my miraculous sure-catch hands up close. Anytime, Jerry. For fun, I decided to have him run the same route I did for the Young pass. But I made the mistake of mentioning this on yesterday's show. So when we walk outside this morning to do it, the sidewalk is crowded with autograph hounds and football fans and passersby. I hardly have room to throw. We wait for the light to change at the corner. When it turns green, Jerry lopes across the street and then cuts to his left at the sidewalk, just as I had done. I let the ball go—a beautiful spiral. It looks like a cinch. Then something happens that would only happen on our show and in New York. One of the construction workers from the project across the street suddenly appears, leaps in front of Jerry Rice and bats the ball down. I can't believe it. Neither can Jerry. Probably on a bet, this guy has done what so many pro defensive backs cannot do. He denies Jerry Rice the ball. We're all stunned and speechless. But not our associate producer, Rosemary Kalikow, who screams, rushes up to the guy and smacks him across the face. Just takes her clipboard and belts him hard. Now deeply scared, he scurries around the corner and dives into his construction site for safety, while we try it again—this time, successfully.

Next ordeal: Gelman's haircut. The time is drawing near. Monday he will be shorn at last. Right on the air. I can't wait. Lately, he's been looking like Gelman the Barbarian. And that ponytail! It must go! We let viewers vote for the new Gelman look. There are three fax machines to record the votes for three separate haircut options. Actually, I present a fourth write-in option: The totally bald look made popular by so many black athletes. I tell Gelman that he could be the first white man to make it work. He'd be beautiful bald. I'm not sure he buys it. Anyway, three hairstylists come on to each unveil their ideas. One is just a slight trim. Another is a moderate cut, close at the sides and a mop on top. The third is a very close cut that looks terrific on the incredibly handsome model shown in the picture. I point out that Gelman's never going to look as great as that guy, even with plastic surgery. But nobody cares.

Kathie Lee, meanwhile, announces that she will boycott the hair segment. She's upset that our own hairstylist, Bryant Renfro, won't be participating. It turns out that Bryant has to be on the West Coast Monday with Barbara Walters and, therefore, can't be around to scalp Gelman as planned. So he had to be replaced, which doesn't sit well with Kathie Lee. Her relationship with Gelman has been calm lately, but it's always tenuous. This could be the flare-up that breaks the accord. Anyway, she sidelines herself out of solidarity for Bryant. But the show must go on. I give out the three fax numbers and expect the votes to go crazy. Instead, the machines all short-circuit because of the heavy fax traffic. One vote comes in and everything goes dead. One vote! I'm totally embarrassed.

Final ordeal: We cross the street to the new Reebok Sports Center where I'll perform a rock wall climb with a professional mountain climber who also happens to be blind. This guy might as well be Spiderman. We start together and he's up the wall like a rocket. I hoist myself about eight feet up and freeze. The other guy keeps scaling. He's three stories up. He keeps getting smaller. He's in orbit. And I'm stuck. Can't go up. Can't get down. Can't move at all. Pinned against the rock wall. And that's how the show ends. With me stuck. Some days it just doesn't pay to get out of bed.

Friday ☆ *February 24*

For ten years, I've been staring at this handbill pinned on the bulletin board next to my desk. It's an advertisement for a Martin and Lewis engagement at the Copacabana nightclub during the fifties. In fact, I took Phyllis Setzer to see them there on our prom night. This morning I take the ad downstairs to the studio to show Jerry Lewis, our first guest. Jerry looks the same as he did back then, more or less. Now he's about to open on

Broadway for the first time ever, playing the devil in *Damn Yankees,* and he couldn't be more excited about it. But first he says he's got a couple of stories about Kathie Lee and me to tell.

He begins to reminisce about my old San Diego show. Back in the early sixties, Jerry kept his boat docked in San Diego Bay. Every weekend he would come down there and, on Saturday nights, he would sit on his boat and watch my show on his transistor television. Word got back to me that he not only saw the show, but that he wanted to come on as a guest. He didn't specify a date, but I was told when the spirit moved him, he would do it. And, sure enough, one night the studio doors swung open and there was Jerry Lewis. We extended that show by another forty-five minutes to accommodate him. After the show, he stuck around for a long talk. He began advising my director, Tom Battista, with tips on how to improve the look of the show. He was so enamored with the idea of a live Saturday night show, he later got ABC to give him one of his own on the network. He hosted *and* directed that show for a while, with a whole video console built into his desk. As I recall, he had even talked with Tom Battista early on about coming up to direct the show. Tom didn't get the job and the show was canceled fairly soon, anyway. Then, he turns to Kathie Lee and reminds her of the time she interviewed him on *Good Morning America*. Jerry says, "That was the best interview I ever did in my life!" Which surprised her as much as it did me. Great. He had to give me technical advice, but tells her she's a genius!

And speaking of directors: Later, actress Kate Capshaw comes on and I tell her something she doesn't know about her husband, Steven Spielberg. A few years ago,

Joy and I attended a movie premiere at the Museum of Modern Art. Afterward, there was the usual quiche-and-wine party. All kinds of film industry big shots were there—including Steven Spielberg. Publicist Peggy Siegel grabbed me and said, "Come over here and let me introduce you to Steven." But I saw that he was surrounded by several guys, deep in conversation. So I said to Peggy, "No, I don't want to interrupt. And he doesn't know who I am, anyway." I started walking away, but I heard a guy say, "Regis!" I turned around and it was Spielberg. He said, "I wanted to tell you something. You probably would never remember this, but years ago as a kid I went to see *The Joey Bishop Show*. That night you came into the audience with your microphone, asking people to tell you and Joey what their dreams in life were, their ambitions and goals. And you came to me and said, 'Hey, young fella, what's your dream?' And I couldn't talk! I was so shy and introverted as a kid that I panicked. I wanted to tell you that I wanted to be a movie director, and yet I couldn't. And you were very patient and very nice and you tried again. You said, 'Now, come on, don't be nervous. Just tell us what it is.' And I could not tell you."

As he told me this, I could see that he was choking up a little. "That has bothered me all of my life," he said. "Every time I see you on television—and I've seen you now for twenty-five years—it comes back to haunt me. I couldn't speak." And, funny thing was, I remembered that moment clearly. I remember thinking at the time how this trembling kid reminded me of me and my own inability to tell anyone that I wanted to be on television. It's a painful, frustrating feeling—and, unfortunately, unforgettable. And so here was this shy fellow, frozen stiff, who would grow up to become the greatest director of his generation, who would even co-found a giant entertainment company called Dream Works SKG—of all things! I couldn't believe it. And today neither can his wife Kate, who is genuinely touched.

Tonight Joy and I join Claudia Cohen and Senator Alfonse D'Amato for dinner at "21." By now, all of New York knows what Claudia wanted me to keep quiet weeks ago. Yes, Senator Al is her secret love, the guy who's brought a gleaming smile back to her face. And this was the week they told the world. A few days ago, they even held a press conference at the Water Club to talk about their relationship and their plans to be married—although no date or engagement was announced. Still, it made headlines all week—even knocking O.J. off the front page. Throughout our dinner, Claudia and Al are holding hands, which is tough to do when you've got to cut your own chicken. This continues to look like the real thing.

Senator Al is a real New York kind of guy. And he talks like one, with a great New York accent. Naturally, much of the talk is about Washington and politics. I get a kick out of him when he makes small talk about his friends Bob Dole, Newt Gingrich and company: "So I said to Dole, I said, 'Look, Bawb, you gotta listen to me here . . . ' " He sounds like any other guy who tells stories on a New York street corner. You find yourself forgetting that he's a U.S. senator and a powerful one at that. He talks about the great and mighty the way Freakin' Finelli probably talks about me.

Part III ─────────────────────── ☆

We do it today. What the country has demanded! What the viewers have voted for! A haircut for Gelman. Even though the fax machines kept breaking down, their choice was clear: number two. The moderate cut. Nick Berardi, of the Vidal Sassoon Salon, will do the job. Gelman is ready—or, should I say, resigned. It's time for a change and he knows it. So he sits down, braces himself, and Nick grabs the ponytail. I step between them and say, "Excuse me—I've got to have the honor!" Nick says, "Absolutely right." Gelman starts panicking. He says, "Now don't cut it on the wrong side of the rubberband!" I say, "Don't worry, Gelman!" I take the scissors and start cutting proudly. Meanwhile, I have hidden in my pocket an enormous clump of hair. So I pull it out just as I remove the ponytail. "All right, Gelman," I say. "Here it is!" I show Gelman the clump and he looks terrified. For a second there, he almost had a seizure. But what a moment of triumph! And when Nick finishes, Gelman looks younger and more handsome than ever. He seems unsure, but he'll get used to it.

Anyway, a rare pleasure tonight: I get to drive my car

in town. I have a five-year-old gray Jaguar. And it still drives nicely, even though it doesn't get much use. We only take it up to Connecticut and back once a week. For that, it costs me $388.98 per month to store it in an Upper East Side garage. Growing up in the Bronx, my family paid only thirty-five dollars a month rent. My mother would have killed me if she knew. No doubt, she'd just repeat her famous warning: "Remember this, Mr. Big Shot—the poorhouse is just around the corner!" But I love that car. And I love driving around New York, especially at night. Television producer Sonny Grosso, one of the New York cops who broke the famed French Connection case, asks us to join him for dinner up in East Harlem. Every Monday night for twenty years, he's been eating at Rao's on 114th Street. He swears that it's safe to drive up, that no one will touch the car, that he drives there all the time. So we park across the street and go inside.

There are only seven tables in this legendary restaurant. The decor hasn't changed since the forties when Rao's served as headquarters for gangster Dutch Schultz. Nobody's even touched the ancient Christmas ornaments over the bar. It's a wonderful, musty old place, full of memories, with a jukebox that never stops playing Dean Martin and food that never stops coming from the kitchen. The waiting list—if there really is one—is years-long. You simply can't get in. It's for regular customers only, like Sonny, and they can come only on their designated nights. For Sonny, it's Monday. He always likes to fill his table with an eclectic group. So tonight there's author Ed Torres, who's also a judge for the Bronx Criminal Courts; my cardiologist (and Sonny's), Dr. Jeffrey Borer; smoldering actor Armand Assante; and Joy and myself.

Sonny is a marvelous storyteller—spinning cops-and-robbers tales about the mob, the wiseguys. He grew up around the corner from Rao's and he remembers everything, every character. Since his days as a hero cop, he's been a major producing force in television. He's warm and gregarious and you've got to love him. Especially in this environment.

And there's Joy, seated smack between Sonny and Armand Assante, smiling and enjoying herself immensely, surrounded by all of that raw charisma—or, as Kathie would say, all of that *testosterone*. Being next to Armand must be a thrill for her. I've kidded her for years about him. She and her girlfriend Susan still get worked up whenever they talk about Armand wearing that white suit in *Mambo Kings*. So I have my suspicions about her feelings toward him. Armand has also been a guest on my various shows over the years. Now he confesses to me about his shyness and reticence regarding interviews. This, of course, melts the redhead. He also tells me, quite sincerely, that he watches our show faithfully. I wonder if he knows that everytime I mention his name, I've always included the word *smoldering*. Armand's that way—intense, passionate, and, yes indeed, smoldering. And there's Joy—forty-eight hours away from being married twenty-five years—gazing soulfully at this remarkable hunk. Life is funny. I'm trying to laugh. At least, nobody stole our car.

I go hunting for Joy's anniversary present. I won't go alone. I'm not that secure. After the show, I pick up a friend who knows more about jewelry than practically anyone and he will guide me through this shopping expedition. He is Lawrence Krashes, vice-president of Harry Winston, Inc. I think Joy wants a certain pair of earrings, but you really never know with her. Lawrence has been involved with selling jewelry to the savviest customers all over the world. But he states, unequivocally, that Joy is the toughest, most unpredictable shopper he's ever known. Once she returned some bauble he had highly recommended for her. Lawrence never got over it. He seems nervous as we meet in the early afternoon, like this may be too much for him. I feel exactly the same way.

It wasn't always like this. I used to be very confident about purchases. But then, about twenty years ago, I came home with a gift for her. I can't remember if it was a birthday or anniversary. But I do remember Joy sitting at the dining room table with her sister, The Winds of War. I made the presentation right there, so The Winds could eat her heart out. Tentatively, Joy opened the package. And there they were—a gorgeous pair of earrings. Joy smiled. The Winds remained expressionless. I expected that. But then she began smiling, too. But it was a certain smile that I have only come to know after I have committed a faux pas. My blood began to run cold. What could it be? What had I done now? Yes, The Winds smiled broadly, as if to say, "Look what you've done now, you jerk." There was silence. Then Joy patiently explained, "These earrings are for pierced ears." And her ears weren't pierced. How could I not know that? How had that escaped me? That was the turning point. My confidence faded. Frankly, I've never been sure of any purchase since.

And now, even with this wise old pro with me, I'm still nervous. I can see in his worried eyes the same paralysis gripping him that has gripped me all these years. Well, nothing looks good enough today—until the saleslady tries on a certain pair of earrings. She isn't any spring chicken, but they look great on her. Lawrence quickly nods yes, and that is that. Now they are secreted in my desk drawer. Tomorrow I'll know if we did the right thing.

Wednesday ☆ March 1

Our anniversary day. Twenty-five years. Silver. I remember her, and that day, like it was last week. She was the sweetest and the savviest and the sexiest. She had perfect posture, the greatest pair of legs I had ever seen, and a walk that instantly captured your imagination. She was charming, friendly, and always smiling. And so efficient. She could cut to the quick of any problem and solve it instantly. She was independent and proud and had just enough of a temper to keep you on your toes. She was the greatest package of femininity I had ever encountered.

We met on *The Joey Bishop Show*, where she worked as Joey's executive secretary. She had worked at a variety of jobs in television production, and had the talent to produce behind the scenes. But I also thought she had all the ability anyone ever needed to make it on camera as well. Of course, she was too self-effacing to ever think about that. After our marriage, she chose to stay home so she could be there when the kids left for school and when they came home. She was never afraid to work, and I'm not talking about just doing a TV show. I mean physical labor, like the time we bought a house and couldn't wait to fix it up. She was eight and a half months pregnant, but got down on her knees with me to pull linoleum off the floor. She would cook a dinner for four practically every night, give the kids a bath, put them to bed, and then do it all over again the next day and the next month and the next year.

We met in the middle of my life's low cycle. She was in her prime. She could have had anyone she wanted. Some of Hollywood's biggest stars were wooing her. She could have wound up with any of them. But it turned out to be me. I wasn't so sure about her choice. There were so many problems. The future looked bleak. Once I remember stopping the car and advising her to get out and run as far and as fast as she could. Luckily for me, it was in a rather shabby part of Hollywood and she wouldn't leave. I never knew for sure if it was because she was afraid, or too much in love to get out and run. Then, March 1, 1970, we were married. Of all places, we did it in Forest Lawn. One of the most famous cemeteries in the world. I wondered if that was an omen. Johnny Carson even made a joke about it in his monologue the next night. But the wedding chapel was charming. Despite a driving downpour of rain that lasted all day and all night, we had a lovely wedding. Tom Battista was my best man and her sister Marilyn, The Gentle Breeze, was her maid of honor. It was done around four in the afternoon. It was all ahead of us. The next twenty-five years. And now, a quarter century later, she remains exactly the same as I found her. Only sweeter. And savvier. And sexier.

☆   ☆   ☆

Now, to get through the day. It doesn't start well. I had hoped that Kathie Lee wouldn't remember. She's very demonstrative, and an anniversary can bring out the worst in her. I mean, she can proclaim her love from the mountaintops. It's second nature to her. It's not that easy for me. Guys don't shout from mountaintops unless they're falling to their death. It's embarrassing! But she begins: "This is a very special day for you." I knew it was coming. The grilling: Where are you going? What did you get her? And then, finally, do you still love her? Well, of course I still love her! What am I doing here for twenty-five years! But, yet again, she's put me on the spot.

Here's my defense: I have to bring some balance to the show. When she gets so effusive, I try to play it down. And I can see that she's working herself up into one of those gooey-love, teary-eyed modes. So I make a little gag out of "Do you still love her?" I sit there and think it over. Kind of like a Jack Benny pause. Just for a second or two. And then I mutter, "Yeah, I still love her." Okay, so I'm ad-libbing and I'm not doing a great job of it, all right! But what else are you going to do with her? Naturally, Joy is watching at home and she isn't too thrilled with my response. Then the Lennon Sisters come out and sing, "The Anniversary Waltz." I can't stop wincing. I'm just not cut out for these things.

We celebrate our anniversary with dinner at Le Cirque, one of New York's classiest restaurants. As usual, the place is packed with a high-powered crowd. We take a corner table. I've got the earrings in my pocket and a special note for Joy, telling her how she remains the greatest thing that ever happened to me. I wait for the right moment. I'm nervous. I haven't picked out jewelry for her in twenty years. Finally, we run out of small talk. This is it. I reach for the velvet box and bring it to the table. And she produces a small box for me. I open mine first. A gorgeous set of studs and cuff links for my tuxedo. I'm knocked out. This might be tough to follow. At this point, I've almost forgotten what the earrings look like. But there's no turning back.

She quietly opens the box. I study her face for the reaction. She looks at them and, unless she's fooling me, I think she loves them! She puts them on and they look great on her. What a relief. They're a hit! I slump back in my seat and relax. After all these years, my confidence is back. Also, my dignity. Yes, I can still knock her out with my taste. But wait a minute. I see that look on her face. Something's on her mind. What now? "Well," she says, "I hope they weren't too expensive." Uh-oh. The challenge. I guess every wife, sooner or later, wants to know "How much?" I should have known this would come up. I'm not sure how to handle it. I stall for time. "Why don't you guess?" I say. This is turning into a tense moment. The ball is in her court. Finally she takes a stab: She guesses a figure less than half of what I paid! I can't believe it! I'm stunned! She sees my reaction and quickly raises her price. But it's too late. Her number wasn't even close. And she knows jewelry! I wonder, Did I get taken? Who knows what this stuff is worth, anyway? *New York* magazine recently ran an article about how even the savviest customers get ripped off.

Just then the waiter comes over with a big smile and my favorite dish on the menu, the flounder in mustard sauce. Maybe the waiter should guess what the earrings are worth. I think, Stop it! Don't let your confidence ebb away! Be strong, Don Pardo. Don't let it shake you. Take the high road. Never tell her the price. Never give in. Just smile and eat your flounder, stupid. But the first chance you get, go back to that jeweler and ask him if he's sure you paid the right price. Yeah, that's what I'll do. Till then, happy anniversary, darling.

Thursday ☆ March 2

Trivia nightmare. Usually our trivia questions on the show are embarrassingly easy. Not today. Tomorrow's guest will be Jeff Goldblum, and we like using the trivia contest to plug the next day's bookings. But this question is ridiculous. Name the 1977 Oscar-winning movie in which Jeff starred with Woody Allen and Diane Keaton? First of all, Jeff was just a struggling young actor back then. He had exactly one line in this movie! One line. He was an extra in a party scene—not a co-star! The right answer is *Annie Hall*, but this is the wrong question. The phone contestants are stumped. Two guess *Sleeper*, one guesses *Bananas*, two others are clueless. The segment won't end. We give up.

I remember giving a similarly impossible question years ago on *A.M. Los Angeles*. Unfortunately, I came up with the question and decided it was so hard, I'd raise the stakes. "If anybody gets this, I'll come out and clean your house!" I said. Dumb. The question was, Who gave Deanna Durbin her first screen kiss? Who would know that? Nobody, I figured. Except for the first caller. *Robert Stack*, she said instantly. Damn. It took me three hours to clean her house. I wore an apron and mopped, dusted, scrubbed. I broke a glass and cut my hand. I bled because of a trivia question! And that was the last time I made an on-air promise.

But today it drags on so long, I see our first guest a few feet away in the wings, impatiently shuffling his feet. Peter Falk. He's over there watching. Waiting. Muttering to himself, just like Columbo. He's enjoying the chaos and carrying on a running commentary. I'm getting bored with this trivia nonsense, so I start doing my Columbo impersonation and, for the first time, it's not bad. Kathie is impressed. Even Peter Falk is impressed. Later, we talk about his wedding seventeen years ago in Beverly Hills. I was a guest and I'll never forget it.

The late John Cassavetes was his best man. Ben Gazzara was an usher. The three of them had been lifelong friends, and all three were very nervous on this day. Especially Peter. There was nervous laughter in the church hallways and now the wedding had progressed to the vows, always a tense moment. The priest asked Peter to repeat after him. Suddenly Cassavetes began to shake uncontrollably. Then he began giggling. He couldn't stop.

It escalated to full-blown laughter. Gazzara went next. Deep laughs. All nerves. The priest asked Peter if he would take this woman as his lawful wife. His bride, Shari, looked at him expectantly. The man couldn't speak. He froze. Cassavetes and Gazzara were howling, trying to fight it back and failing. The whole church started to titter. Unforgettable. But somehow vows were exchanged—between laughs—and Peter is laughing all over again now as I remind him.

From cracking up to crackers: After the show, I meet Joy and we proceed over to the Silver Cup Studios to make another Harvest Crisp commercial. This will be our third set of commercials for the hard-to-pronounce cracker. Now there's an Italian herb-flavored Crisp and, as usual, I love 'em. Tastes like a tiny pizza. Unfortunately, we have to speak Italian in the commercial. I even have to sing an aria from *Rigoletto*. But, as always, the real test comes at the end of the spot when I have to say, "Harvest Crisps crackers—I love 'em!" For years, I've worked on this account, but I still can't spit out that slogan. Something about all those *s*'s. It's a killer. And I only have a second or two to say it. Joy tries it and she's perfect. "Harvest Crisps crackers. I love 'em!" You try it right now. It ain't easy. What's worse, I'm being watched by Ed Bianci, who's directed all of my spots, and by the great cinematographer Gordon Willis, who shot the *Godfather* movies. I ask Gordon if my Italian-speak reminds him of De Niro or Pacino or even Brando. Gordon just nods, but I don't think he means it.

Finally, the commercial is done. I conquered the slogan, if barely. And I'm still not proud of my sibilance. On the way out of the studio, the guy who stands in for me—and also works as a speech teacher—tells me the key is to have your tongue firmly in place behind your lower teeth. Great. If only he had told me at the beginning, we could have saved an hour and a lot of embarrassment.

Friday ☆ *March 3*

I'm a commercial machine. Today it's off to Florida to do Kathie's latest Carnival Cruise Line commercial. I'll be one of five guest stars in this batch of commercials. Kathie's been doing these spots for eleven years, and has become synonymous with the product. So we fly out of Newark for Miami with the usual contingent—her kids, husband, nanny, secretary, hairdresser, makeup artist, and co-host. It's a jumbo jet, and we fill almost every seat in first class. The kids are on good behavior. After a couple of hours, Cody does go on a march and, at one point, I see him scaling the wall above the window. But for the most part, he's fine. Cassidy is never a problem. We screen the episode of *Coach* on which Kathie Lee and Frank were guest-stars. I missed it on the night it had aired. Very funny. For a while there, Kathie was thinking about a sitcom for herself, but after doing some of these guest spots and seeing all the work involved, that idea has gone away.

We arrive to find the ship packed, proving how effective these commercials have been in the cruise line's success. We're aboard the M.S. *Ecstasy*, which eases out of the Miami harbor around sunset. I'm in the Penthouse Suite, originally built for the owner. It's a beauty, but unfortunately perched above the Lido Deck, where the band plays into the night and the passengers have a ball. So I expect to toss and turn and get no sleep.

But first there's dinner, and a very funny occurrence: Kathie excuses herself from the table and goes to the ladies' room. When she returns, she looks shaken. She tells me she encountered one very excited fan in the bathroom. A woman just overwhelmed to find Kathie in there. Then Kathie went into the stall and when she came out a few moments later, the woman was still beside herself, jumping up and down. She looks Kathie in the eye and says, "I can't wait to get home and tell all my girlfriends, 'I took a sh— with Kathie Lee!' " Kathie tells her, "But I didn't do that!" Too late. If you could see her *now*! Mortified!

Saturday ☆ March 4

Gorgeous morning. Breeze is gentle and sweet. We're listing in Nassau Harbor, along with a fleet of cruise ships. I meet Kathie Lee and the commercial people at seven on the running track, near the top of the ship. We'll shoot the last scene of our commercial first: Kathie Lee and I are jogging. She's asking me about my favorite things on the cruise—the service, the food, the shows. "So what don't you like?" she wonders. "Going home," I answer, according to the script. But I have a better line. Instead of "Going home," I want to say, "Going back to work with you!" It gets a laugh from everyone I've tested it on. But Bill Dryer, the advertising chief, says he took it to the top guys at Carnival Cruise Lines and they prefer "Going home." We shoot it both ways, but I know what will end up on the air. Anyway, it's a fast shoot and we wrap a little past noon.

Tonight I fly to Fort Lauderdale, where I'll meet Joy before we begin a holiday cruise Monday on the M.S. *Staatendam.* To get there, I head over to the airport on Paradise Island, where Merv Griffin once had a resort complex. I remember the many family vacations spent there with Joy and the girls. Driving by these places makes me very nostalgic for those days when the kids were so young and small. Did I appreciate it enough back then? I thought so, but now I wonder. That phase of our lives together is long gone, and I truly miss it. At the airport, I sit outside watching the magnificent sunset and reminisce and feel terribly sad. Life is going by very quickly.

In the customs line, the guy behind me says he saw yesterday's show and now demonstrates how he can put his tongue behind his lower teeth and say "Harvest Crisps crackers" five times fast. What a show-off. But can he sing *Rigoletto* in Italian? Later, I check into the Pier 66 Hotel in Fort Lauderdale and call Joy, who'll fly in tomorrow. She sounds subdued. Finally she says, "I have some bad news." I brace myself. She says she had returned to the same store this afternoon to replace the purse stolen there five weeks ago. "Suddenly," she says, "I noticed my purse was open and my wallet was missing." Bad news, all right. Same place, same time, same thing. Another wallet, more credit cards, more cash—all gone. She never felt a thing. They opened the purse, took the wallet, and were probably heading home on the sub-

Early Don Rickles on
my Westinghouse Show.

The night I sang to Bing Crosby and got a record contract.

A ballet lesson on
the St. Louis show
with Marty "Hello
Dere" Allen.

Jerry in Las Vegas in the 70s.

Photos: Regis Philbin Collection

My stage manager, director, producer, general manager, and lifelong friend, Tom Battista.

Johnny looking at me with amusement.

Once Sara Purcell tried to drown me while checking my body fat by weighing me under water...only she wouldn't let me up.

The Champ, Muhammed Ali, and the King.

Burt Reynolds trying to tackle me in the mud on the *Semi-Tough* movie. Naturally, I was too fast for him.

Paying off a bet that no one would guess our trivia question that day. I never made that bet again.

One of my heroes, Notre Dame football coach Ara Parseghian.

Watching a replay of Gelman's cannon firing. Look how happy he is in his cape and tights.

A visit from David. She got flowers, and I got an old sandwich he found in a cab.

The Halloween epic. I love her but what a strange-looking guy.

Photos: Steve Friedman/Buena Vista Television

Me and Bobby and director Irwin Winkler before our scene in *Night and the City*.

Perry Como has been with us all our lives. What a thrill to have him on our show.

way before she noticed it. I used to worry about Joy wandering around New York. Now I'm getting terrified. And we're scheduled to leave on a Holland America Cruise on Monday without any credit cards. But she's made arrangements to have replacement cards sent immediately to the hotel. What next?

Sunday ☆ March 5

I can't hide anywhere. Hotels used to be safe havens, where you could escape the maddening crowds and just relax. Those days are over. This morning, the maid misinterprets the privacy sign on my door. Actually, it wasn't all her fault. The door handle is such that you can't tell if the sign reads "Privacy" or the flip side —"Please make up the room." So she is the first to knock on my door. I tell her to come in anyway and get it over with. It's done, and now for some peace and quiet.

But there's another knock on the door. The guy who checks the mini-bar. Okay, come in. Take a look. Done. A few minutes later, another knock. I don't believe it. The hotel sends up some complimentary fruit and cookies. Very nice, but what I need is sleep. Please! Now the phone rings. A messenger is looking for Joy Philbin. Can she sign for the delivery of an American Express credit card? "She isn't here," I say. "Can her husband sign for it?" A pause. They have to call headquarters to see. A few minutes later, phone rings again. Yes, her husband can sign. I'll be right down. Messenger's in the lobby. I sign.

He gives me a big brown envelope. Inside, there's one card with her name on it. We're supposed to have two cards with the same account number, but now she has the card and I have nothing. Great.

I return to the room. Turn on the television. The Suns are playing the Warriors in Oakland. Good game. Charles Barkley, Kevin Johnson, the whole gang. This could be their year. Phone rings again. "Can Joy Philbin sign for a delivery?" More credit cards, probably. "No, she's not here. Can her husband sign?" They have to check. Can somebody just kill me now and put me out of my misery? I get back into the game. Phone rings. I give up. The world wins. Why don't I just go sit in the lobby? I go down there again. I sign. At least there are two Master-Charge cards. Back to the room. I try again to concentrate on the game. But no. There's a knock on the door. This time, it's Joy.

Monday ☆ March 6

Another lovely sun-splashed Florida day. Makes me want to get a little hideaway down here to escape those terrible winter months. Barry and Susan Glazer have joined us for the cruise and we get in a couple of tennis games before going aboard ship. Barry Glazer is, of course, the opponent I like to call "my meat." I must beat him and I will, thus he is my meat. No exception now. Joy and I win three games and head for the showers and then finish packing. It's a ten-bag trip for the four of us. As usual, I fill only one bag—and I've already made a commercial here!

Eventually, we board the M.S. *Statendam*, a gorgeous two-year-old ship. Magnificent antiques and paintings everywhere. Joy and I get the owner's suite again. Talk about an upgrade! But when you're the king, why not? I've never seen a suite like it on a ship before. Living room, dining room, bedroom, walk-in closet, kitchen. This could be a great trip.

Tuesday ☆ *March 7*

I can't seem to finish reading a book anymore. To keep up for the show, I'm busy day and night reading newspapers and magazines and guest bios. But I've got one going for the cruise—a novel called *Jump* by New York sportswriter Mike Lupica. Now at *Newsday*, Mike used to write for the *Daily News*, where I especially loved his Sunday column. On that day, he compiled random observations about life, sports, and the world, which always reminded me of those great Jimmy Cannon columns—"Nobody asked me, but . . ."

As a kid, I delivered the *Bronx Home News*. The first thing I did after picking up my stack of papers was to sit on the curb outside the office on White Plains Road and read Jimmy Cannon's column. Everything he said was so wise and true, and I loved the way he wrote. On my newspaper route, I delivered to the Bronx home of boxing champ Jake La Motta, whose life was made into the

Martin Scorsese masterpiece *Raging Bull*. Jake was a great tipper. I can still see him in his underwear top, swinging a stickball bat—actually an old broomstick—goofing around with the neighborhood kids. And his pretty, young, blond wife, Vicky, would watch him from the sidewalk. Later, his brother Joey would wander over and hang around. So I was fascinated to see Robert De Niro portray Jake on-screen and Joe Pesci play Joey. That really was the way they talked, the way they fought, the way it was.

When I returned to New York in the eighties, Jake guested on one of my shows and I thanked him again for those big tips. Vicky La Motta also came on a couple of times hawking a beauty product. Still very sexy all those years later. I asked her if Bobby De Niro included her in his research. He's famous for doing thorough homework. She said, "Oh, yes, indeed. He was *very* thorough." Oh, that Bobby!

Wednesday ☆ March 8

Plenty of O.J. on board. CNN beams in, and there's no getting away from the Simpson murder trial. I began these diaries three days after the bodies of Nicole Brown Simpson and Ronald Goldman were found. And now, nearly nine months later, the case rages on. Strange to watch it at sea, so far away. At the moment, L.A. Homicide Detective Tom Lange is on the stand while defense attorney Johnny Cochran punches away with his cross-examination. Cochran ends every statement with the phrase, "Isn't that correct?" Must have said it ten hundred thousand times since this all began. Lange remains remarkably poised through the pummeling, but Cochran is on the attack, trying to illustrate police incompetence at the crime scene. This could go on forever.

Gale winds are whipping across the decks of the *Staatendam* and the seas are very rough. But the ship remains remarkably stable. No sign of seasickness here. That's the worst feeling in the world. That woozy state. I know it well. In the navy, I'd be aboard those little LSMs out on the Pacific, being tossed around like popcorn popping. I'd get that sinking feeling, turn green, and believe the world was coming to an end. But in these angry seas, there is no sensation at all. So far.

Thursday ☆ March 9

Curaçao. Our first stop. The water is so peaceful here. We dock and take a car over to the New Sonesta Beach Hotel for tennis, lunch, and a swim. The resort is crawling with Americans. Two burly guys from Philadelphia come over. They want a picture for one's father, Ralph. Usually it's for a mother or a grandmother. So it's a pleasure to pose for Ralph in Philly.

Curaçao is an architectural gem and so picturesque. The influence is Dutch; you'd swear you're in Amsterdam sailing past these gabled storybook houses painted in every pastel color. Twenty-five years ago, this was our first stop on a cruise we took shortly after our wedding. For that trip, we sailed from New York, where all the cruise ships docked before the economy and unions forced the business to Florida. Another stupid loss for New York. I remember my uncle Willie and my father's sisters, Peggy and Nancy, came down to see us off. They threw confetti while the ship's band played farewells. Ships don't shove off the way they used to. Funny that Willy, Peggy, and Nancy still look exactly the same as they did twenty-five years ago. Curaçao does, too.

After lunch, we play hearts with Barry and Susan. That's our favorite card game. Joy, by the way, is a terrific card player and very competitive. At one point, I am forced to feed her the queen of spades for thirteen unwanted points, which startles her. She leaps from the chair and smacks me hard on my shoulder and the sunburn stings. Did I ever tell you about her temper? The Glazers get quite an eyeful.

Later, as the game nears an end, I see I can win it. I give Joy the ten of hearts and that's ten more points she doesn't want. Things get quiet. She now has ninety-eight points. Two more and I win. And that's when she really gets into the game. She actually wants to see me denied! Next hand, she gives me the queen of spades, then the ten, then I get heart after heart from her. She engineers it all, and when she is finished, I lose and Susan wins. Maybe we've been married too long.

Friday ☆ March 10

Caracas, Venezuela. Mist hangs low over the mountains that loom above the port of La Guaira. It's a half-hour taxi ride to the city of Caracas, and most of the passengers are on their way. But it's probably the worst day of the year to tour Caracas—the president's birthday. Parades are everywhere. Little school kids in uniforms. The Venezuelan army, not much older, bearing semi-automatic weapons. Twenty-five years ago, Joy and I made the tour: the glass-blowing factory, the mountaintop country club, the million-dollar homes. Then you descend into the city and into reality. The air gets hotter and more humid, houses get smaller, then become shacks, and traffic is snarled to a crawl. Could it be any better now? My guess is no. We stay put. Passengers return exhausted and tell me that headlines in the Caracas papers say Michael Jordan is forsaking minor-league baseball and will play again for the Chicago Bulls. Who would think an American basketball player could make headlines in Caracas on the president's birthday? Jordan really is the Babe Ruth of our time.

After seeing Grenada yesterday, we arrive in the port city of Fort-de-France on the island of Martinique. Partly sunny day with a gentle breeze. Sinatra songs waft across the deck where we lounge. Martinique is bigger and more impressive than I imagine. Fort-de-France, they say, is a combination of New Orleans and Nice, but it's Sunday and closed for the day. So we skip going ashore. But Sinatra sure sounds great. Particularly in this setting.

This far south, CNN becomes CNN International. Suddenly, instead of the O.J. trial, you get the price of bananas in Bolivia. It burns me up. Just when controversial detective Mark Fuhrman is about to take the stand. At this point, the only source of news is the fax taken from the pages of the *New York Times*. It's slipped under the cabin door every morning. Today, there's a short article slugged "Killing After Talk-Show." Sounds like a Movie of the Week, but it's the real thing: Last Monday, on a *Jenny Jones* show about secret admirers, a young man surprises another man by confessing his love. A few days later, the object of the crush shoots the other man dead. The suspect said he was angered and humiliated, particularly because the show's producers told him the secret admirer was a woman—not a man. Just another lie, but in this case, a deadly lie. Lucky for Jenny and the producers that he didn't come after them.

Why am I unsurprised that this happened? The psychological repercussions of these televised ambushes must be devastating. The audience goes home and the producers move on to the next show, but these guests keep all the scars for life. Now one of them has finally flipped. I wonder how often this has come close to happening before.

Monday ☆ *March 13*

Heading for St. Thomas. The cruise director has asked Joy and me to do a question and answer session for the passengers. So far, everybody aboard has been pretty restrained about asking for autographs and pictures and Kathie Lee's whereabouts. On the other hand, maybe they just don't care. Maybe they've never heard of me. Maybe they hate my guts. I'm getting worried! So I quickly agree to the session, which is set for tomorrow.

Tonight, the four of us have been invited to dine with the ship's captain. This is a Dutch line, and he's as Dutch as they come. Usually, these seafaring people love their work, their ship, their sea, and he's no exception. Very jolly guy, but he's told the same joke at least three times now. "I follow the seafood diet. I see food, I eat it." We're joined by two other couples from Chicago, and the dinner is better than the captain's material.

$\mathbf{A}$t sea all day traveling north. The Simpson trial is back on CNN. It's great television. Opposing attorneys Marcia Clark and F. Lee Bailey are going at it. Detective Fuhrman is simply a rock up there on the witness stand. This guy could be the next John Wayne. Bailey can't rattle this witness. He can't show that Fuhrman is a racist. He can't show that Fuhrman planted the bloody glove on O.J.'s property. All the defense strategy was outlined months ago in a *New Yorker* article by Jeffrey Toobin. Obviously, it was leaked, but why? All it did was prepare the prosecution. So far, the prosecution seems way ahead. But that really doesn't mean anything. Everybody expects O.J. to walk away from this whole thing, anyway.

We get a full house for our Q & A session in the Van Gogh Lounge. Somebody asks if I miss Cody when I'm on vacation. "Of course," I tell him, "I always miss the little guy when we're apart." I do all my Cody jokes and get nice laughs. Afterward, a woman approaches me and says, "I watch you all the time, but who's Cody?" She isn't kidding, either. If she doesn't know Cody by now, she hasn't watched all the time. She hasn't watched at all.

Later, another passenger brings me a message: The ship's Protestant chaplain has challenged me to a game of Ping-Pong. He's watched our games with the Glazers, and wants a piece of me. I meet him at the table and we go at it. The chaplain has an amazing assortment of slice shots and trick shots and he seems very intent on winning. So what am I going to do—beat the chaplain? A man of God? Of course not. I let him win. The truth is, I couldn't have beaten him anyway. Then he takes on Barry Glazer, who was once the Indianapolis Hebrew school champ and happens to be much better at Ping-Pong than at tennis. And the chaplain beats him, too. This chaplain doesn't care who he beats! A Catholic, a Jew, whoever! I kid him about charity and the meek inheriting the earth, but he doesn't care. He just wants to win. And he does. Repeatedly.

Wednesday ☆ March 15

We arrive at Nassau, our final destination. Cloudy here, but we grab our rackets and head for the Ocean Club on Paradise Island, Merv's old place. The new South African owners have poured three hundred million dollars into renovating the Ocean Club and the Paradise Beach Hotel. But the same great tennis pro is there, John Farrington. He once toyed with me on the court at one of Merv's tournaments. Come to think of it, everybody toyed with me that day. But today, we beat the Glazers again. Three straight sets. This makes ten consecutive wins since Fort Lauderdale. My meat Barry is beside himself. He should have stuck with Ping-Pong.

Back to Nassau, where the three of them decide to go shopping. I long ago gave up shopping with Joy on these islands. At one point, she leaves them to make a phone call from the dock, but has to wait her turn. Everything is an adventure with Joy. A mysterious Bahamian stands uncomfortably close to her for a while, pretending he's waiting, too. Never takes his eyes off of her. He shuffles away and a college kid, wacked out of his mind, comes up to her with a marijuana cigarette and asks for a light. She doesn't have it. When she finally gets to the phone, she can't reach the mainland with her credit card. She has to round up the right change, then gets through, only to hear a little kid answer and he can't speak English. Wrong number. And you thought these things only happened to me.

Thursday ☆ *March 16*

Cruise over. We say goodbye to the Glazers at the Fort Lauderdale airport. After ten days together, it's tough to part with good friends. We fly home uneventfully. Mail is stacked all over the kitchen table. Unbelievable accumulation. We spend the night going through the pile, paying bills, unpacking clothes. Back to real-life drudgery. Tomorrow, back to the show for St. Patrick's Day. Always a big day in New York. I wonder what Gelman has in store. Will Cody dress up like a leprechaun?

St. Patrick's Day. A sunny day in New York. An odd day on our show. Gelman, in one of his more mysterious moves, begins the show with a bagpipe band blaring upstairs in the control room. Then they march down two flights of stairs and out onto the set. The men in the band are all wearing kilts. Music is great. Very Irish. But why pack them all into our tiny, cramped control room? Do we even have insurance for that kind of thing? All day long, people keep asking what that was all about. Why the control room? I have absolutely no answer for them. I just got back from a cruise. What do I know? And now Gelman has slipped away on vacation. Maybe that's why he left so quickly. No reason for some of these things.

What a day. Bright and sunny. People running through the streets in their shorts and T-shirts. Spring is officially only a few days away. Joy and I are driving north to Connecticut; along the FDR Drive the city looks sparkling. Mayor Rudy Giuliani is making a difference with his Quality of Life campaign. No ambushes from the guys with squeegees. Less graffiti on the overpasses and the walls. On the radio, Jonathan Schwartz is playing all those great Sinatra hits. New York might just make it after all.

It's clear sailing on the Bruckner Expressway through the Bronx, normally a traffic nightmare. Then on to the Hutchinson River Parkway, speeding past Pelham Parkway and the signs for Orchard Beach, where I swam as a kid. Freakin' Finelli country. The laughs we had as kids— Harry Walsh and Albie Bertolini and Dom Sasso, my pals on Cruger Avenue. Kick the Can, ring-a-levio, baseball and football in Bronx Park, basketball in the auditorium of Our Lady of Solace. Year after year. I thought it would never end.

The trees are still brown, but you can almost see them turning green. I want to shout out loud about how good I feel. We made it through another winter. New York made it, too. Funny how I never had this exhilarated feeling in Los Angeles, where it's always sunny, always the same. Maybe it's because days like this don't come often enough here. Or maybe it's because you wonder how many springs you have left.

Monday ☆ *March 20*

I'm watching a man spread his wings. Because he's a man who actually enjoys wearing a cape, this could be a big wingspan. Art Moore is emerging from the shadows. Gelman is on vacation, so Art steps forward today—

just a little tentatively—to assume the Gelman position on the sidelines. Art is WABC-TV's program director, which also makes him the executive in charge of our show. For years now, he has stood quietly behind Gelman, looming large and mysterious, arousing curiosity. Occasionally, we've drawn him into the Host Chat, but he sort of blinks back the limelight. So many people have said, "What does he do?" One of my standard jokes, when I go out into the audience during commercial breaks, is to point at him and say, "Don't look now, but do you see that guy standing over there? Does anybody know what he does?" Always gets a laugh. Even from Art.

At one time, before Gelman, Art was being pitched for the executive producer job. He'd been working for ABC-Cap Cities in Philadelphia and came to New York for a meeting with me. I liked him a lot, but Gelman had been with me in the past and knew our show intimately. Then, shortly thereafter, Art was hired as program director. So I got them both, anyway. And the three of us end up having lunch together almost every day. That's how I first glimpsed Art wearing his big black cape. Here's this conservative lifelong bachelor walking the streets, looking like Zorro. I think he enjoys the theatricality of it. And, I confess, he does look great in a cape. Gelman wouldn't look good in a cape.

Anyway, midway through this morning's show, I notice Art has moved to the console, where the phone to the control room is located. Art is slowly moving into position! Taking charge! After the show, audience members always file past for autographs. And that's when I see it! There it is, on the same piece of paper given to me for my signature. There it is—bold and proud: "Art

Moore." I've always included my producers in the mix of the Host Chat. It gives the show more of a personal dimension. As a result, Gelman has become a celebrity in his own right. And now, right before my eyes, another star is begging to be born. Ladies and gentlemen, Art Moore!

Tuesday ☆ March 21

I t continues: Art Moore opens the show at the console and never relinquishes his position. Looks happy about it, too. He and I go to lunch at Il Tinello, with the Buena Vista programming execs, Mort Marcus and Janice Marinelli. They tell us about the new talk shows on the Disney launchpad. Their hopes are sky-high for Danny Bonaduce, formerly of *The Partridge Family*. He's all grown up and enjoying a radio career in Chicago. Buena Vista found him guesting on the pilot for Stephanie Miller's show. Stephanie also came from radio, in Los Angeles, and now she'll be Disney's late-night entry, going up against Snyder and Conan O'Brien. Danny made such an impression on her pilot that now he's getting his own show. I always like to keep the Disney execs on their toes. So I begin to register my concern that perhaps Disney is following this grim trend of salacious talk shows. "What is Danny Bonaduce going to do?" I ask. "Will he do our kind of show?" They hedge and say, "Well, no." Uh-oh. Then I ask, "So he's going to do an audience kind of show?" They're not sure. "Well," I say, "what kind of show will it be? If he's not Regis and Kathie Lee, he's got to be Ricki Lake." Mort and Janice shift uncomfortably in their seats. They've stopped eating. I can't stop asking. "You mean Disney is going into the TV sleaze business?" No, no, they scream. Never! But the way this business is careening downhill, who really knows? Things have changed dramatically since the Partridges were little kids.

<hr>

Wednesday ☆ March 22

Cat trauma. Haircut day for Ashley. Compared to haircut day for Gelman, this should be a breeze, but it's not. Ashley is a white Himalayan. He has big hair problems. It's an ordeal for him and for us. Because no one brushes him much, his hair clumps together in braid-like mattes. That is, the hair that remains on him. The rest is shed, in equal parts, on every chair, bed, and countertop in the apartment. So he's due for a clip job. Before heading to the station, I do the dirty work. The drill goes like this: I scoop him up, deposit him in the bathroom, close the door quickly, and fetch his carrier—a huge pink bubblelike conveyance that he hates. If he sees the bubble first, he will simply vanish. I'm not kidding. You can hire an army to tramp through that apartment, but they won't find Ashley.

But now there is no escape. I place the bubble next to the bathroom door. I open the door, grab him, hustle him inside the bubble. Done. Now to get him downstairs. I hope and pray the elevator is empty. The bubble is so big, other passengers become sardines. It's embarrassing! But the coast is clear. Next—through the lobby. The doorman smiles and says, "Goodbye, Ashley." But Ashley is meowing so loudly, who can hear? Now to get a cab. New York cabdrivers have seen it all, but this bubble is ridiculous. Finally one stops. We drive around the corner to Lexington and I deliver Ashley to the technician and continue on to work.

After the show, I return to the scene of the crime. And there he is. Or what's left of him. There's a colorful little sash around his neck. He's still meowing. Like a banshee. I carry him up the street in his pink bubble. The apartment is just a block and a half away, but the streets are crowded with shoppers and schoolkids. And the bubble with the crazed white cat inside catches everyone's eye. Then they look at me, nudge each other and whisper, "You know who that is?" It's the longest walk of my life.

Finally we're home. I free Ashley from the bubble and get a good look at him. He looks fifty pounds lighter. He does have a little gut on him, though, which reminds me he's in his seventies, in cat years. But the real problem is that he doesn't know where he is. He's punchy, dopey. Doesn't recognize his own house. Doesn't remember Scarlett, with whom he's grown up and lived for most of his eleven years. Every day, every night, they've been together, and now he is arching his back and hissing and threatening to attack her. Wait until he sees himself.

By the way, Freakin' Finelli and his wife, Carmen, were in the audience this morning. Freakin' looks good today. Just the same as he did when we were kids, hanging out at Mac's candy store, across the street from Our Lady of Solace elementary school. That was our greatest joy, especially on those hot summer nights. Standing around Mac's with the guys, then crossing over to the school steps, talking, singing, laughing. And what laughs we had. Our gang included Ed Treratola, Bob Lynch, George Brennen, Willie O'Shaunnessy and, of course, Freakin'. And Freakin' is one of the few who has never left the old neighborhood. He's a retired sanitation worker, now a U.S. postal carrier. But he's still Freakin'. Growing up in the Bronx back then, there was only one major cussword in usage. And that was "freakin'," which had a worse connotation. To Tom Finelli, everything was freakin', thus his eternal nickname. He was always making freakin' fun of freakin' everybody, telling freakin' all of us to go freak ourselves. Bronx kids talk differently nowadays. But little else has changed all that much in the neighborhood. And whenever I see Freakin', I feel like I'm back on the corner.

Anyway, he's on a freakin' mission this morning. He's asking me to receive the Father Steven Kelly Memorial Award at a fund-raiser for my old school, Our Lady of Solace. Of course, I'll be there, but do I have to receive an award? This could be my least favorite thing on earth. I didn't even know Father Kelly, but I remember the priests before him. Father Smith, the fire-eating pastor. What a serious and intimidating man. Once, after mass on a Sunday afternoon, I saw him at the Polo Grounds attending a Giants game. That really surprised me. It just never occurred to me that Father Smith would ever go to a baseball game. Father Claudwell was another. I was an altar boy, and before mass one day, I told him I had just heard on the radio that Wendell Willkie died. He was so upset, he threw his prayer book across the room. It never occurred to me that priests got angry, either.

Come to think of it, one of the great embarrassments of my life occurred when I was an altar boy. I must have been twelve, but I still get the chills thinking about it. I had been given the responsibility of hitting the chimes during Sunday mass. When struck properly, the chimes made that sweet, beautiful, hollow sound: *bung bung bung*. But nobody had ever shown me how to do it. How hard could it be, anyway? You just hit them, right? So at the proper moment, I tapped the chimes and the church froze. I had made the worst atonal noise in the history of religion! *Bak! bak! bak!* No Catholic had ever heard such a miserable chime. All at once, the congregation cringed and glared at me in horror. Even the priest, Father Bidgood, shot me a hot glance. I wanted to die. I tried again. Same thing. Only worse. *Baakkk! Baaakkkk!* Here I was, playing the Big Room, right in front of the Big Guy, and I'm making chimes sound like a flyswatter hitting wood. How humiliating. I was tapping too high on the chime. Should have hit it below the center hole. Anyway, what a freakin' nightmare.

Thursday ☆ March 23

Joanna's home for mid-semester break. It's hard to believe that she'll graduate in a couple of months. Suddenly, all of her energy is devoted to the next phase of her life. Get a job, get an apartment, just get going with her life. I remember that panic. She's a fine writer, and wants to pursue a career in magazines. I was kind of hoping she'd consider broadcast journalism, but that's not for her. Anyway, her primary concern at the moment is finding an apartment. I try to explain, "First the job, then the apartment." But it's too late. She's digging into the real estate section of the *Village Voice* and finds something that sounds fabulous. Of course, all those ads *sound* fabulous. Until you see the real thing. But this one is perfect—right price, right location, right street. There's just one slight drawback—that is if you're fussy. The bathtub is located in the kitchen. How unique. The search, I fear, has only begun.

Friday ☆ March 24

The redhead is red hot. Joy's into her second day of shooting this season's cycle of *Haven* shows. Each night, she conscientiously reads the next day's script, works on her interview questions, narrows down her approach to topics, and makes notes endlessly. What a doll. For the most part, that's all we talk about during these taping days. Makes me realize that I rarely talk about our show at home. I know I should work harder at it, but I just can't anymore. But then here's Joy, seemingly just starting out and gung-ho about it. I like that about her. And, frankly, her *Haven* show is getting hotter and better, with a much wider syndication next fall. Maybe we'll even see it in New York again. All of those weekend infomercials make it tough to find a proper slot before the wee hours of the morning. But, then again, she's always worth staying up for.

Meanwhile, the media critics are now moralizing over the Jenny Jones Talk-Show Murder, as it's being called. Where were they when this sleaze began? All they did was churn out stories about the popularity of these shows and the giant ratings. Now it's gotten out of control and they're angry. Unfortunately, they helped create this monster. And I doubt they can stop it.

Monday ☆ March 27

Oscar night. Dave Letterman is hosting. For me, his performance will be the most intriguing reason to watch. I remember asking Johnny Carson last year, "Wouldn't hosting the Academy Awards be a perfect vehicle for your return to television?" Johnny shook his head. "Absolutely not," he said. "That show has the toughest audience in the business. It's an audience of industry insiders all sitting together, and they're a tough laugh." So he'll be feeling Dave's pain.

I know that crowd. During my Los Angeles years, I always hosted a pre-Oscar hour show from the red carpet outside the Music Center. I stood there facing a camera, as the stars tripped up the aisle behind me. But since my back was to the action, I never knew who my next interviewee would be until they were standing alongside of me. Suddenly, I would turn around and there would be Richard Burton staring at me with that blank expression. Or Robert Duvall. Or Michael Jackson. Diana Ross. Luciano Pavarotti. There would be no time to prepare. The crowd noise was overwhelming. It was impossible to hear anything. But we were the only game in town in those days. Nobody else covered the stars entrances, and viewers loved the spontaneity of it and that first chance to check out the fashions. Some people thought it was more entertaining than the Oscar show itself. But it did have rough edges and, the next day without fail, Howard Rosenberg, the *Los Angeles Times* TV critic, would roast me unmercifully. He ranted, raved, and had a field day beating my brains out. He hated that preshow with a passion. But for some reason, every year, he watched faithfully.

Like last year, there's a major Oscar-watching party here at Elaine's restaurant. *Entertainment Weekly* is footing the bill. Publicity king Bobby Zarem is in charge of the festivities. Because Joy is tied up taping her show, Joanna joins me. The place is packed with all those famous New York faces—Walter Cronkite, Morley Safer, Mike Wallace, Hugh Downs. Even Gelman and his girlfriend, Laurie Hibberd, who co-hosts a morning show on fX cable. We take our seats and Joanna is lucky enough to find herself next to Jim Seymour, the managing editor of *Entertainment Weekly*. It's a good table—with Gay and Nan Talese, *Vogue* editor Shirley Lord and husband, Abe Rosenthal of the *New York Times*, and Betsy and Walter Cronkite. The Oscar cast begins with a welcome from white-haired Academy president Arthur Hiller. But hardly anybody here recognizes Arthur. Suddenly, Walter Cronkite grumbles in that distinctive voice of his and says, "God, Johnny looks old!" Does he really think that's Johnny Carson or is this another of Walter's sly foxisms? It doesn't matter. The table breaks up with laughter.

Arthur Hiller is no ball of fire, but things get worse

during the confusing production number that follows, "Make 'Em Laugh." Nobody is laughing. So it's a cold audience when David Letterman comes out. These New Yorkers at Elaine's want to see the hometown guy make good at Hollywood's biggest show. Unfortunately, our crowd is more receptive than the Shrine Auditorium audience. His bit with New York cab-drivers plays well in this room. But it's a slow start for Dave who gets better as the night drags on into eternity. Still, knowing Dave as well as I do, it has to be difficult for him to be harnessed so rigidly into a situation where there's no way out. Regardless of what he does, the show will grind along for another three hours. It's a tough job, all right. But Dave hangs in there. I guess Johnny was right again. Anyway, Joanna and I leave early, but not before Jim Seymour tells Joanna to come see him about a job after she graduates from school. She is thrilled. Maybe now she can get an apartment without a bathtub in the kitchen.

Tuesday ☆ March 28

Rosie O'Donnell pinch-hits for Kathie Lee. She's done this before, and every time she comes back, she's more entrenched in her acting career. Has two movies coming out. One with Demi Moore and Melanie Griffith. Not bad. Rosie even turned up last night in Letterman's Oscar montage of actors auditioning for his role in the film *Cabin Boy*. Everyone from Paul Newman to Tom Hanks to Steve Martin to Rosie, all reciting the line, "Wanna buy a monkey?" I think Rosie stole the bit. We have a ball talking about the Oscars with Claudia Cohen, who is on the scene out there. Then we get a surprise trivia winner in the studio audience. Turns out to be the reporter from *People* magazine who is doing a story on Gelman. Can you believe it? Gelman profiled in *People*! I tell him it took me forty years to get into *People* and Gelman is doing it in twenty minutes. Maybe it's a slow week for *People*. Or maybe Gelman is ready for his own show.

For weeks, I've been getting calls from a friend named Roy Rifkin. Roy is a charming guy, but it's hard to pinpoint exactly what he does for a living. Whatever it is, there's a lot of investing involved. He's been after me to join a new restaurant venture called Television City. It will be a broadcast-themed restaurant right across the street from Radio City Music Hall, anchoring a corner of Rockefeller Center, home of NBC. Possibly the greatest location in the world. Anyway, several television personalities have come aboard for a small piece of the action. So I've asked legendary entertainment lawyer Burt Padell to check out the details for me. Got to be careful. I had a taste of restaurant ownership once already. Some years ago, Mikhail Baryshnikov and I had a limited partnership in the Columbus restaurant on Columbus Avenue. We had hoped that Robert DeNiro would also come aboard, but Burt Padell advised him against it. Eventually, Bobby opened his own successful Tribeca Grill. Meanwhile, Columbus is long gone—although it was fun while it lasted, and I even made a few bucks.

Now I follow Bobby's example and go to Burt before making a move. We meet for the first time at lunch with the restaurant operators. Burt looks mild-mannered enough approaching the table, but what a tiger! He begins firing numbers, clauses, questions, and I just keep eating. After lunch, we walk up Broadway and I hear about his life and his famous clients like Madonna, Faye Dunaway, Jackie Mason, and on and on. Burt himself was a New York Yankee bat boy during the Joe DiMaggio era. Later he even became a Yankee player until he broke an ankle, then went on to get his law degree and a degree in accounting. As we approach 56th Street, he asks if I would like to see his office, which is like a museum of popular culture. I've never seen more baseball and show business memorabilia in my life. Really extraordinary. Cooperstown could build a whole annex for Burt's baseball collection—rare pictures, legendary bats, signed balls, antique jerseys, private correspondence, all framed and mounted beautifully. And he has miles of entertainment posters and artifacts—everything from all of Madonna's platinum albums to a 1936 letter from a homesick Jimmy Durante to the pipes from Lon Chaney's original organ in *Phantom of the Opera*. Every inch of wall space is covered with history, old and new, and easily worth a fortune.

At lunch, I had mentioned to Burt the odd saga of my lone recording album for Mercury, *It's Time for Regis!*, released during the Bishop years. Mercury was eventually bought out by Polygram, which last year re-released the album on compact disc. Now Burt asks about royalties. I laugh. "In twenty-seven years, I've never seen a dime," I tell him. He wants to check into it. I tell him not to waste his time. It wasn't a big seller in the first place. "No," he says, "I'd like to pursue it." So I tell him he can keep everything he finds over $70,000. I mean it as a joke, but he just nods okay. Maybe I'll go into this restaurant venture, but I know there are no royalties from that album.

Computer lesson today. Progress has been slow. Too much time has lapsed between lessons. I've forgotten everything—if it's two clicks or one on the mouse, how to make an edit, which icon is which. Sure, it's a marvelous invention, this little box crammed with all that stuff. But it's not all that user-friendly. I mean, if these guys are smart enough to get all that information inside there, they ought to be smart enough to make it simple for the rest of us. Anyway, J. D. Reid from *People* magazine drops by to watch my lesson and take a picture. They want me to put a letter in e-mail. I've heard about e-mail, but have no idea how it works. I decide to write to Lou Holtz about this year's recruiting class for the Notre Dame football team. I tell Lou how thrilled I am to hear we have the biggest, baddest, best group of freshmen ever assembled. I struggle through the letter and keep misspelling the word *the*, of all things. It's embarrassing. And in front of *People* magazine! (Let's hope this won't reflect poorly on that big Gelman piece.) Finally, I get it done. Now to send it. I need the Notre Dame football office e-mail number. So I call them to learn they don't have an e-mail number. It figures. This tech revolution might be a little overhyped. I fax Lou his letter and continue my lesson. I write another letter. This one to Gelman. It says, "Dear Gelman, You are fired. Your pal, Regis." We all laugh. The *People* photographer takes a picture of it and then Gelman walks in. He doesn't think it's so funny. "You'll have to go through some other people to get that done," says Gelman. He's bugged. Come on, Gelman. Lighten up. Anyway, I don't have his e-mail number, either.

Thursday ☆ March 30

Joanna and I have lunch with my Notre Dame friend Harry McQuillan from K-III Communications at Il Tinello on 56th Street. K-III publishes magazines like *New York*, *Seventeen*, *New Woman*. Since Joanna made up her mind about working in magazines, I'm trying to introduce her to as many people in that field as I can. Harry is an old publishing hand and a die-hard Notre Dame fan who played tackle on one of Ara Parseghian's teams back in the sixties. Like me, Harry lapses into stony silence when the team loses. Anyway, he's going to set up a day of appointments for Joanna with the various K-III editors. Real life is getting more real for her.

Tonight we attend the premiere of *Arcadia* at Lincoln Center, primarily to see John Griffin, the son of my agent Jimmy Griffin. Jimmy is one of the few Irish agents in the business, and I got him. I call him the Irish Street Fighter or the Bulldog—and that's when he's *easy* to get along with. But tonight is for his eighteen-year-old son John, who has been suddenly cast in this Tom Stoppard play, directed by Trevor Nunn. The big time. And how he got to Broadway in his first legit play is one of those great show business stories.

Jimmy got him a summer job in the William Morris mailroom, where so many moguls got their start. One day a call came in from the coast. Could they put a certain New York actor on tape reading some lines and send it back out to the coast? John was asked to help the actor and feed him dialogue. Hollywood called to say they liked the actor fine, but who was that reading with him? They were impressed, and John was inspired. He went around to some auditions in town and wound up reading for Stoppard and Trevor Nunn. He beat out two hundred other young actors for the part in *Arcadia*. Naturally, Jimmy and Linda are thrilled, and so arc we.

We take our seats at the Beaumont Theatre and the play begins. Every time John comes out, I sneak a side-long glance at Jimmy and Linda, who are beaming. The only odd thing is that John never says a word onstage. I wasn't exactly expecting this. He keeps coming out, but has nothing to say. No dialogue. I'm worried he's not going to have any lines. But it doesn't bother Jimmy. He's still beaming. Then in the second act, as another character, John speaks and I'm relieved. And he keeps speaking and he's terrific and it's a great opening night.

All day long, I've been thinking about a postcard I received from a fan who offered another title for this book. It's a line I've muttered on the air for years, usually when my exasperation level is soaring: *"I'm only one man!"* I like it. It feels right. Tonight I mention it to Jimmy, who says he'll run it past the Hyperion people. Time to unleash the Bulldog once again.

Getaway day for Kathie Lee. She'll leave after the show for a week in the Caribbean. There's nothing like the last show before a vacation. It always flies by. Everything is easy. She's even smiling at Gelman. Our guest is Lawrence Taylor, the great New York Giant linebacker. Lawrence is embarking on a wrestling career. He's scheduled to do battle with Bam Bam Bigelow, a fearsome 390-pound wrestler who has a head full of tattoos and a mouth not quite full of teeth. It's an absolutely brilliant move by promoter Vince McMahon. Taking the most famous football player in recent New York history, offering him a million bucks to climb into the Wrestlemania ring, and stoking this blood feud between him and Bam Bam. Even the sportwriters, who normally wouldn't mention Wrestlemania under their breath, are writing reams about it.

All of this inspires Gelman. He's ordered up a fake beard, some washable tattoos, and a bald skull-cap tattooed with a skull-and-crossbones. Before the show, I pull on the outfit, including wrestling togs, and tape a piece as Bam Bam, verbally ripping Lawrence Taylor to shreds and attempting to fight my way past security guards to get into the studio and at Lawrence. It looks pretty funny, but I hope Bam Bam doesn't see it. I don't think he has much of a sense of humor.

Meanwhile, Jimmy Griffin calls to tell me that the Bulldog has struck again. *I'm Only One Man!* will be our new title for the book.

Apil Fool's. We're in Connecticut for the weekend. We decide to see a movie. But which one? Always a monumental decision. Joy votes for *Outbreak,* with Dustin Hoffman, which is racking up big box-office grosses. But we recently had Randy Quaid on the show, plugging his latest movie, *Bye Bye Love.* The travails of three divorced men. The clip looked promising. Joy concedes to see it. So we drive over to Mount Kisco and the local cineplex. As we enter our little boxlike theater, I notice the first nine rows are taped off. And there are only eighteen rows in the whole place. To my horror, I am told that the seats are reserved for a birthday party of ten-year-olds. Twenty-six of them! Each with his own bag of candy! In they troop, laughing, giggling, scratching, rattling candy wrappers. Just our luck. But twenty-six kids here to see a comedy about divorce? What an odd choice. I wonder how many of these kids are going through that trauma, or have been through it, or will go through it. The movie is just fair, except for Janeane Garofalo, who turns in a very funny performance. Maybe it's all of these kids or maybe it's Joy, who sits strangely silent, but I have a feeling I blew it. We should have seen *Outbreak*.

After the movie, I go get the car. I'll pick up Joy in front of the theater. To get there, I take a route from the parking lot I've never taken before. It's very dark, and suddenly I realize I'm going the wrong way on a one-way street. But nobody's coming, so I proceed a half-block to the corner. I look to my left, see nothing coming, and edge into a right turn. Just then a black blur whizzes in front of the car. Just a few more inches and I would have slammed into a kid on a bicycle! No reason for him to expect a car coming down this street. I jam on my brake so hard that I have to catch my breath. I'm really shaken. Man, that was close. All I need is to injure a kid on a bike. I'm too upset to even tell Joy. Bad enough that I picked the wrong movie.

Monday ☆ April 3

On the way to work, I see a jogger emerging from Central Park with a dog's leash tied to his belt. Never seen that before, but I guess if you're going to jog with your dog, that's one way to stay together. I take a second look at the jogger. I know him! It's Tom Brokaw! Being pulled along by his dog! Peculiar sight.

Christina Ferrare is back all week pinch-hitting for Kathie Lee after a year's absence from the show. And she's fired up for the occasion. She knows the routine of our opening segment well—the free-flowing exchange, the anecdotes and stories about what's happening in the world or in our lives. Sometimes what goes on in the world comes second. I start to tell everybody what happened last night at Wrestlemania between L.T. and Bam Bam. Then I hear Christina blurt out, "Don't you want to talk about me?" After a year's wait, she was itching to bring us up to date on her life, her children, her husband, and her new venture—painting dishes. She is fully primed. Stories, pictures, dishes—she has it all for us. Wrestlemania will have to wait. And it does.

Later, I get to lift the lumber and swing for the fences. Michelle Smith, the probable starting pitcher for the U.S. Olympic women's softball team, is here to face me down. We go out to Columbus Avenue where all of our athletic challenges are fought. Her mound is in the center of the street, forty feet away from home plate. I'm at bat. She does a double pump in her windup, takes two giant steps and fires away underhanded. Wow! What blinding speed! Incredible. She's almost on top of me before she lets the ball go. Usually I'm okay out here on Columbus, but this is embarrassing. She's merciless. I decide to go for a bunt and lay a nice one down. It feels good to make contact, but there's not much glory in a bunt. Otherwise, it's strike, strike, strike. I only hope George Steinbrenner's not watching.

Tuesday ☆ April 4

Christina comes in like a lamb this morning. Yesterday she was on fire, exploding out of her chair. Now she's much calmer and as good as ever. And it's a lovely spring day in New York City. I duck out early for a workout at Radu's, then meet Joy and Lawrence Krashes for lunch at the Trump Tower. Lately, Joy has been getting antsy about our apartment. We've been there eleven years and took it because it had three bedrooms and was close to all the schools. But Joanna is on the verge of leaving the nest. J.J. has become a world wanderer, but she'll be out of there as soon as she graduates next year. So Joy is looking for a fresh start. I tried and failed to interest her in that high rise across from our studio. Now, after lunch, we all admire the magnificence of Trump Tower and Joy says, "Hey, why don't we look for a place here?" I think she might be kidding, but she isn't. "Well, why not?" I say. We ride up to the real estate office, get a saleswoman, then return to the lobby to walk over to the residential side of the building. And there he is—the Donald himself—striding toward us in his black overcoat, blond hair flying, red power-tie peeking out. I call out to him, "Donald, I'm here to buy your apartment." Only kidding, of course, but he's thrilled to see us. "Come on, let me show you my place," he says. This is crazy. How can I look at his place and then look at another apartment? Anything else will seem like a hovel. I try to back out. He won't hear of it. He can't stop himself. He's got to make a deal. I beg him, "Please, Donald, don't disillusion me!" But there's no way out.

Elevator takes us to the top floor. Of course. And there, behind what must be solid-gold doors, is the most majestic apartment we've ever seen. It's a masterpiece with a thrilling view of Central Park and the Manhattan skyline. Gold everywhere in sight. Donald says, "Look at this." He pushes a button, and fountains at the end of an enormous living room leap and dance toward the ceiling. And this ceiling! It may be the closest thing to the Sistine Chapel you could imagine. Donald leads us from room to room, walking, talking, pitching. It's the art of the deal all over again, live and in color. Then he goes in for the kill. "This," he announces, "is the most extraordinary living space in the world." And he may be right. Then he sends us on our way to inevitable disillusionment.

But we go look at an apartment that actually seems perfect. Not that it even approaches Trump's, but it catches our eye. Who knows? By tomorrow, we'll probably forget it. We leave the Tower and I'm ready to go home. But Joy wants to go across the street to buy someone a wedding gift at Steuben Glass. We make the purchase and now I'm really tired. I've been through the show, Radu, Donald Trump, glassware, and I want to go home. But no. Joy says Tiffany is next. She promises, "Just ten minutes and we'll go home together."

Finally, we're out of there. But I can tell Joy doesn't want to go home. She's just warming up. I look for a cab to make my escape. I flag one down, run over to it, and before she has a chance to talk me out of it, I give the cabbie the destination. He flips on the meter and we wait for the red light to turn green. I glance back at the sidewalk and there's Joy with Christina Ferrare! Where did she come from? What's she doing here? Too late to find out. The light is green, I wave to them, and the cab takes me home.

We make dinner plans and decide to invite Christina along with us. She's away from her family in California and alone. Must need a night out. We pick her up at her hotel and drive over to restaurant 222 on the West Side. Christina talks about the reaction she's been getting to her appearance. Deservedly good, but some friends offered her pointers—you know, that devastating, well-meaning advice. Never mind that she's been co-hosting for years. One thing about being on TV—everybody's got an opinion about how you're doing. Years ago, I used to let even the most well-meaning criticism get to me, but now it just stings for a second and I forget about it.

But Christina is still sensitive. And now I'm finding out just how sensitive. She's recalling our chance meeting on the sidewalk earlier—how she had seen us walking toward her, how I darted suddenly into that cab, how badly it shook her up. Joy had made a joke at the time, telling her, "I don't know what's wrong with him. He never runs away like that. It must be you. It can't be me." She was only kidding, but Christina took it seriously and went home in tears. Still crying, she called her husband, Tony Thomopolous, to say I must hate her. Her eyes are glistening, just telling us all this now in the car. I'm so stunned, I almost hit two different pedestrians. Makes me realize just how fragile we all are and how tough it is to go onto that firing line of daily television without winding up a schizoid.

Wednesday ☆ April 5

Christina is funny during Host Chat, talking about our dinner last night. She tells the story of the sidewalk misunderstanding and the tears that followed. Our audience boos me. So I made my co-host cry! I'm sorry! They don't want to hear my explanation. They don't care that Joy was shopping me to death! Or that I never saw her until I got in the cab. Anyway, before dinner, Christina had mentioned to her husband that we arranged for her to have a tablemate—writer Bill Zehme, who's coaching me through this book. Tony Thomopolous, who is one of those dashing, confident show business executives, had an attack of Greek jealousy. He was about to leave California for a convention in France, but called her twice before boarding his overnight flight. He wanted to hear all about his wife's dinner companion. She got his messages upon returning to the hotel. But it was too late to catch him. Must have been a long night for Tony on that plane. Not so confident, after all. Hey, who is?

Alan Thicke comes on to talk about his critically acclaimed work on the new sitcom *Hope and Gloria*. He plays an egotistical talk-show host. Do all talk-show hosts have to be egotistical on these series? Who writes this stuff? What do they know, anyway? We run a clip in which he's imploring his producer to take better care of him, to improve his lighting. "Like Regis and Kathie Lee," he says. "Come on! Be my Gelman!" Shows you how important Gelman is becoming these days. Hey, I can't even get *Gelman* to be my Gelman! If I had to wait for him to get the lights fixed in our studio, we'd still be in semidarkness.

Friday ☆ April 7

The best laid plans always backfire. But what happens today is insane. Why do I bother? I must be on a plane for Orlando this morning. Must get down to Disney World to tape tomorrow's Easter Parade—even though Easter is next week. But who cares? I have everything under control. If I leave immediately after the show, I can make it to La Guardia for my flight at ten-forty. My bags are packed and a car will be waiting. So I go down to the studio to do the show. Gelman is off in Canada somewhere being a celebrity, and his audience warm-up is sorely missed. I sense a dead crowd. And the opening segment is a struggle. It's Christina's last day, and she wants to thank some people whose names she can't remember. Ouch. Meanwhile, a few feet off-camera, there's an animated conversation going on between two crew members. Maybe they forgot we're on the air. The audience is distracted and restless. The trivia contestants, both retired, don't know that Julia Roberts was in *Pretty Woman*. We are going downhill fast. Dolly Parton is our first guest, always up and funny and cute. But next comes three supermodels—Claudia Schiffer, Elle MacPherson, and Naomi Campbell—who want to plug their new restaurant, Fashion Cafe, opening tonight at Rockefeller Center. It's always tough to interview three guests at once, and this is no exception. It's just one of those shows.

We go to a commercial and I'm eyeing the clock, planning my departure and the subsequent rush to the airport. That's when Art Moore motions for me to meet him alone. He has a stricken look on his face. Very uncommon for him. "What is it, Art?" He tells me, "We've had a bomb scare and the building must be evacuated. Everybody out. We've got three minutes." *Bomb scare?* This hasn't happened to me since the Walter Winchell interview thirty years ago! Suddenly, we're back on the air. I make the announcement to the audience and they think it's a joke. They don't move. I explain it again: "We have to go outside! The show is over." The models look confused. It's about nine forty-five. Fifteen minutes of airtime left. The control room switches to a backup show, a repeat of an interview with Tony Bennett. We all leave the building. My car is waiting, but everything I need—my bags and plane tickets—is upstairs in my office. Now I can't go up to get them! What a fiasco.

So I'm out on the street with the audience while the NYPD bomb squad races through our building. We can't get back in. People are coming up to me for pictures and autographs and stories about how I met their aunt twenty-three years ago in Paducah. Finally, my assistant Jennifer gets someone to retrieve my bags, but the guy forgets my pants which have my wallet inside. Another trip upstairs. Valuable minutes tick by. It's now five past ten. Thirty-five minutes until take-off. I should have been well on my way by now. The pants and wallet arrive and I'm in the car. Changing my pants in the backseat! The driver says it's going to be close. We race through the park, but crawl along Madison Avenue. Third Avenue is a little better, but not much. We'll never get there. Finally, traffic loosens up. We're on the FDR Drive, over the bridge to La Guardia, and onto Delta Airlines. My plane is parked at the last gate in the terminal. Every time I fly, it's always the last bloody gate. I'll just make it. Three minutes to spare. I take my seat, still panting.

Joan Lunden is right across the aisle with her hairdresser. She's studying her parade script. Twice a year, we co-host Disney's Easter and Christmas parades, and Joan loves to be prepared. No one is more thorough and conscientious. She wants to be informed about all aspects of the parade. I'm not kidding. I've seen her stop a meeting cold to ask which of the Seven Dwarfs will march by first and then the exact order of the Dwarfs to follow. I admire her tenacity. Me, I can barely get on a plane.

The woman next to me is flying to Orlando to meet her husband for an insurance convention. Her name is Marlene. She lives in Greenwich. When she moved there two years ago, she thought she would meet and become best friends with Kathie Lee. It never happened. I tell her about the bomb scare. She says, "Will you be back on the air by Wednesday? I have tickets." I assure her we will, unless—well, let's not even think about that. I notice she's wearing glasses. I brought a ton of reading material for the flight, but of course my glasses are on my desk upstairs on the fifth floor. All of this aggravation because some jerk wants to play games. Marlene offers me her spare pair of magnifying glasses, which I will return to her Wednesday at the show.

Orlando is warm and overcast. We get settled, then have a script meeting with the parade staff. Tonight I'm on America Online, a first for me. Computer people get online to send questions and I answer them. A moderator and a typist are on the phone with me. He reads me the question, she types my answer into the computer. The only problem is, I have to give my answer so slowly for her to type it that I keep forgetting where I'm going with the answers. It's awkward. Frankly, it would save time to just conduct phone calls with each person. Most people want to know about the bomb scare. I tell them nothing was found, but it did interrupt my conversation with four beautiful women. "I resent it very much!" I say. Others want the inside scoop on the feud between Gelman and Kathie Lee. One suggests I get a cat named Kathie Lee, since she has a dog named Regis. Funny, I say, but I don't need another cat! It's a long hour, but somehow I get through it.

Saturday ☆ April 8

Our bomb scare story makes the *New York Times*. Also the morning *Orlando Sentinel*, which I read. Apparently, the call came from someone with a Middle Eastern accent who wanted to promote world peace, claimed he wasn't a terrorist but, nevertheless, said he planted a bomb in our studio. Isn't that great? This nut wants to plant a bomb to promote world peace! We tape the Easter Parade at noon and I make my way to the airport immediately afterward. No delays today, unlike last Easter when I embarrassed myself in front of Joan Lunden.

What a story. After that parade, I made my escape—only to find that my Delta flight back to New York had been postponed by bad weather. So I stupidly ran to all the other terminals to find another flight. I lugged my heavy carry-on bags from airline to airline, but the weather had grounded every flight to New York. Totally exhausted, I returned to the Delta terminal for my original flight. The lounge was packed. Everyone waiting. Finally, a flight attendant spotted me and let me preboard.

I walked onto the plane and decided to have a drink. I usually order Diet Sprite on the plane, but after all that running and disappointment, I wanted a real drink. Vodka tonic. So it's me alone with three flight attendants, whom I regale with funny Regis and Kathie Lee stories, as I woofed down the drink. I had them screaming. And that drink hit the spot. Let's have another. I hadn't eaten anything since breakfast, and never have more than two drinks. Except that another delay was announced. So I went for a third. The attendants were still laughing. I think. And I'm still the only passenger aboard. Midway through the third drink, it hit me like a ton of bricks: *You're drunk, you dope.* And I never get drunk. Never. But here I was all alone on the plane, totally loaded. I asked for a pillow. My plan was to go to sleep and, well, sleep tight until we got home. I closed my eyes. It had been a hectic day. I was dead tired. I began drifting off. Then I sensed that passengers were finally entering the plane. Who cares? I was almost asleep. But someone nudged me. I opened my eyes. It was Joan Lunden. My seatmate. And she wanted to talk. Since we only see each other a few times a year, there's always so much to catch up on. Joan was all geared up. And I was drunk.

I looked at her and saw her face come in and out of focus. My eyes spun in my head. I wondered if she could tell. Finally, I blurted out, "Joan, they let me on early and I've had three drinks and I'm sorry to tell you this—*but I'm drunk out of my mind!*" To this day, I don't know if she heard me or not. But she kept right on talking and didn't stop until we were over Washington, D.C. For the whole flight, I just stared at her with my spinning eyes and nodded when I thought it was appropriate, laughed and frowned when I felt it was necessary. I did the best I could to act civilized. I think it worked. At least, she never stopped talking. And she never said a word about it again.

Tanned and rested, Kathie Lee is back from vacation. She spies her cousin in the audience. A fine musician, she says. She brings him up for an impromptu session at the piano. He takes his place at the keys. She stands alongside him, gets that starry look in her eyes. Somehow I feel a song coming on. He noodles a bit. She says, "Can you lower it a third?" Now I know a song is coming on! She's mugging. She's belting. She's very funny. Year after year, I see the headlines on the women's magazine covers. Same story—she's leaving, she can't take it anymore, she wants to be home with the kids. Come on! Take a look at her now. She's having a ball. The woman is on fire. She'll never have fun like this again. She must have missed it like crazy while she was gone. This is her life. Where is she going?

Back to the Host Chat. I ask her about her vacation. Big mistake. Some woman at their resort made disparaging remarks about Cody and Cassidy, who were apparently having too much fun, just being boisterous. Kathie Lee chased the woman down and gave her a tongue-lashing. The story goes on. Meanwhile, we're running out of time fast. Gelman is shifting from leg to leg. Even Art Moore begins to panic. But Kathie cannot be stopped. No one can say things like that about her kids! Finally, she ends her tirade by telling the woman that she'll pray for her. Always a good way to end an argument. But we don't have a prayer catching up for the rest of the show.

Dinner tonight at the Monkey Bar with Gelman, his girlfriend Laurie Hibbard, and Mary Kellogg, our Disney liaison. Mary is in charge of all of our remote broadcasts and now outlines the plan for next month's shows from Branson, Missouri. Then we talk about where we'll go next year. Gelman suggests Africa. Not a bad idea. I've heard so much about it, why not? Stay tuned for Gelman in a pith helmet.

Tuesday ☆ April 11

From my cab window this morning I spot huge tents going up next to Tavern on the Green in Central Park. Tonight I'm supposed to be in there, attending the annual PEN dinner, the year's biggest formal bash for esteemed New York writers. Last year it was held in one of those enormous waiting rooms at Grand Central Terminal, a novel site for a black-tie affair. I spent most of that night in a Grand Central bathroom, doubled-over in pain. Do I know how to have a good time or what?

Actually, it had been a nice party, until I felt that familiar catch in my throat and darted from the table. I am told I have a hiatal hernia, which can at any time become a major regurgitation problem. That means, one moment you suddenly realize that your food isn't going down correctly, followed by a moment when you know that it wants to come back up again. It's a terrible sensation and very unpredictable, and that night it arrived without warning. A waiter quickly pointed me toward a men's room at the far end of the station. I raced in there and hoped to find an empty stall. Not a chance. There were twelve stalls with twelve pairs of feet under each door. I happened to be the only guy in the john wearing a tux, but nothing's too unusual for Grand Central Terminal. I held it back gamely and waited for a stall to open up. Little did I know that those twelve guys were planning to spend the night in there. I'm like a cat with a hairball and these guys are bedding down for the night.

But I was trapped with no place to go, no place to hide: a sick celebrity in a tux. Even the stall occupants came out—only to back away in horror. And I was really sick. I had to use every paper towel I could find. Finally, I stepped out of the men's room where Joy waited in her evening gown, talking to NBC weatherman Ira Joe Fisher, on his way to a train. I managed to say hello, but then realized the worst wasn't over. I headed back inside, where a concerned security guard stood watch over me while I did what I had to do. I'll never forget his kindness and recently saw him again, but managed to hold myself upright this time.

Anyway, so much for my fond memories of the PEN party. Claudia and Senator Al have invited us along to-night, so that I can make up for what I missed last year. Already they've become New York's most talked-about couple, and the senator's presence at the party is bound to stir up controversy among the writers who are angry about the proposed end of funding for the arts. What most of them may not know is that Senator Al has been at the forefront of trying to save that funding program. But by five o'clock, none of that matters, anyway. I get a call telling me that the senator has not responded well to a stress test and will be spending the night in a Long

Island hospital. Claudia is heading out there now and, all of a sudden, it looks like we're not going to any party.

_____

Wednesday ☆ April 12
_____

J erry Seinfeld once said Kathie Lee and I do *nothing* better than anyone else on television. He meant it, I guess, as a compliment. After all, his NBC sitcom is famous for being about "nothing." But it took me a while to get his point. Which is, during our Host Chats, we have a lot of fun talking about nothing all that important and nothing in particular. We just cover the little incidents and minutiae of life. To Jerry, that's nothing. If he thinks we've elevated it to an art form, what am I going to do? Argue with him?

What's ironic is how our Host Chat segment seems to work its way into various television plots year after year. We've popped up on a couple of *Seinfeld*s (including the time Kramer came on our show to plug his stupid coffee-table book), one *Mad About You*, a *Cosby Mystery*, and today it's Delta Burke's *Woman of the House*. According to the formula, we usually banter about something going on in a program's fictional storyline and then we turn up in that episode on some character's TV set, somehow advancing the plot. Sort of a "Look! Even Regis and Kathie Lee are talking about it!" moment. We always tape these bits right after our live broadcasts. I'm just glad there aren't any costume changes. The writers of this *Woman of the House* episode have tried to capture our spontaneous style and actually have done it well. We ad-lib slightly around their dialogue and it looks okay. Once again, we did "nothing" perfectly, I guess.

Afterward, I join Joan Lunden for a grueling three-hour satellite interview tour of the stations carrying the Disney Easter parade this weekend. We meet at the National Video Studio on 42nd Street, where sex therapist Dr. Ruth Westheimer used to tape her show. I remember once doing that show against my better judgment and thirty minutes later reminding myself to never go against my better judgment again. Dr. Ruth liked getting up close and very personal. I've already blocked from memory the lurid questions she asked me, but I stumbled out of there in a sweat, humiliated to the core. Anyway, today I'm exhausted by trying to give different answers to the same questions over and over again. I marvel at Joan's ability to keep her responses so fresh. She's a real pro who always moves straight forward, never looks back and never gets tired (especially on long plane trips, but that's another story).

Screening tonight of *Kiss of Death*. After the movie, Joy and I head for the exit as the credits roll. Always try to get out early. Easier to get a cab that way. We're outside when Joy discovers she forgot her umbrella inside. Weatherman Al Roker predicted rain tonight, so I had grabbed my raincoat and she brought along the umbrella. So Joy turns around and works her way back through the exiting crowds to retrieve it. "Forget it!" I yell, but she's gone.

Thirty seconds later, a guy comes up to me with the umbrella. He found it near her seat. So now I have the umbrella, but no Joy. Meanwhile, the crowd pours out and so do the questions: "Where's Kathie Lee?" "How's

Gelman?" "What are you doing here?" "What exactly does Art Moore do?" I can't take it anymore! Finally, I turn and face the wall to avoid being noticed. Next person walks by and says, "Regis, why are you looking at the wall?" Nothing helps. At last, Joy returns. I don't say a word —just show her the umbrella. Let her figure it out.

Now for the trauma of hailing a cab in the middle of a postmovie rush. First, no cabs are in sight. Then no cabs on our side of the street. Then somebody jumps in front of us and takes the one we've flagged down. Then Joy bumps into someone she knows and engages in a long conversation, while two empty cabs whiz past. I break up Joy's conversation, and again there are no more cabs. What a New York nightmare.

Finally, we catch one and head over to Nino's on First Avenue, a great boisterous Italian restaurant that makes living in this town bearable. We have a great dinner and head home. As we approach our apartment, the rain begins. I say, "I'm glad we've got that umbrella." Joy looks stricken. She doesn't have it. Yes, it's back at the restaurant, safe and sound in Nino's checkroom. "Well," I say, "at least I've got my raincoat." But, of course, I don't have that, either. The coat is with the umbrella in the checkroom. Sometimes I wonder how we make it home night after night.

Thursday ☆ *April 13*

Doggone it, who are we kidding here? I hope this isn't a bad omen: Comedy writer Al Franken is with us today, plugging his film *Stuart Saves His Family*. Stuart, of course, is Al's long-running *Saturday Night Live* character, Stuart Smalley, the self-described "caring nurturer and a member of several twelve-step programs." Stuart is kind of a touchy-feely guy, famous for leading himself and others through daily affirmations—positive statements that build up self-esteem. And the funny thing is, these affirmations can work and really make you stronger. So I say, "What we need around here are some affirmations of our own!" Because Al is such a good writer and always prepared, he agrees to give us the Stuart Smalley treatment. He's brought along two small hand mirrors, which he passes to Kathie Lee and me. "Don't look at me," he says, in Stuart's nasally voice. "Look into the mirror—only you can help you!" So we gaze into the mirrors and are told to repeat after him—which we do: "I am a *great* talk-show host!"

Maybe I'm imagining things, but I notice the tenor in Kathie Lee's voice is quite strong as she says this. "I think she's done this before," I point out. She nods, guilty as charged. The second affirmation is: "I have the best partner in the business!" This time her voice is less confident than in her first affirmation. I think she actually muttered. And then finally: "And if I don't win the Emmy this year, I don't have to get angry." We both say this gritting our teeth, then finish: "Because I'm good enough. I'm smart enough. And, doggone it, *if they could see me now!*" Great. Now we're doing a Carnival Cruise commercial! As for that Daytime Emmy Award, forget it, Stuart. We never win. After years of rejection, my only fun is feigning anger. But I have no expectations. At this point, I know better.

In fact, Gelman recently picked one of our shows and submitted it for Emmy consideration. How do you pick just one show from a daily program like ours? How can you isolate a single day? A single hour? As usual, we have no idea. He finally settled on one and sent it in. It's the show where I go nuts over how beautiful the bathrooms are in the American Renaissance restaurant. I never saw that show, can hardly remember it now, but Gelman thought our chemistry was especially good that day. So, if we lose—and we will—it's Gelman's fault. Of course.

My daughter Joanna has, meanwhile, considered several entry-level job offers in the magazine business and, after some sleepless nights, decided on *Seventeen*. She's terribly excited. I've heard back from some of the people who interviewed her and all of the reports have been excellent. It's funny how you can think the world of your kids, but still hold your breath whenever they go out for a job interview. Her excitement reminds me of my own—way back when I landed my first job, after the service, as an NBC page. It's a thrill to get started. But, first, let's just get her graduated.

This is J.J.'s last weekend abroad. But forget about her coming home. First, she and her friends will travel around Europe for a couple of weeks. It still staggers me to think about her roaming around that continent. I must have been almost forty when I first went to Europe. And now she's hoping to get Joy to come over to Spain and spend the final week with her. Getting Joy to commit to something is not easy. Up to now, she's been leaning against going. As we drive to Connecticut, I offhandedly ask whether she might do it. Suddenly, she thinks she will and later swings into action. She gets on the phone and makes arrangements to fly to London Sunday night, where she'll meet J.J. and then go on to Spain. Airline schedules and fares change by the hour, so Joy hammers away at a ticket agent and quickly works it out. Only one problem: She isn't so sure whether she should go. She wonders, isn't this a little sudden? Can she pull off such an impromptu trip? Can she pack properly? Take-off time is forty-eight hours away. This could be close.

Morning. Time is running out on Joy's decision. Should she or shouldn't she? Will it be another fiasco? Neither Joy nor J.J. has ever been to Spain. What's the weather there like? Will it rain on the plain in Spain? Joy is waiting for a sign that might convince her of what to do. The sign comes—and God only knows what it is—but it tells her not to go. She places another long-distance call to London. So far, the phone bill has eclipsed the tuition for this semester. She breaks the bad news to J.J. Just yesterday she told J.J. that she was coming. But now she hears J.J.'s disappointment. Guilt overtakes her during breakfast. Last year, Joy made a similar trip to Italy with Joanna during *her* European study abroad. She doesn't want to slight J.J. So she makes another call to the airlines—and now she is going after all! Another phone call to London to share the good news. But the travel plans are terribly complicated. She's landing at Heathrow and then taking the speed tram to Gatwick, London's other airport, where she'll meet up with J.J. for their flight to Spain. I cringe with terror over the whole ordeal. And I'm not even going!

A milestone this afternoon: In twenty years of playing tennis with Tom and Elaine Battista, we've lost repeatedly. Because Tom's so large and has tremendous reach, I call him the Big Berzerker. And with Elaine's smooth, consistent stroke, they have proved unbeatable to us. Sure, once in a while we may get lucky, but it's usually a miserable wipeout. And, naturally, I have yelled and screamed and broken rackets and not conducted myself at all in a sportsmanlike manner. But you've got to understand—I'm talking about twenty years of humiliation! And every year it only gets worse.

But today that streak ends! I'm equipped with yet another new lightweight Weed racket inscribed once more with a message from owner Tad Weed, imploring me to take deep breaths, relax, be happy, and not slam this racket down too hard. I take the court a new man. I feel it. Net Man is back. He feels strong. He feels good, Don Pardo! He's ready to end this twenty-year jinx. I tell Joy: "Let's do it. Let's stay focused." We do, and it's 4–4 in the first set. That's when we usually choke, but not today. We win it 6–4. Let's play another. No water break today. No idle conversation. We go right into another set and win it easily, 6–1.

Now it's the Big Berzerker who's having troubles. The Berzerker is yelling. We begin a third set. Can we complete a sweep of the Battistas? Joy remains focused, even though her tennis elbow pains her. She makes some great shots and with Net Man quietly gliding over for an occasional poach, we do it. We win our third in a row! It's an incredible sports moment! One I'll always remember. Later after dinner, we play hearts and I win that game, too. Yes, today Net Man is holding all the cards! As Marv Albert would say, *I'm on fire!*

Joy is going to Spain. She can't believe it. Neither can I. All of this started Friday on our drive up to Connecticut. Just a chance remark to make some conversation—and a mother's love and guilt does the rest. But J.J. has not called back to confirm at which airport she will meet her mother. I can't believe that in the course of six transatlantic calls yesterday they still don't know where to meet! Were they just talking about the weather?

Suddenly, Joy is having more second thoughts about all of this traveling. I don't want to sound pessimistic, so I don't say anything—but in my heart I'm glad it's not me. Travel isn't what it used to be. At one time, it was adventure. Now it's just a pain. And I can experience more than enough pain without ever leaving New York.

We join the Battista family for Easter lunch and then head back to the city. Still no call from J.J. Kids are so unpredictable. A packing rush job as soon as we hit the front door. Joy actually gets everything she wants into two bags. I guarantee it would be four bags if she were traveling with me. And now she really has those butterflies in her stomach. No hotel reservations made anywhere. Never been there before. Doesn't know a soul in Spain. It's just her and J.J. I keep saying it's going to be great. But still no call from J.J. What if she doesn't show up at either airport? Joy's car for the airport is here. We head downstairs. Joy climbs into the car, I kiss her goodbye and she's off to JFK.

I tune in to the Bulls-Knicks game. Just before eight o'clock, J.J. nonchalantly calls to say hi. Why didn't she call earlier? Who knows? But Joy has both tickets, which means J.J. won't be able to get past security to meet her at the gate. How about meeting at the British Air check-in counter? Good plan. I immediately call Joy, who's on her way to the American Airlines gate at JFK. I hang on until they track her down. I finally get her and give her the latest. She feels better, I think. We hang up. I hope she'll be okay. Me, I'm exhausted.

Monday ☆ April 17

Phone rings at four-forty A.M. That's always a chiller. Got to be bad news. You always think of the kids—but now Joy has been in England for about an hour, and that's long enough for anything to happen. It could be Scotland Yard, for all I know. I hate to answer, but I have to. It's the security company up in Connecticut. The burglar alarm has gone off at the country house and the police are on their way. This has been going on since we got the house. If there's a breeze blowing southeast to northwest, between the hours of four and five A.M., the alarm will go off. Never fails. The cops must hate us by now. I'm sure it's nothing serious. But it's impossible to get back to sleep. Besides, I feel a case of the grippers coming on in my stomach. Those searing abdominal cramps from hell. Oh, the dreaded grippers! What a way to start the week.

I do the show in pain. It's calm and uneventful. Usually when I'm not feeling well, something extra seems to kick in to cover my unease. I wonder sometimes if the viewers can detect when you're having a problem. Anyway, the grippers continue gripping me throughout the day. Before the show, I'd taken a big dose of Immodium in the prop room. Took a second swig right after the show. Gelman warned me that it's pretty potent stuff, but I did it, anyway. Claudia's office calls to say there's a party tonight for architect Charles Gwathmey. She'd like me to join her. By late afternoon, my grippers have gotten so intense that I'm thinking I should call her and cancel. But I don't want to leave her unescorted. She calls just before she leaves her apartment around eight, and that's when I learn Senator Al is with her. If I had known she had an escort, I would have canceled. But she's on her way and there's no way out.

They pick me up and we proceed to the party at the Racquet Club on Park Avenue. Senator Al is in good spirits, having survived his heart scare and also the controversy surrounding his recent joking remarks about Judge Lance Ito, who presides over the Simpson case. (In a radio interview, Al lapsed into a mock Japanese dialect, which nearly got him crucified. The guy is, after all, irrepressible—tough quality for a politician.) He and Claudia are still holding hands and giggling. My grippers are getting stronger by the moment. Paparazzi make a rush toward the senator and Claudia as we get out of the car. Lightbulbs are flashing and popping. Crowd is stirring. No need to prompt Claudia or Al to smile. They're always smiling. Ah, new love. Everywhere we move at the party, cameras keep going off. We leave and head to Elaine's for a little dinner. I'm feeling terrible and also

Ethel Senese, Joy's mom. "WELL HELLO, LET'S EAT!" On the show and working the cameras.

My guy, Notre Dame football coach Lou Holtz, in our studio at our thirtieth anniversary show.

The day Jack Paar walked on.

My son, Danny, and daughter Amy.

Early days in L.A.

It's not really a job. We just meet every morning, have a few laughs, and go home.

My pal Ashley. Can you see the tooth that made him famous?

Photos: Steve Friedman/Buena Vista Television

Stop looking at my daughters!

Another black tie at the Waldorf.

My day with the empathy belly.

Photos: Steve Friedman/Buena Vista Television

We can still make each other laugh.

Kissing up to Joy.

Our family Christmas Day show, 1993.

The Aspen skiing expedition in January 1995. Two skiers, one snow-boarder, and three cracked ribs.

angry with myself for going out. I just want to go home. That feeling is never stronger than when we zoom right past my apartment house.

At Elaine's, we sit at the same table where Joy and I shot our scene with Bobby De Niro. Even that memory doesn't help. Claudia orders fried calamari and fried zucchini, while I sip a Perrier. Finally, she takes mercy, realizes I'm sick and starts suggesting remedies for my problem. Claudia is very health-conscious and doctor-oriented. If you have a hangnail on your little toe, she knows exactly which doctor you should call. Anyway, it's plain to see that I am blocked—or constipated, as they say. Claudia prescribes an enema for me. I'm in terror. An enema! I haven't had an enema in half a century!

Senator Al nods and says, "A Fleet enema. Absolutely no problem." I can't believe one of the most powerful senators in the country is weighing in on the enema vote. But he's deeply concerned and calls over one of his security men who's lingering at the bar. He tells him, "I want you to take Regis home and stop at the drugstore on the way and buy him an enema." The security guy's eyes widen and he bellows, "AN ENEMA?!" I shrink in my seat. A nearby table of ten stops talking and turns to look at me. I wave a little. But there's no sense arguing with a senator. I decide to just get out of there and take my chances on the way home.

In the car, I tell the guy I really don't need an enema. "Oh, no," he says, overruling me. He's a retired homicide detective who has his orders from Senator Al. "He said an enema, we get you an enema!" We pull up to Love's Pharmacy on 86th Street and go inside. It's around ten o'clock, but the store is more crowded than I'd hoped. And, of course, the customers are surprised to see me—

and even more surprised to see me take a Fleet enema off the shelf. Why didn't I just stay home? Why am I standing in a line waiting to pay for an enema? This is ridiculous. I get it paid for, but not before the cashier takes a good long look at me. Back to the car, on to home, where I get out and try to hide the purchase from the doorman. I can't wait to get inside my own apartment. All of this aggravation has intensified my grippers. I need relief!

And now for that green and white Fleet box, with a diagram of two suitable positions in which to administer the product. Well, what do I have to lose? I assume position B and, let's just say, I try and I fail. That's right. I fail at my own enema. Sue me, mock me, I don't care. Believe me, it ain't that easy!

Tuesday ☆ *April 18*

Still miserable. I sleep fitfully through the night. No let-up from the pain. I wake up around seven to call Gelman. No answer at our office number. I remember that the staff holds a meeting around this time. I try another number that is supposed to be the control booth. I wake up a woman somewhere in New York who tells me in no uncertain terms, "This is not Channel Seven and never call this number again!" All right, sorry, lady! I call the ABC operator and ask to be switched to the prop room. The guys are always in there plotting their day. Success. I give them a message for Gelman. "I can't make it. I can't come in. What about Claudia hosting?" A few minutes later, Gelman calls back and wakes me up again. He says, "Are you sure you can't come in?" I groan, "Gelman, you don't know what I've been through. No, I can't!"

Back to sleep. Another call. It's Claudia. She's now pinch-hitting for me. Can she tell that funny enema story? "Absolutely not," I tell her. It's not funny and, besides that, it didn't work. She says, "Please? Please? Please?" She is pleading. She is begging. Can you imagine me asking if I could tell an enema story about her? Finally, I give up. I tell her to go ahead, do it. I go back to sleep. I wake up around nine-forty and watch the rest of the show. Then the phone starts ringing. I should have known better. I should have known that Kathie Lee and Claudia would take that story and run with it. My two aunts are very embarrassed. My friends are appalled. Gelman doesn't even want to discuss it. Why hadn't I guessed that Kathie Lee—who loves to tell bodily function stories—would pry every last detail from Claudia, who was only too eager to reveal everything. Together on the show, they have a long hearty laugh over it. What a scream. As I lay crumpled. If only I had just stayed home and kept my mouth shut.

Around noon, I call my pharmacist and tell him my problem. He strongly recommends a magnesium citrate oral solution. The most powerful, fastest-acting laxative you can take. Relief could come within a matter of moments after swallowing. "Send it quickly," I say. It has a lemon flavor. It's not too bad. But will it work? Moments pass. Nothing. A few hours go by. Nothing. People keep calling me, urging me to see a doctor. But doctors are always a last resort for me. I'm skeptical. Joy recently went to a doctor who took numerous X-rays for her painful shoulder and elbow. He concluded that she had tennis elbow. Told her to take two Advil and gave her a bill for $1,700. What a genius.

What I hate most about seeing a doctor in New York is the inevitable wait in the waiting room. But now I force myself to go. As always, I do it just before closing time. But the waiting room is packed anyway. When I enter, there's a flurry of excited whispers and glances, which always makes me feel right at home. I've known this doctor for a long time. He's a good man, but sometimes I wonder. He pokes me in the abdomen, draws some blood and guess what he gives me? A Fleet enema! Two of them. I put them under my jacket and slowly walk home, wishing it would all go away. But wait! As I enter my front door—could it be? Yes! The magnesium citrate kicks in and goes to work. Within minutes, I'm feeling better.

Wednesday ☆ April 19

I'm still not one hundred percent, but decide it's much too risky to allow Kathie Lee and Claudia another chance to have a field day with my condition. So I go in, hoping to preserve whatever shred of reputation I have left. Kathie Lee is wide-eyed and incredulous about viewer complaints that she went too far. They were just having some fun, bashing my brains out. What could be wrong with that?

Upstairs on my desk, I find the new issue of *GQ* with

an article lambasting the talk-show sleaze craze. Written by Norman Shad, it's called "Talk Stupid to Me." The subhead: "Daytime talk-show hosts are starting to look more and more like the deviants, morons, and murderers they celebrate." Shad begins: "It is dark in America and, every afternoon in broad daylight, it's getting darker. It is daytime talk." He cites a speech given by Jeff Greenfield, ABC's political analyst and media specialist, at the National Association of Broadcasters convention in Las Vegas. Jeff has been one of the first few voices to decry the craze. He opened the convention saying: "The question is: What are you doing producing such programs? Or airing them? Or sponsoring them? The question is: Granting your legal right to air such shows—what about my right? The public's right to draw the appropriate considerations about your sense of taste, your restraint, and ordinary common sense?"

Later in the morning, I notice the staff staring in horror at our office TV. Oklahoma bombing disaster. Details are unfolding. Our director, Dave McGrail, reminds me that today is the second anniversary of the Branch Davidian fire in Waco, Texas. But I tell him it's just coincidence. Somebody has just blown up the Federal Building in downtown Oklahoma City and the devastation is staggering. Why Oklahoma City? People move to places like Oklahoma City to avoid things like this.

This is the kind of day when it's almost impossible to do our show. Being live gives us the opportunity to react to what everyone in the country is talking about. But this morning the full horror of yesterday's explosion is the only story in America. Nothing else to talk about. Nothing else matters much. Every newspaper I hold up has that poignant picture of the fireman holding the bloodied body of that little baby. That picture said it all. What a heartbreaker. So it's a tough opening to get through. All you can do is share your own feelings about it. Everything that can be said has already been said in the last twenty-four hours. And everytime I look at Kathie Lee, her eyes are filled with tears. And then when you've finally said it all, there's the trivia question which sounds more trivial than ever. There's nowhere to go with this opening.

First guest out is ABC anchorman Peter Jennings, a perfect booking for a day like this. But it's just luck and happenstance on our part—Peter's been booked for a couple of weeks now to promote his special on schoolkids and their education. He's been with us a number of times, but never for something this big—where the who, the what, and the why are still unknown. He is unflappable and smooth as always, despite the limited facts available. He holds up a picture of a devastated building in Beirut that looks so similar to the Federal Building in Oklahoma City. But he warns everyone not to jump to conclusions about the suspects. During the commercial, he asks if he sounds too preachy. Even Peter Jennings worries about how he's coming off on such an emotional day.

Gelman and I convince Peter Lassally to join us for a farewell lunch outdoors at the Saloon on Broadway. Peter rarely leaves his office, from which he oversees the Letterman organization. But now he's moving back to Los Angeles full-time, where he'll continue to stay the course of Dave's future and also Tom Snyder's show. He and his wife, Alice, are here to pack up and close down their New York apartment. The movers are in there right now. So we sit in the sunshine and reminisce. But he's leaving tomorrow. And it's sad to lose a good friend to the West Coast. I hate to see him go.

Friday ☆ April 21

I'm feeling the grippers again. But I dare not mention it on the air for fear it may trigger another sordid inquisition. After the show, I attend a meeting about our upcoming prime time Mother's Day Special at Disney World. We'll tape it on the Friday night of Mother's Day weekend, then air it Saturday night. We'd like to do it right. Gelman has ordered in lunch for the staff from his list of inexpensive neighborhood take-out places. It'll be roast chicken and some rice dishes from Afghani Kabob, a perennial Gelman favorite. His assistant Cynthia goes to fetch soft drinks on the fourth floor. We all dig in. The chicken is not only roasted and delicious, but it's heavily seasoned. I mean, really hot. Afghanistan hot. I don't want to sound like a wimp, but I'm wondering what's taking Cynthia so long with the drinks. My mouth is burning. I'm dying for a cold Diet Coke, but can't even form the words to complain. David Mullen, the associate producer, softly groans, "Where is she? I'm dying!" Gelman, who loves hot, well-seasoned food, says exactly what I thought he would say: "You should never mix liquid and food. It's not good for your digestion." Blah blah blah. He goes on. Please! The *Live* staff is sweating bullets and near revolt. The Afghani Kabob chicken is taking its toll. We're dropping like flies. Finally, Cynthia returns just before I expire. The office Coke machine was empty and she had to go outside for the drinks. Meanwhile, I notice Gelman is the first to open his can and take a good long gulp.

Rain pours later. A depressing night in town. I'm a man alone. Joy is in Spain. My pal Peter has left town for good. The grippers are gripping me once again—right where the hot chicken burned a hole through me. The cats are staring at me. I made the mistake of giving them a second meal the other night and now they expect it every night. But I don't feel like it. It's not a good night for anything. I'm going to bed.

Phone rings at seven-twenty this morning. Great. That's ten minutes earlier than I get up during the week. All week long you wait for Saturday to sleep in. Why do I bother? And guess who's calling? The security people in Connecticut with another alarm going off in the house. What else is new? Isn't this how my week started? Must be that southwest wind again.

I can't get back to sleep, so I get up and raise the blinds. I'm happy to see the sun shining brightly. Now to gaze down at the sidewalk to see how people are dressed—a big city temperature check. The joggers are in shorts, pedestrians in sweaters. It's going to be a great day. Have to go to Connecticut. I promised Joy I would water the plants up there. Plus, I can check out the alarms, get a little sun and just relax. It's strange to be alone on a Saturday. The cats are silent in the kitchen, still eyeballing me. I mix their food and serve them breakfast. What a life they lead.

In the car, I play a tape of Dean Martin songs put together by writer Bill Zehme. What a great collection: Dean singing in nightclubs. Dean singing with Frank and Sammy, even Bing Crosby. Dean cracking sly jokes—nobody funnier. Dean from his great Dixieland album, smooth as a southern julep. I can still see him on that album cover wearing checkered riverboat duds, straw hat, and a giant smile. Now I'm driving past Yankee Stadium, opening day only four days away. Another season coming up. I look through the buildings a few blocks away and spot my old high school, Cardinal Hayes. Still standing proud on the Grand Concourse. Now I'm passing Macombs Dam Park, where I played CYO football for Our Lady of Solace School. All these memories as Dean sings "Carolina in the Morning." Suddenly, I decide to cruise the old neighborhood. Why not? It's a gorgeous morning and everything looks great. I'm on the Bronx River Parkway, passing Bronx Park. Out there on the same fields on which I played as a youngster, dozens and dozens of Little Leaguers in bright jerseys and helmets are deep in their games. My God, it's been more than fifty years since I was doing the same thing! I can't believe it. The world keeps changing, but the kids are still out there playing baseball and enjoying it. It's a reassuring sight.

I swing off on the Boston Post Road exit and onto the streets of the Bronx, past the apartment houses where I delivered the *Bronx Home News*, laying papers on every doorstep on every floor. There's the playground where my mother took me when I was a toddler. Still looks like a good time. Now I'm on Cruger Avenue, my old street. My old house is still the same, but with different siding. It's up for sale. Street looks tired. The empty lot where we played so many games into dusk is fenced-in, apparently a city-owned repository for old, rusted heavy machinery. What a shame. And the lot next to my house, once bursting with flowers and vegetable plants, is paved over—just another parking lot ringed with barbed wire atop a tall fence. But there on the corner is my street sign—Regis Philbin Avenue. That was the work of Freakin' Finelli and Gelman, who conspired to surprise me a few years ago. And across Bronxdale Avenue is the old swimming pool, once gleaming and white and filled with kids escaping the city heat. Now it's blackened and dilapidated with every window smashed and broken.

Next: Holland Avenue, where I'm happy to see the well-kept homes remain nicely intact and freshly painted. Then, the corner of Holland and Morris Park: Our Lady of Solace elementary school, the church, Mac's candy store—still the hub of the neighborhood. I worked in that candy store as a kid. For the last twenty-two years, it's been run by a neighborhood girl, Lorraine Kelly. And she's maintained it as the hangout for regulars it always was. I decide to go in and see if Freakin' might be there. Turns out Freakin' is off on his rounds delivering mail. But there's his father, Anthony Finelli, alias Freakin' Senior. We have a cup of coffee and some laughs. Across the street, I notice the door to the school hall is open. We go over to take a look inside. Bronx kids are signing up for next fall's football season—the next generation of Morris Park Lions. Just like always. The Solace school hall, then and now, triples as a basketball court, dance floor, and auditorium. I played for years on that court. Did the annual class play for eight years on that stage. Only now, it looks a little older, a little smaller.

Freakin' Senior and I visit the church, now under renovation. I step up to the altar, the same altar where I served as an altarboy. How well I recall those early seven A.M. masses in the dead of winter, pulling robes on in the dark, the days of Latin masses and haunting hymns. Bittersweet times. We wander into a few of the old stores: the meat market; Conti's pastry shop; and the Italian deli next door. Suddenly, a crowd is gathering. Word is getting around the neighborhood. I knew I should have shaved this morning. A cop car pulls up: Santana and McDowell, two of New York's finest. Somebody's got a camera. It's picture time. I'm with the cops. I'm in the deli with a loaf of Italian bread in my mouth. The deli guy wraps me a big ball of mozzarella cheese. Conti gives me a box of cookies. People are swirling around. It's getting wild. I better leave.

I say goodbye and walk back to the car, which is parked in front of the beauty salon. One of the hairdressers is on the sidewalk: "You gotta come inside and say hello." There's no escape. I go inside and see that the place is much bigger and deeper than I expected. There's a sea of women in here: women in curlers, women with towels on their heads, women with color in their hair—all yelling and shoving. The owner proudly walks me through his shop. Somebody has another camera. I'm posing again. Three women, six women at a time. I'm kissing. I'm hugging. Now I *know* I should have shaved. They carry on like I'm a superstar. It's becoming a scene out of *Moonstruck*. These people are so warm and giving. I stay and I joke and I take more pictures, and now it really is time to leave. I hug Freakin' Senior goodbye and take off.

I open the rooftop of the car and let the sun stream in. Dean is now belting out "Mississippi Mud." I push the volume to the max just like a kid with a boom box. It can't get any better than this. I head up White Plains Road, past the old firehouse, and realize that all kinds of emotions are rising up inside of me. In fact, I have to fight back the tears. Somehow a spur-of-the-moment decision to wander the old neighborhood turned into a riotous lovefest. I'm deeply moved, very touched. There's a saying that goes: Whoever winds up with the most toys at the end of life is the winner. That's wrong. It's whoever winds up with the best memories.

Tennis with Elaine Battista. Big Berzerker Tom is in Russia on business. She brings another couple—Olga and Jann from Austria. And they're pretty good. They crush us in the first game. But we're warmed up for the second game and doing better. Then, at one point, they have us down again, 5–3, when I go to my last resort, my sacred ritual. I've done this in the past and it always works. I look up at the blue sky above and I shout out loud, "Lou! Lou Holtz! I need you now! I dedicate this game to you, Lou!"

Olga and Jann are looking at each other like I'm insane. They've never heard of Lou Holtz, but it doesn't matter. I have implored the spirit of Lou Holtz to enter my body and help me win this game. Now it's 5–4. Then 5–5. Then 6–6. And all the time we're playing, I'm crying out for Lou to help. At 7–7, we decide to play a tie-breaker. And Lou does it again. We win, 8–7. After the game, I explain to Olga and Jann who Lou Holtz is. They still don't understand, but who cares? We won, and I thank Lou for his guidance!

J oy is home. Spain is behind her. So is Enrique. More about him in a minute. After eight great days traveling with J.J., she's exhilarated and exhausted and full of stories. She'd flown from Barcelona to London to New York, getting in late this afternoon. What an adventure. Joy doesn't travel lightly—except with the kids— and she likes to stay at the better places. But, like a trouper, she skipped all of Spain's five-star hotels and settled for the four-stars. They did rent a little red Fiat with a stick shift to get around in. Of course, the stick didn't help her tennis elbow. Especially given the rugged terrain of the Spanish countryside, which gets mountainous at times. But they covered four cities—Marbella to Seville to Madrid to Barcelona. Quite a tour.

Since Joy is known in our family as a stickler, there were a few tough moments. J.J. reported on the phone, "Mom did quite a job on the concierges in every hotel, challenging them, changing rooms, and driving everybody crazy." I do love the way she knows how to get what she wants. But will the Spaniards ever recover? In Seville, they managed to get last-minute tickets to the bullfights. Their concierge Enrique secured the tickets at 40,000 pesetas apiece. Later, they saw the actual price was 30,000 pesetas apiece, which may explain why Enrique was also at the bullfights that night. But Joy and J.J. became quite fond of Enrique.

At one point, they took the Ave, a high-speed train,

across part of the country. At the next hotel, J.J. played a little trick. While Joy was out of the room, some red roses were mistakenly delivered to them. J.J. spread the roses out on the bed and wrote a little note saying, "Dear Joy: Maybe the next time you and I can take the Ave together? Enrique." When Joy came back to the room, she was thrilled with the flowers, couldn't wait to find out who sent them. She opened the card and her jaw dropped. J.J. started to laugh and gave it away. But for a minute there, it could have been Joy and Enrique and rose petals in Spain. Please! I don't think I like that guy. Finally, she left J.J., who's headed off to Florence to meet her girlfriend for a week of adventure in Italy. Meanwhile, Joy is here, Enrique is there and that's the way I like it.

Wednesday ☆ April 26

Opening day for baseball here in New York. The Yankees and the Texas Rangers up at Yankee Stadium. I want to be there. Gelman isn't much of a baseball fan, but he's the only one available to drag out to the game. So I bring it up during Host Chat. As usual, he's noncommittal. Something about another Mother's Day meeting. Give me a break. How many more meetings can we have!

After the show, I keep working on him until he finally says, "Okay, let's go." We've been invited to watch the game from George Steinbrenner's suite. George is home in Tampa, recuperating from a detached retina operation, but the invitation is here. According to the New York papers, Steinbrenner is a terror. But when I spent a weekend with him at the Indianapolis 500 a few years ago, George was a prince. We had an awful lot of laughs. And he held his own at an old-time baseball trivia quiz I concocted. Even named the Cleveland Indians first baseman from the forties—Hal Trosky. The guy's no slouch.

Anyway, Gelman and I finally leave the station around noon for the fifteen-minute run to Yankee Stadium. We had two transportational choices. Either take a cab to the East Side and then go down to a subway train to the Bronx—or just get a private car to take us all the way. We're too lazy to switch to the subway, so we take the car. Big mistake. Impossible to reach the stadium without running into a monumental traffic jam. Our driver compounds the problem by picking all the worst roads. So we're stuck in the traffic jam from hell. Gelman has brought along one of those disposable cameras to record our day at the ballpark. Something to show during tomorrow's Host Chat. But whenever we grind to a halt in traffic, which is frequently, I jump out of the car and shoot pictures of the long line of cars locked at attention ahead of us, behind us, all around us. It's photojournalism at its best!

Almost an hour after we got in the car, we're finally getting close. Meanwhile, I'm shooting passing cars, vans, billboards, cop cars, whatever—just to keep from going crazy. At one thirty-five, it's game time and we're still on the highway. If we'd taken the subway, we'd be eating hot dogs by now. Never again. A couple of blocks away from the park, we just get out and walk. We take an elevator up to the owner's suite. A security guard checks for our names which, of course, are not on the list.

Finally, somebody recognizes us and lets us in. The suite is filled with Steinbrenner associates and friends. The game is now in the second inning, but who cares? It's a beautiful day and the stadium looks terrific. And despite the unpopular strike, the crowd is loud and boisterous.

Gelman and I are famished. There's a buffet with lobster tails and petite filets, but we head straight for the hot dogs. Lobster tails just don't make it at a ball game. I scan the seats outside the suite. There's Mike Wallace, always looking good. And *60 Minutes* producer Don Hewitt. And then I spot him. Joltin' Joe DiMaggio. He'd thrown out the first ball, but we missed it. I nudge Gelman and tell him, "Take a peek at Joe." I tell him what it was like to watch DiMaggio lope out to centerfield with that magnificent stride of his. As a kid, I studied the way he hit like a god and made the most difficult plays look easy. He was the classiest, and still is. Quiet. Powerful. Joe D. The Yankee Clipper.

I tell Gelman it would be great if we got a picture with Joe to conclude our story in the Host Chat. Gelman agrees, but I stall for time. "What's the matter?" Gelman says. "Just go over and I'll take the picture." But I'm paralyzed: "You don't understand, Gelman," I explain. "It's Joe DiMaggio! The Yankee Clipper! You just don't walk over, slap him on the back, and say, 'Do you mind, Joe, if I take a picture?'"

Gelman can't get over my reticence. "I've never seen you like this," he says. And it's true. I sneak another peek back at Joe. Everyone else is peeking at him with the same awe, and I feel sorry for his lack of privacy. Why don't we all just go away and leave him alone? I tell Gelman about Joe's famous line after his wife, Marilyn Monroe (*Marilyn Monroe*, for God's sake!), had returned from entertaining the troops in Korea. She told Joe about the tumultuous reception she'd gotten there. "You should have heard them cheer," she said. And he simply replied, "I have." No human had ever heard more cheering than Joe. Now he's eighty years old. Silver haired, still handsome with those deep dark eyes. A real icon. Gelman has the camera ready. He's too young to know what a big deal this is for me—although he's beginning to get the idea.

Okay, here I go: I work my way into Joe's presence. Introduce myself. I'm not sure if he knows who I am. I tell him we met years ago in Joey Bishop's dressing room the night he stopped by with a young Reggie Jackson. Joe nods vaguely. God, how I hate to ask him to pose for this picture. But I have to. I have to have this picture. I put my arm around him gently. We both look at Gelman. I hear the camera click. It's over. I have my picture. It was worth the hour and forty-five minutes in the car. We leave in the fifth inning. This time we take the subway and make it back in seven and a half minutes.

Back home. I have an hour before we leave for Greenwich, where there's a Hyperion dinner for their salespeople and authors. This author is beat. I lie down for a minute and fall asleep immediately. Suddenly, I'm awake again and with Joy in the car. I'm so fed up with car travel today. First stop is our Greenwich house. We get there at six. I take a workout in the downstairs gym, while Joy inspects the plants I watered Sunday. And then I hear it. The scream. She has stopped in horror at the coffee table in the living room. The big, beautiful, handmade table fitted with a heavy glass top, where the plant sits. Every other plant was watered to perfection—except for this one. This one had looked thirstier than the others. I over-watered it. Water ran out of the plant, onto the glass, into the wood under the glass. The table looks like a lake. There's no way to lift up the glass and dry the wood. Joy says it's ruined. She is very annoyed. It doesn't look good. Fortunately, I point out, we never go into the living room. Never. Sportscaster Warner Wolf, the house's previous owner, told me he sat in that room just once in eight years. Maybe we can wall off the room altogether. I'll propose this to Joy later.

I go on to the dinner at Valbella restaurant. The publisher has assembled its sale force to get them charged up over the fall lineup of books. I'm just one of the authors here and we all take turns, hopping from table to table, visiting with the salespeople. But just when you get the table warmed up, it's time to move on. Not everyone there knows that much about me or the book. Someone wants to know if there would be anything controversial in the book. I say no. Anything titillating? No. Any sex? Absolutely not. He seems disappointed. Makes me a little nervous. Who cares about Gelman and me trapped in traffic or how I gave a plant too much water? Yeah, I'm getting very nervous. I go back to the house, pick up Joy, and head back to the city. Another car ride! I'm dead tired, but cheer myself thinking about that picture with Joltin' Joe.

We get in bed and flip on the Letterman show. His first guest is Kathie Lee. I'm drowsy, but let's see how she does. It's a tough seat next to David's desk. She tells a funny Donald Trump story, but in her second segment launches into what she calls a "willie story." Uh-oh. She doesn't mean a guy's name, but a British expression for . . . Well, Dave is scared. Dave thinks she's getting gamey. I see his back arch. Willies give him the willies. Before she's halfway through the story, he says it's time for her to go. Kathie says no and it becomes a standoff. She's not through with her willie story, but Letterman is looking at her like she's Madonna. It's getting very heated out there. Hang on, Kathie Lee! She does, but still no willie story. It's over. I can still see the sparks crackling when I turn out the lights.

Thursday ☆ April 27

As always, Gelman pops into my office at eight forty-five. But this morning he has that sheepish look in his eye. I ask, "What is it, Gelman?" He's holding the pictures we took yesterday. Wait a minute. Don't tell me! He says the film was wrong. It was only for shooting outdoors. "You mean we don't have Joe's picture?" He shrugs: "No, wrong film." I don't believe him. I quickly riffle through the pictures and they look great—except for Joe and me. It's dark. Black. Unbelievable. I'm sick. After all that. Thank God I still have Kathie's Letterman appearance to kid about. Ten minutes and they're at each other's throat. I yell, "Try it for ten years, David!" I taunt her, "You better stay here with me where you belong!" But she isn't so sure on how she came off last night. "Are you saying I died on the show?" I rarely have an opportunity like this. Kathie having a moment of self-doubt. I never do answer her question. And it makes her nuts. So, for once, I'm in control and it feels good.

We also have a women's swimwear fashion show,

which goes pretty well. The models are young and thin. From what I can see, I think Joy has most of them beat. Tomorrow, we'll do the men's bathing suit fashion show. We plan to use our own staff as models. No pretty boys. And all of the anticipation centers on Art Moore, who's become a great on-air character. All week I've been asking him to strip down, flex that unbelievable physique and give American women what they want. But Art has been reticent. Gelman has an idea. Why not superimpose Art's head over a rippling body-builder's body? It's a simple camera trick.

After the show, they go to work taping a young, well-tanned, well-built weight lifter, strutting around in a tiny suit. Then they shoot Art, who plays along and makes the appropriate faces for each pose. The plan is for the rest of us to model our suits—then finally go to the tape, in which the Moore Man will bring down the house and possibly earn himself the Mr. America crown. Our audience is already in deep suspense. Peter Lassally calls from the coast. You'd think he'd be above all this, but even he is curious. "Is Art Moore going to model tomorrow?" he asks. "You'll just have to wait and see," I say. "Art hasn't made up his mind."

Friday ☆ April 28

The studio is electric. Will Art Moore pose? Could he? Upstairs before the show, I take a look at the finished tape. It's a perfect match: Art's head on this young stud's body. And when the guy begins to flex his massive muscles, Art's face contorts in perfect sync. He's smiling. He's grimacing. This posing is tough work, but Art Moore is up to it. He turns and spreads those lats. Art has that confident look. The look of a winner. His pecs are pulsating. Delts are devastating. Biceps are bulging. There he is—Mr. America! I love it! Now let's do the show. Kathie Lee doesn't know any of this. We want her to be shocked!

Our opening is very strong. She's full of dread, on her way to the dentist for the extraction of two wisdom teeth. Again, I plead with Art to join us in the swimsuit segment. Art remains elusive. He will not commit. Then, at last, it's time for the fashion show. I slip backstage, get into my suit and matching robe, and put on some sharp sunglasses. On cue, I make my entrance. I feel like a ditz coming out, dropping my robe to show off the suit. Naturally, I do a little posing myself. Got to look good, you know. Especially when I know what's coming after me. Julian, our stage manager follows. Looks great. Then Mullin, our associate producer. Awfully good. And then Bobby Orsillo from props. All the guys look great. The men of *Live*, unafraid to show their bodies.

Gelman is up there now. I know he's dying to wear a thong, but I've talked him out of it. We go up to the booth. Larry Kantrowich, our assistant director, stands up, peels off his clothes and displays his hunky physique. Then cameraman Allan Van Hoven, a real weight lifter, shoots himself in the mirror with his own camera. Allan is pumped. Everyone is on fire. What suspense. And then I make the final big introduction and we roll tape. Here he comes: Art "The Body" Moore. Holding a briefcase over his middle area. He pulls it away, shows off his bikini briefs, and goes into his posing routine. Kathie Lee is screaming. It's a riot. And Art Moore keeps flexing. Who could stop him? It's one of the funniest segments we've ever done.

Now for the weekend odyssey: Late in the afternoon, I take a two-and-a-half-hour ride to Cromwell, Connecticut, to attend the UConn Football Banquet. Skip Holtz, their new head coach, has invited me—and his parents, of course—to the event. From there I will fly back to Notre Dame with the Holtzes on a private plane. I'll be up there alone with Lou for two hours! No phone calls to interrupt us—as we plan the Irish attack for the next season. I've got a million ideas for Lou, and I know he'll appreciate them! The banquet goes smoothly. I'm impressed with the look of the Connecticut football players. The school wants to build their program. Skip Holtz—who's beginning to act and sound more and more like his dad—will fix that. Ironically, Lou Holtz was an assistant coach at the University of Connecticut thirty years ago. Skip was born here and now returns from Notre Dame as the head coach. I sit with his lovely wife, Jennifer, and we listen to the guest speaker for the night—her father-in-law and my hero—Lou!

Lou is one of the country's most sought-after dinner speakers, and tonight he's at his best. Not afraid to tell you what's right and what's wrong and how to accept life's surprises and disappointments. How to never lower your standards for anything or anyone. He's around five-ten, reed-thin, with a shock of blond hair and eyeglasses—but when he speaks, it's all fire and you have to listen and learn.

Once, I took my son Danny to a Notre Dame–Navy game in Philadelphia that was preceded by a team dinner.

He sat next to Lou at that dinner. They chatted quietly and then Lou got up from the table. Dan thought he was going to the men's room or something. At first, he couldn't see that Lou was beginning to pace through the player's tables, getting ready to speak. Then he started. The words came out loud and clear and decisive. I'll always remember Dan's head snapping around to see who was talking like that. It was Lou—getting his game face on. Getting his team stoked. It was only Navy—not the toughest of opponents—but Lou wasn't taking any chances, and Dan was very impressed. And so is this crowd tonight in Connecticut. I look out over a sea of faces, players and fans alike, all eyes riveted on Lou. They won't forget this banquet for a long time.

Saturday ☆ April 29

Lou needs me early! He doesn't waste a minute of his life. We meet in the lobby of the Radisson at six-fifteen. He can't wait to get up in the morning and get to work. I'm in the lobby by six-ten. I don't want him waiting for me. Not for a second. We board a private plane and take off for Indiana at seven. I look at the Holtzes—married thirty-four years; five children, all college graduates, all successful. I wonder how they maintain their schedule. Lou has another speech at ten-thirty this morning on campus. Then at eleven-thirty, he will do someone a favor. He'll step outside the football office, as planned, hand over a small box to a young man and his girlfriend, who will then repair to the campus grotto where she'll open the box, see her engagement ring, and receive a marriage proposal. An engagement blessed by Lou! This afternoon, we sit in the coach's box, high above Notre Dame Stadium, to watch the annual inter-squad Blue-Gold game which concludes spring practice. This team is highly motivated after four losses last year. "The defense looks terrific," Lou tells me. Quarterback Ron Powlus is ready. Former Notre Dame coach Jerry Faust now joins us in the box. He is irrepressible, chatty, always laughing. Not a mean bone in his body. Even though he is gone from coaching, he still loves this place with his whole heart. The game is sluggish. There is no scoring, no intensity.

Lou is getting restless. He never coaches this game. Prefers to watch it from upstairs, but now he's on the phone, growling. Even calling a few plays, hoping to ignite the team. It doesn't work. At halftime there's still no score. During the halftime ceremony, Lou surprises me at midfield and presents me with a beautiful gold Notre Dame wristwatch. The students in the stands give me quite a cheer. It's a thrill to thank them over the microphone. Always feels like I'm at home in that stadium.

Now it's back to work. Second half. Lou does not return to the booth. He stays on the field. He'll call the plays and get this thing going. And, almost immediately, he does. Powlus fires two touchdown passes to Charlie Stafford in the first four and a half minutes and Lou isn't finished. Powlus throws three more to Stafford before it's over, and everybody leaves feeling strong and happy. See the difference one man can make? Call it leadership.

Tonight is a special night for my friend, associate athletic director Roger Valdiserri, who for many years was the best-known college sports-information director in the country. Roger started working as a student secretary for Frank Leahy in the fifties. He's been at Notre Dame ever since—outside of a stint with the Kansas City Chiefs. A few years ago, he lost his lovely wife, Elaine, to cancer. A terrible blow to him and his family. But tonight he's surrounded by his five great kids and all his friends and we're holding a retirement roast for him. The only problem is everyone loves this guy. He has no enemies and is the best there is at his job. So what's there to roast? As the emcee, I wonder aloud how we can roast a man everyone truly loves. Roger is admired and revered and may be unroastable—and that's why, ladies and gentlemen, it's always good to have Jerry Faust at events like this. When in doubt, just go after Jerry! I'm hoping this sets the tone for the evening. But the speakers are funny and to the point. Faust has a hysterical story about hunting with Roger. Chicago Bear Chris Zorich tells an emotional story of how Roger was like a surrogate father to him at Notre Dame. Finally, up comes Lou again. His fourth talk in the last twenty-four hours! I marvel at him. And then Roger takes the podium with his children. I've watched them grow up and now I'm watching them beam at their father, their hearts wide open. A memorable night for a special guy.

Sunday ☆ April 30

Light, gentle rain falls on campus. I leave the Morris Inn at Notre Dame. I see the golf course ripped up to make way for yet another group of university buildings. The construction explosion here has been awesome in the last ten years. The stadium that Rockne built in 1930 will be next. They're adding twenty thousand more seats, but won't touch the original structure. I fly to Cincinnati for a change of planes to New York. Cab ride home. When we turn off the FDR on 96th Street to go into Manhattan, I know I'm not in South Bend anymore. The contrasting worlds just tug at my heart strings. How can the two places I love best be so different?

Monday ☆ May 1

Regis has the mange. Not me—the dog! Kathie Lee gives us an update on the newest member of her household. I think she's trying to make me feel responsible! Anyway, in addition to all of his other maladies, Regis has now developed patches of mange. She knows he's a great dog, but I think she may have a touch of buyer's remorse. And now I'm insulted that she ever named him Regis in the first place. I didn't mind a leaky eye or a funny rash—but the mange? Come on! Don't blame that on me, too!

After the show, she hosts a luncheon party at the Fashion Cafe at Rockefeller Center. This is to celebrate the publication of the new book she's done with Cody, *Listen to My Heart*. That's right, Cody has co-authored a book! Like I keep saying, Cody can't write, can't spell, and can't read—but he's written a book, ALL RIGHT? Kathie takes the stage and makes two more startling announcements: The Cody book will be on next week's *New York Times* best-seller list. I don't mind Cody getting his book out before mine, but does he have to rub it in by being an instant best-seller, too? Kathie's next announcement is that she's started her third book, *Don't Mess With Me— I'm a Mother!* Remember when she said she was going to cut back and take it easy? Please! There's no end to it. And what about Cassidy? She probably has something in the works, too! Why not?

How well I remember her first pregnancy, with Cody, five years ago. We all went through that pregnancy together on television. Just like a daily version of *I Love Lucy*. Every day she'd tell me what it felt like. The discomfort. The heft. The appetite surges. The nausea. Of course, I pointed out that it couldn't be so bad, that women have been doing it for years. I mean, she acted like she was the first woman to ever bear a child! But she'd just scoff at me. And women in the audience would hiss at me. So Gelman, who's always willing to make me the sacrificial lamb, went out and found a contraption called an *empathy belly*. It's a device that simulates pregnancy. Expectant fathers are urged to wear them to better understand what their wives are going through. Okay, fine. So, one morning, I strapped it on and did the whole show pregnant. The thing weighed about thirty-five pounds. Practically tipped me over. And, yes, my back *was* killing me! But I started getting used to it. I'd point to this distended bloat and call it my Li'l Puddin'—the same name she called her own stomach. For the rest of the day, I took my Li'l Puddin' everywhere I went—as a camera crew followed me. I felt like I'd joined the circus. I waddled down Broadway to a business meeting, thinking I would stop traffic: Look! A pregnant man! Of course, nobody noticed me at all. Nobody cared! New Yorkers are used to strange sights. Why would a pregnant man cause heads to turn? And Gelman had wanted me to wear it for twenty-four hours, too. I said, "Sure, Gelman, you can bet that I'll be sleeping with Li'l Puddin' tonight!" But once I got home, I had to take the load off. Okay, so she made her point!

After lunch, Joy and I meet our real estate agent, Eva Moore, and walk up Fifth Avenue to take one more look at that apartment in Trump Tower. Yes, we're still thinking about it. The place is really different. Great eye-appeal. But is it us? We don't know anymore.

Tuesday ☆ May 2

J.J. finally returns from Europe with four loaded bags. Home at last. Remember how she felt on New Year's Day? Had to be pushed aboard the plane for London. Then came the homesick calls. Those lasted for about five days and then came calls from all over Europe.

Happy calls! Excited calls! J.J. going skiing in the Alps. J.J. in Rome. J.J. from Wales. J.J. in Paris. J.J. having a ball.

At dinner time, she regales us with her travel adventures. She's a wonderful storyteller and has us screaming with laughter. Like the time she was late for breakfast at a bed-and-breakfast house in Wales. She hadn't known breakfast was served at nine sharp. The strict owners were very annoyed that she didn't make it down on time and told her so. She finally got her breakfast, but found the sausage and breakfast meats inedible. Tasted awful! So, rather than incurring further wrath from these people, she wrapped them in paper napkins and stuffed a wad in each front pants pocket. Then she took her empty plate into the kitchen to be washed. At the same time, the family German shepherd bounded in through the backdoor. The dog smelled food on J.J. and began jumping up and down, nuzzling against her pockets. The family had never seen the dog behave like that before. They figured it was just an outpouring of affection. But this dog must have been starving because it never stopped mauling her. J.J. was scared to death that it would paw a sausage right out of her pocket. So she fought her way to the bathroom to dispose of the food. Tossed it right out the open window. When she came out, the dog never noticed her again.

Then there was the saga of the amorous young Italian cop. J.J. and her Notre Dame roommate, Jama, were on a ten-hour train trip from Florence to Sicily. They had to share their compartment with this dark, seductive fellow who seemed very interested in them. Immediately, they were suspicious of his intentions. But for the first six hours, he was on his best behavior. He would remind them that he was a police officer, flashing a badge, chasing away anyone who dared to enter their compartment. Finally, the girls fell asleep. Then, hours later, J.J. awoke with a start to find him cuddled up against Jama, softly whispering to her, "Oooh, *Bella Mia* . . ." Jama was sound asleep, so J.J. gently nudged her awake. Jama jumped up and they both read this guy the riot act. Must have scared him as much as he scared them. Another Lothario shot down!

Wednesday ☆ May 3

Gelman and his girlfriend, Laurie, came up to the apartment for dinner. J.J. and Joanna have personally requested Gelman. They've known him since they were nine and ten years old, respectively, and they get a big kick out of him. They think he's quite a character. And because he knows everything, I'm already nervous about what kind of wine to serve. Gelman took a wine-tasting course, only adding to his bachelor mystique. Now if only he could afford the good stuff! I pull out three bottles for him to inspect. He dismisses two, but says the third will be satisfactory. Thank you, Gelman. Why do I have to indulge him like this? But he's still a growing producer and needs his sustenance. Joy prepares a beautiful dinner, but makes the mistake of removing Gelman's plate before he's finished. He'd already polished off his second helping and there was nothing left on the plate. "Thank you, Joy," Gelman says. "You're bringing me a third helping, right?" Of course, Gelman. Eat me out of house and home! What do I care?

At dinner, J.J. has one more story for us. As an introduction to English life, each transfer student spent the first two days abroad with an English family. J.J.'s host family seemed typical at first: mother, father, young daughter, living in a suburb of London. The first night was uneventful, but on the second night Mom and Dad had to go out. They said they wouldn't be back until three in the morning. A little strange, but okay. But their twenty-three-year-old son, Neal, who lives in town and works as a chef, would come over to cook for J.J. and the little sister. That afternoon, J.J. had been looking for a closet upstairs when she opened a door and discovered a small bedroom with an empty crib. The room hadn't been lived in for years. Very strange. Anyway, Neal showed up ready to cook and right away J.J. knew something was wrong. Neal was wearing black leather leggings and kept leering at her while cooking. J.J. got a little nervous and announced that she would go visit her friends down at the town pub after dinner. That way, she could make a quick escape. But at the end of dinner, Neal said, "Come on, J.J. Let's go to the pub." There was no escape. At the pub, Neal drank heavily and, at closing time, was waiting to take J.J. home. But it was only eleven o'clock—which meant Mom and Dad wouldn't be back for another four hours. Four more hours alone with black-leather Neal!

At this point, I'm at the edge of my chair at the dining room table. J.J. had to think fast. She told Neal that she'd been invited to a party at a friend's house in town. Neal was by now quite wobbly, but said he'd love to join her. Then he asked what she thought of his family. "Very nice," J.J. replied. "Yes," he agreed, "but you know that little girl is not really my sister. She's been taken in by my parents after a life of abuse." He described some of the abuse. J.J. was getting more scared by the minute. And then Neal said, "Did you see the crib in the upstairs room? Let me tell you about that!" "No!" J.J. cried. She didn't really want to know, thank you anyway. So they went to the party.

By this time, I'm beside myself at the table. The trick would be to outlast Neal, who was just about on his last leg. Finally, he gave up and left. Then J.J. waited till three o'clock before returning home by cab. The parents had returned and hoped she'd had a nice evening. They told her to sleep well. Which she couldn't. That crib was right in the next room. She kept her eyes open until morning. God. Even I'm a total wreck now. Gelman is gulping his wine nervously. Joy is staring at J.J. with disbelief. After all these stories, I ask her to rate her trip abroad—from one to ten, ten being the highest. J.J. gives it a solid ten. Loved every minute of it. Even her night with the Addams Family. Where's that wine, Gelman? I need it now.

Thursday ☆ May 4

I can't take any more tears! Now Kathie Lee is weeping on me. We are in the middle of our Host Chat when she brings up a recent interview we did separately with the same reporter. We were both asked the same questions, more or less. And she tells me her answer to the question, "What would you do if Regis couldn't do the show anymore?" She repeats what she told the reporter: "Well," she says, "I wouldn't do the show at all." She would just walk away from it. But she says she found out how I responded to the idea of her leaving the show. And she wants to tell everyone. But first she starts to cry. Big tears in those big eyes. Lower lip trembling. Sniffling and dabbing at the corners of her eyes.

Please! This is twice in the last two months that Big Bad Regis has made his co-host cry! Christina Ferrare thought I had purposely avoided her and wept. Now, it's Kathie Lee! For twenty years, I've been working with these co-hosts—and never did I engender a dark moment. A tribute to my goodwill and infinite patience. But now, suddenly, I have supposedly made two co-hosts cry. For a minute, I wonder if Kathie means it, but there's no time to lose here. Let's set the record straight immediately: The reporter asked *two versions* of basically the same question. What I heard was this: "What would I do if Kathie Lee left to go do something else, *as she has threatened to do so many times?*" My answer was—depending on what year it was and if I were able to continue working—I would probably get another co-host or do the show alone or get a new format or whatever. What am I supposed to do? Drop dead? Become a bee farmer? Come on!

My argument makes sense to me, but she's getting all the sympathy. The audience looks grim. One woman is actually sobbing in her seat. And Kathie keeps sniffling. So I say to her, "You mean you'd want me to just stop? Just drop dead?" She quivers a little beneath her Kleenex, nods, and says, "Well . . . yes . . . uh-huh. Otherwise my feelings would be hurt." Oh, that bad boy Regis! He's been so terrible for his co-hosts all these years.

Saturday ☆ May 6

Tennis day in Connecticut. But, wait! I left my new beautiful Weed racket back in the city. All I have here in my broken Weed. Grudgingly, I opt to use another racket, and Joy and I lose. Big mistake. I have no choice: I'll try the broken Weed, anyway. Already I feel better. I'm my old self again! Even broken, the Weed is superior. We win the second and the third sets. I can't lose with my Weed. Net Man is back. Thank God, because next week I face an undefeated amateur on our show. She's a seventy-four-year-old grandmother who's gone back to college and has beaten all comers on the college conference schedule. Now she thirsts for the blood of Net Man. Come and get me, Grandma! I'm ready for you!

Dinner tonight at Valbella in Greenwich with the Charles Grodins and the Jack Paars. Stories are flying. The topic is humiliating engagements—those invitations that turn into disasters. I have had my share, a fact that seems to be well understood by all present. Chuck recalls a bankers convention at which he once appeared as a special guest. Nobody told him exactly what they expected him to do there. He even sought out a relative who was a banker for some guidance—and got none. But he went anyway and took the floor and made an open plea. "What exactly do you want from me tonight?" The bankers just laughed. Chuck wasn't kidding. He was baffled and kept asking, "What do you want?" And the bankers kept laughing. He filled ninety minutes this way, but never did get an answer. At least, they paid him a lot of money to be confused in public.

Jack, meanwhile, remembers an engagement he took during his *Tonight Show* years. He was told only that it involved cars and would take place on a Saturday night at Soldier Field in Chicago. That's all he knew. As he usually did for these affairs, he brought along a tape of funny announcer fluffs, which gave him material to talk about. So he showed up at this raucous, jam-packed stadium. Only then did he realize that he had been booked into a demolition derby! This crowd couldn't give a damn about his cute little announcer fluffs. They wanted action, crashes, accidents! But first, Jack had to slowly ride around the perimeter of the field in an electric car. The impatient crowd got worked up. A chorus of boos finally built into a mighty crescendo—a roar of hate. Who was this guy holding up the demolition derby? They wanted to kill him. Jack couldn't get out of there fast enough.

At the end of the meal, Tony the maître d' informs us that he's so honored to have three talk-show hosts at one table that there would be no check. A nice surprise. Chuck is elated. He's beaming. Jack leans across the table to him and points out, "It's still going to cost you at least a buck for the parking attendant outside." And Chuck's face falls. Mournfully, he shakes his head and says, "There's always a catch."

I should have learned something from those stories last night. I make a quick trip to Columbus, Ohio, for a personal appearance at a Home Place store. A huge and boisterous crowd. This is devout football country and everybody's excited about the renewal of the Notre Dame–Ohio State rivalry after fifty years. I ingratiate myself to the sea of customers by announcing my prediction for the score of the next showdown in September: Notre Dame, 28; Ohio State, 7. It is not received well. I can't get out of there fast enough.

Gelman's fear of marriage worsens. The cause? Billy Crystal's new movie, *Forget Paris,* which is screened tonight. Joy and I attend, as do Gelman and his girlfriend, Laurie. This is an important movie for Billy. His last two were not hits. Billy's family from Long Island is all over the theater. Billy says a few words to the audience before the preview. He's been married nearly twenty-five years and says he wanted to make a pro-marriage movie. And it's funny and warm: boy meets girl, they fall in love in Paris, it's all laughs. Then they get married, return to reality, and suddenly there aren't as many laughs. Well, you know. But there's a happy ending.

Gelman looks shaken as we leave the theater. I ask how he liked it. He says weakly, "Well, I didn't think it was so pro-marriage." Laurie says, "Why doesn't anybody ever ask me?" And she's right. Why do we always ask the guy? The crowd sweeps us to the escalator, and Gelman and Laurie can't join us. But if Gelman never gets married, one of the reasons will be Billy Crystal's pro-marriage movie. We go on to the party at Gabriel's. The crowd is optimistic about the film's chances, but Billy remains cautious. He says he'll wait and see how the paying customers feel about it. I don't even tell him about Gelman's reaction.

Wednesday ☆ May 10

My tennis showdown day with the bloodthirsty grandma. Of course, I have to beat her. But if I beat her, I'll look bad. How can I crush a nice old lady? People will hate me. Then again, if I lose, I'll look like a wimp. Why did I ever get into this? Gelman and his big ideas! I should call in sick. It's raining and that's bad news right off the bat. It gets worse. I go downstairs and find out that Phil, my regular driver, has told the doorman he can't make the trip today. For the last few months, Phil has been shuttling me across the park. I met him one day when he was hired to take me home—on somebody else's dime. But he moonlights in his spare time and made me an offer I couldn't refuse. And, for the most part, it's worked out well. He's always there—especially when the sun is shining and cabs are plentiful. But today, at the first drop of rain, Phil can't make it and there isn't a cab in sight. Naturally.

So I walk over to Madison Avenue to find a cab. Nothing doing. I go to Fifth—same thing. Walk to 79th Street and wait. Forget it. I'll walk all the way. Why not? It'll loosen me up for the big tennis match. A light rain is falling. I've got my tennis bag, plus my big briefcase—and, midway through Central Park, they start getting heavier and heavier. But all my work on the treadmill is paying off. I make it and I'm not even breathing hard. Still, it would have been nicer if Phil had shown up.

Show goes well and we meet Lucy Dettmer, my formidable opponent, who couldn't be sweeter or more likable. She's seventy-four, a grandmother, a college student, and a tennis star. The woman's an inspiration! After the show, we head over to the Vertical Club for the game. And I'm suddenly thinking of all the reasons why I can't and shouldn't win. First off, I never play singles. Second, I still can't find my new Weed racket. So I'm stuck with my broken Weed. Third, I've got a brand-new pair of sneakers, which feel strange and unfamiliar. Fourth, the combination of that walk through the park and Kathie Lee's opening have worn me to a pulp. And fifth, how can I beat a grandmother and still be politically correct? As I keep telling everyone, I'm only one man!

Gelman, meanwhile, has gone all out to produce this sports spectacular. He rents a limo for me and loads it up with a huge entourage. Our arrival is staged to look like one of those circus cars out of which pours an endless army of clowns! One by one, there's Art Moore, with shades and earpiece, as my security detail; Steve Friedman, my personal photographer; Bobby Orsillo, my trophy carrier; my four cheerleaders (two pairs of comely twins); Radu, my personal trainer; Gelman, my producer; and me. I'm wearing my Notre Dame warmups, my sunglasses, and my best game face. Meanwhile, Lucy has already arrived in an old cab with her husband.

Next comes an elaborate warmup. I'm being fussed over by all of the aforementioned, as the "Theme from *Rocky*" blares out. Lucy just rolls her eyes and says, "Come on, can we just play?" I don't blame her. Gelman has pulled out all the stops. Then it's game time. But first I have to go to the men's room. I have never been to the Vertical Club, which is a mazelike, multilevel sports complex. Naturally, I get lost. I see an open door that looks promising. I go inside, prowl past the empty showers, and find what I'm looking for. On my way out, I walk into a locker room—and there's *a naked woman with her back to me*! God help me—I'm in the ladies' locker room! She hasn't seen me. I turn quickly. But here comes another naked woman out of the shower! She screams. Hoping not to frighten her further, I stupidly say, "It's me—Regis!" It doesn't help. She yells again and a heavyset attendant comes rushing around the corner to eject me. I'm totally embarrassed. Finally, I escape and run smack into one of the Vertical Club guys who says, "I thought you might get lost. The bathroom here isn't easy to find." Tell me about it.

Now I've got to face Lucy, who couldn't be less scared. She's never lost a college match and she isn't about to lose to this loudmouth TV host. She's got a slice shot that's almost impossible to return and she's consistent.

What a role model. At seventy-four, she's enjoying life and beating my brains out to boot. I lose easily, 6–2, and slink off the court, humiliated, and grumbling. I cast a withering look at Gelman and tell him to fix it in editing.

Black-tie event tonight. We go to the Plaza Hotel where the Make-A-Wish Foundation is honoring Marla Maples Trump. The Donald is there and makes one more sales pitch about that apartment in his Tower. He never stops. He never forgets. He never gets tired. "Great security!" he keeps saying. But what we need is more space. Joy looks particularly beautiful tonight. She's knocking me out. Sitting next to her is a handsome young Italian movie producer who doesn't stop talking. Even for a breath. I wonder how he's getting oxygen. By the time we get home, she's exhausted. The guy talked her to death. Thanks a lot.

Thursday ☆ May 11

En route to Disney World to do our Mother's Day special. Gelman is sitting next to me, and surrounding us are Kathie Lee, Cody, Cassidy, two nannies, secretary, etc. Gelman surprises me by ordering a mimosa. It's eleven A.M. and Gelman never eats breakfast. He's got nothing in his stomach, but gulps down the drink and orders another. Now that's gone, too. Right before my eyes, it has happened: Gelman is a little loaded. And I've got him for a two-hour flight. I'm writing this as he flips through *People* magazine—the issue containing a fabulous profile of famous talk-show producer Michael Gelman. Now he's come across a story about a Philadelphia man with the same name as one of his college girlfriends—who also happened to be from Philadelphia. He speculates that the guy might be the father of the girl. So he begins a long, rambling reminiscence of his days at Colorado University in Boulder. What a wild place. Was he there for an education or a party?

Anyway, Gelman is getting very nostagic. The stewardess has just been by. He's ordered a ginger ale, but I've asked her for a mimosa and a Sprite. The Sprite is for me. I want Gelman totally wasted. The mimosa arrives and Gelman is trying to regroup. He's sipping his ginger ale. Oops, there goes a sip of the third mimosa. Gelman is a goner now. He asks if Tim, my Disney tour guide, will be there to meet us. I say yes. He says, "It's probably a thrill for Timmy to be with you and guys like Alan Thicke. Probably more so with Alan Thicke." Gelman's getting nasty. I'm reading *Electronic Media*. Apparently, the Jenny Jones murder incident hasn't frightened Jerry Springer. According to this article, Springer recently had on a female porn star who had sex with 250 men over a ten-hour span. I read this to Gelman, who pauses to think about it. Then he says knowingly, "That's a lot."

Our special will celebrate six or seven mothers whose sons or daughters sent in their stories. I've asked to read their letters as background on each lady. Gelman had said we would look them over together on the flight, but he forgot to bring them. We are staying at the Grand Floridian Hotel at Disney World, but our production office is located at the Contemporary Hotel. I'm hoping Gelman will send me the letters when he gets over there. But tonight, there is no Gelman and no call, either. And, it goes without saying, no letters. How did we ever get on the air, anyway?

I decide to call the production office. The hotel operator has no idea what I'm talking about. I ask for the *Regis & Kathie Lee* production office. She's never heard of it. I hang up and try a different operator. Nobody knows anything about the office. There's no phone number to be gotten. Can you believe this? We're putting on a TV special in less than twenty-four hours honoring six women about whom I know nothing—and I can't get their letters because there is no telephone number. Finally, around ten o'clock, Gelman calls and promises to leave the letters at the front desk of our hotel, so I'll get them first thing in the morning.

Friday ☆ May 12

This morning, I go to the front desk. Gelman happens to be there. Guess what? They can't find the letters he left the night before. I ask you again: How did we get on the air? Disney guide extraordinare Tim Wolters arrives on the scene and locates the letters. But at this point I don't care anymore. The stories of these women are long and complicated and usually very sad. You can't imagine the kind of hardship so many people withstand.

Tonight, we do the show which will air tomorrow night before Mother's Day. And we have the usual audio problems. It's almost impossible to understand the narration of the sons and daughters as they reminisce about their mothers. Somehow we get through it and never look back. The crew comes out of the remote truck saying everything looked good. So who knows?

Late dinner at Victoria's restaurant with Kathie Lee, Claudia, and Senator Al. No date set for them yet, but they're still holding hands and still managing to use utensils at the same time.

Monday ☆ May 15

Emmys this week. Friday night, the year will culminate in another loss. Believe me, I know it's coming. Why should this year be any different? Still, that Emmy would be a nice way to commemorate our ten years on the air together. No, stop it! Kathie Lee and I both know better. There's no chance. Gelman isn't so sure, though. And he's supposed to know everything. Forget it, Gelman.

Tonight, Joy and I go to the Greenwich Country Club for a fund-raiser to benefit Ara Parseghian's Medical Research Foundation. The great Notre Dame coach is deep in a heartbreaking family crisis. A few months ago I learned that the three youngest Parseghian grandchildren were diagnosed as having Neimann-Pick type C disease—a rare genetic disorder that prohibits the metabolism of cholesterol. The excess storage of cholesterol damages the nervous system, resulting in the deterioration of the body and, eventually, death. Currently, there is no treatment. Scientists figure to find it within the next ten years, but Ara doesn't have that kind of time. If he could raise enough money, research can be speeded and his grandchildren might be saved. So, it's one more challenge for this legendary coach and his lovely wife, Katie. And tonight, they'll be presented with a check for $115,000 to brighten their hopes and dreams.

Terry O'Neil from ABC Sports has brought in an array of speakers for this event—myself included. They even replay my thirty-one-year-old interview with Ara on the fifty-yard-line at the Coliseum, the morning after a tough loss to USC. Joy sits next to Mike Ditka, the former (but always) head coach of the Chicago Bears. Up close, Ditka looks like he can still go. The face we've seen so many times scowling on the sidelines looks even more awesome just a few inches away. But he's uncharacteristically mellow tonight. In fact, Iron Mike confides to us that New York fascinates and even frightens him. He says this big city truly intimidates him. If New York scares Ditka, then what chance do the rest of us have? Anyway, we all need a boost here. So I decide to risk my life and tease Ditka. I cannot suppress the urge to chant, "Ditka! Ditka! Ditka!" Over and over again. And he plays along, craning his neck and yelling out, "Where is he?! Where is he?!" I'm relieved he didn't throttle me.

By some odd quirk of fate, Joy seems to have given in. I can't believe it, but I'm not going to question it, either. This afternoon, we revisit that new building across the street from the station. My dream residence. We look around a terrific apartment that I've shown her before. Beautiful views of the city. I'm almost embarrassed to bother the real estate lady one more time. But now Joy actually says she likes it. She thinks moving to the West Side might make for a new beginning. A new nest won't feel as much like an empty nest with the girls gone. So we agree to put in a bid. Who knows if we're going to get it? But if we do, she says I'm still not allowed to come home for lunch.

Check-up day at New York Hospital with Jeffrey Borer, my heart doctor. Haven't seen him since our tremendous dinner at Rao's with Sonny Grasso. But first, let me tell you about New York Hospital. Yes, it's a great medical center, filled with dedicated people. But whoever designed the place should be sent back to school for remedial architecture. It's just a horrendous maze of hallways and doorways and corners. I've been going there for three years and still cannot find my doctor's office. I'm not kidding. By the time I do, I'm usually a raving maniac. And today I'm so upset, I warn everybody that I'm planning to close down New York Hospital in tomorrow morning's Host Chat. So, naturally, my blood pressure turns out to be very, very high. Dr. Borer waits a few minutes for me to calm down, then takes it again. And again. And again. Until it's finally back to normal. He could save a lot of time by meeting me anywhere in that hospital!

As I am writing this, Dr. Borer's office calls with my cholesterol results. Not good news. I had it down to 222 from a previous high of 305, but now the number is back to 285. Either I'm not taking my medicine right or I'm not eating right, but something is wrong. Maybe it's trying to find his office. More tests in a few weeks. What a drag. How I hate those needles.

Thursday ☆ May 18

Perry Como is eighty-three today. I want to wish him a happy birthday by calling him on the air. But I don't want to scare him to death. So, before airtime, we call his Florida home to see if he'd be receptive. But Perry's still asleep. Let's not bother him then. I'll just wish him well in the Host Chat and he'll hear about it. But before the show ends, Perry wakes up, finds out about our plan, and calls us. He sounds great—and ageless.

Eternally the calmest man in show business. I say, "Perry, I thought you got up early?" He says, "Oh, no, sometimes they just make the bed around me."

Also this morning, we discuss how we'll handle losing the Emmy tomorrow night. Kathie Lee and I begin to rehearse our reactions. I want to go into a weeping mode. First anger, then sorrow. She suggests we dab our eyes with Kleenex. She's always been good at that. But never at the Emmys. She always smiles stoically and applauds as we lose. Not me. I'm tired of being so magnanimous. I mean, it's out of character! Anyway, Kathie Lee didn't even attend last year. But this year she promises to be right there next to me, feigning mock outrage. We'll see.

Friday ☆ May 19

Tonight is the Daytime Emmy Award show. Our annual disappointment. Actually, it's not that important to me. Oprah always wins and why should this year be any different? Last week, Kathie Lee announced that she would attend for my sake. She thought I looked lonely last year. Never mind my loneliness. I suspect the real reason she's coming is because she thinks we might win. But we're also doing concerts and shows starting this weekend in Branson, Missouri. Weeks ago, I even suggested to Gelman that we leave for Branson today to get ready. But he reminded me that the awards are tonight. And there was a glint in his eye that told me that even he thinks we could win. I said no chance, but it looks like we're all going.

At dinner, the staff is excited and having a good time. Segment producer Cindy McDonald is on the loose, taking funny pictures with one of two disposable Kodak Fun Saver cameras Gelman has brought to cover the event. Can you imagine Oprah showing up with a cardboard camera to take staff snapshots? Gelman denies that he's confident we'll win, but why else would he bring the second camera? I take a good look at this group of people who make our show come to life. What troupers. They're at it twelve hours a day, sometimes more, in a single, crazed, one-room office. Television is supposed to be a glamorous business. But you'd think otherwise if you saw our office. Sometimes I wonder how they keep their sanity. The phones never stop. Newspapers, magazines, books, and faxes are piled everywhere. Interns scurry in all directions. And then there's that daily Gelman meeting, which drones on and on until you want to scream. But each day they're all there, battling it out, getting the guests, churning out the ideas. And here they are now, full of anticipation, wearing their best evening attire . . .

I see all of our segment producers, starting with Joanne Saltzman—who's always smiling, always up. And since she married Mr. Saltzman, she's relentless. I'll take a little credit for that. A few years ago at a Kathie Lee Christmas party I had a warm chat with him and later that night he proposed.

Delores Spruell-Jackson—who's been with me longer than anyone here. A sweetheart. Nobody has a better time than Delores when the ladies are out lunching together.

Barbara Fight—who doggedly pursued Gelman from Washington, D.C., where she taught grammar school. She wanted this job desperately and eventually wore him down and got it. Immediately, I nicknamed her "Wanna Fight." But she's really a soft touch who falls in love with every guest she preinterviews.

Terri Palumbo—who likes to check herself out in the makeup room mirror while briefing me on her guests. In fact, she can't take her eyes off herself while she talks to me. It's fascinating.

Cindy McDonald—gutsy, unafraid of any assignment or anything or anyone. Legend has it that, just for the heck of it, she once goosed Gelman and he was too frightened to protest.

Rosemary Kalikow—tireless, funny, colorful. Nobody dresses like Rosemary. Nobody would dare. But, on her, everything looks great. She gives me a gentle shoulder rub each morning in the makeup chair, just before the big Basque hands of stage manager Julian Abio come in for the kill. I look forward to it.

Kate Crane—a touch of class on the staff, with that British accent going for her. She came to this country, got a job, got a husband, got a life—what's the problem? Nothing stops her.

Then there's audience coordinator Isabel Rivera—who, like Gelman, was an intern too valuable to lose. She handles our show tickets and a ten-month waiting list, which makes for more headaches than you could imagine. She makes it look easy.

And assistant producer David Mullen—nicknamed "Mullenmania." A great detail man, totally organized, his desk is as clean as a whistle. But every now and then he's still capable of giving me the wrong year for the show intro.

And Cynthia Lockhart, our production secretary. Before her arrival, there was only chaos. Whenever she's gone, chaos again. She is unflappable, sweet, and cannot be derailed, no matter how hard life tries.

And Tony Pigg—the booming voice of *Live!*, our announcer, unseen at his own request. But he's always there, reading that copy and bringing it to life. The show just wouldn't sound the same without him.

And last, but hardly least, our indefatigable director, David McGrail—no director in television history has as little time to rehearse a show. Granted, some days there's not much to rehearse. But, once in a while, he'll have a musical number, a fashion show, and a sports event out on Columbus Avenue to prepare for—and only fifteen minutes between two local newscasts during *Good Morning America* to do it. That's when he has to wing it like the rest of us. I appreciate what he does up in that booth.

So here they are—our brave little staff. I realize how important this is to all of them and how much they deserve it. They fly in the face of all the darkest trends in talk shows and make me proud that we're doing a program that's different by being simple and timeless. I wonder if I have ever thanked them enough for their efforts. An Emmy *would* be so satisfying. And there is an undercurrent of optimism around our tables. Even Gelman confides to me that he has counted twenty-four people he should thank if the show wins. I advise him to condense it to the word *staff*—if he wants to continue working in this business.

We take our seats in the Marriott ballroom. First row, same as last year. Even the same seats. (Uh-oh. Another omen?) Kathie Lee is on my left, Joy on my right. On this morning's show, we had gone through one final rehearsal of how we'll react. I said I would shake my head in disbelief. Scowl a little. And throw some pieces of paper in the air. Now I'm ripping up a page of the program, preparing my confetti of disappointment. I plan to really pour it on when I hear the name *Oprah* announced. But wait a minute. In my heart of hearts, I have a tiny feeling of hope, too. Maybe we could win. It's probably just the staff optimism rubbing off on me. But I do sense the anxiousness all around me.

Okay, here comes our category. The nominees are read aloud. I slip the confetti into my palm. Kathie Lee is readying her acceptance speech. Joy is smiling. Kathie leans her head on my shoulder. Here we go. And the winner is . . . *Oprah Winfrey*. I knew it! I shake my head miserably. I scowl angrily. I toss the confetti in the air, making a small blizzard of woe. Kathie clutches her Kleenex and slightly dims her smile into a little pout. And that's when I notice that the camera never falls on anyone but Oprah. We're producing a show-business melodrama over here and no one can see us! Even my little bit of fun is denied!

Time to go home now. We head for the escalator of the Marriott and summon up some perspective. Be philosophical. Just smile and keep moving. Tomorrow, we'll leave for Branson. Monday there'll be another show. And again on Tuesday. And the rest of the week. And the week after that. And next month. And next year. There'll be some good shows and some shows we'd all like to forget. Some mornings, it would be wiser to just stay in bed. But I don't think I'd rather be anyplace else for that hour. It's the only place I'm safe! And I'll probably miss it terribly when it's all over. When will that be? I don't know. And I don't have time to think about it. I've got to find my plane tickets, pack my bags, and get ready for the next show. After all, I'm only one man.

Here we go again: Almost a year has gone by since we took that long escalator ride down to the lobby of the Marriott Marquis hotel after the Emmy awards. This book came out in hardcover months later, at the end of August. Finally, I was a full-fledged author! It was something new for me. I wondered if anyone would be interested. I couldn't wait to see the book in stores. That week we were on vacation in the Hamptons and someone told me it was on sale at a bookshop in the Bridgehampton Commons. Tom Battista and I headed right over to case the joint. It was a strange feeling. I was getting nervous. Getting the old heebie-jeebies in the pit of my stomach again—just like in the early days of my television career. We walked in. There it was in a stack near the front door. I wanted to find out how it was selling, but I didn't want the sales clerk to think I cared that much. How could Mayor Koch walk around New York asking people, "How'm I doing?" What masochism! Luckily, the sales girl didn't know me. In fact, it was her first day on the job and she didn't know anything, much less how one book was selling. She called her manager. Now it was getting complicated. I wished I hadn't asked. In fact, I wanted to run out of the store, but it was too late. The manager did recognize me and said, "Well, the first shipment arrived yesterday. Twenty books in all." Now she was figuring out how many were left. You guessed it. Twenty.

"That's it!" I said. "It will never sell. Nobody cares."

I walked out of there a bit shaken. At the same time, it was fascinating to be part of a whole new world: publishing, the final frontier. And from that point on, every time I passed a bookstore I looked for it. Once, on my way to my first autographing party in Boston, I stopped at the bookstore in Logan Airport. I thought the clerks might be amused, so I barged in, shouting in my best out-of-control Dana Carvey voice, "Okay, *where is it?* Where's that best-selling *I'm Only One Man!* book?" The three clerks—all East Indians—looked at me like I was crazy. Obviously, they'd never seen me before, but one of them did track down the book. Three copies, hidden in the deepest recesses of the store. Way in the back. In the dark. No chance to find them without the aid of a bloodhound.

The clerks pacified me by placing all three copies in a prominent position near the front door. As I left, the clerks were smiling and bowing, but they still seemed unsure of who this loudmouth was. The autograph party was a huge success—six hundred people waiting in line since early morning. I was jubilant, getting cocky even. So upon returning to the airport to fly home, I decided— just for some laughs—to pop back into that bookstore. All three books were gone! Already within hours! My adrealine was pumping. Who was hotter than me? "I'm a hit!" I yelled. Until one of the clerks walked back into the dark recesses and, sure enough, reappeared—with three books.

☆   ☆   ☆

Since I last wrote to you, there's been a brand new most frequently asked question in my life. "Where's Kathie Lee?" has been replaced by "Is she really leaving?" My answer: "I don't think so." But it's not really for me to stay. The underlying problem between Kathie Lee and Gelman has always been the issue of booking guests and the situation exploded again last fall when she appeared on CNBC's *Charles Grodin* show. Grodin stumbled into it, asking if the old booking problems had been resolved. No, they hadn't, she said—not in her mind. And, moreover, unless she was given a voice in the production of the show, she would leave. CNBC's publicity department fed the quotes to the Associated Press like it was a burning news story and away we went. What a circus. The columnists grabbed it and milked it mercilessly. *TV Guide* made it a cover story. The more everyone talked about it, the more obdurate Kathie Lee became.

I watched the controversy grow into a swirling monster. She was serious. It would be a major negotiating point in her contract talks. I would be left to answer all those *Is she really leaving?* questions. Gelman, meanwhile, got himself an agent and we all hunkered down for a long cold winter.

As I described earlier in these pages, the producer of a television show, historically speaking, is in charge of booking. That's his or her job. But the hosts can always request a certain guest. That's the way it should be. And, for the most part, that's the way it is around our shop. But sometimes a no can offend. It shouldn't get personal, but it can *feel* that way. I remember once getting a no on Jack Paar, for god's sake, and I haven't gotten over it to this day.

And so Christmas came and, with it, a lengthy vacation for all of us, while tempers cooled. When we returned in January, there was nary a word about the impasse. Not that it's forgotten, I'm sure. But things seem to be on an even keel again and everyone is talking to one another. Occasionally, there's even a smile. I guess all of us realize how long and hard we've worked to make this show what it is and, frankly, how good a situation we all have. Despite all that you've heard, sometimes I feel I'll be the first to go. And I have to smile, thinking of the day I walk out that door, picturing those two looking at each other and slowly beginning to circle one another like a pair of panthers in a cage. I love it!

☆　　☆　　☆

Also, during the intervening months, there's been a new twist in the sleazy saga of daytime talkshows. Somebody finally spoke up and told the television industry to shape up and grow up and stop the shameless exploitation of unwitting (and witless) panel guests. Those ugly daytime shows were rocked hard when former Education Secretary Bill Bennett and Senator Frank Lieberman mounted a campaign against all the TV sex and sleaze. Funny that it wasn't our own industry that made the first move. But I told you they wouldn't do a thing as long as that brand of programming made money. And the media writers didn't do anything about it, either. They sat at their computers and watched the whole charade and reported about all those growing ratings. But the anti-talkshow offense out of Washington finally got the public's attention and only then did the TV executives react. Those ridiculous sexual topics were replaced with "helpful relationship stories." Let's see if it lasts. During the big ratings sweeps periods, somebody will undoubtedly break down and go for the big numbers again with something sensational, sexy, or stupid. Then again, I skated in Central Park wearing tights and a toreador outfit on our show last month. Of course, I have terrific legs and can't blame Gelman for exploiting them.

☆　☆　☆

Remember how I began this book with a story about Dean Martin? I had wanted to see him one more time and so Bill Zehme and I went to the restaurant where he dined every night and we silently watched Dean from across the room. I can't tell you how happy I am that we did it and that I went over to the table to tell him one last time that he was the best. I learned a lesson. If you've appreciated someone in your lifetime, if they brought you a little happiness, and if you have a chance to tell them so—DO IT! It just takes a second and you'll be glad you did.

Dean died Christmas morning—about a year and a half after we saw him at La Famiglia restaurant. His physical condition and appearance had deteriorated dramatically. God, was there ever a better looking guy in a tux onstage, singing, having fun, making people smile? Zehme and I exchanged sad phone calls at Christmas. We had agonized over his condition and wondered and speculated why he had to leave like this. Sometimes the sadness would turn to anger. Where were his friends? What about his family? It all seemed a dark mystery. Since then I have talked at length with his good friend and longtime agent Mort

Viner, who said he tried for years to get Dean out of his shell. Everybody tried. (And few tried harder than Frank Sinatra.) To no avail. That's the way he wanted it to be. Mort was in charge of the funeral arrangements. It was a small, select group who attended—after dark. Army Archerd, the *Variety* columnist, was the only reporter invited and Army wrote a warm, moving story about the services: Dean, he reported, was buried in black tie in the little Westwood cemetary with his music softly playing in the background. It was a beautifully written account by an old pro. And I dropped a note to Army telling him so. He later called to thank me for the letter and to tell me that Dean meant a lot to him, too, but even he was hard-pressed to explain this ending.

I kept looking for answers. I reread Nick Tosches's dark, compelling biography called *Dino: Living High in the Dirty Business of Dreams*. I listened to the tapes and CDs Bill Zehme would send me, all full of songs I never knew Dean recorded. I watched bootlegged videotapes of his old NBC shows brought to me by New York disc jockey Mark Simone. There he was—on my TV, in my ears, and in my head, bigger than life, bigger than ever. I guess I went into a little bit of a Dean twilight zone. Finally, Zehme and I met with Nick Tosches at a Greenwich Village trattoria for lunch and a two-hour reminisce about Dean. Tosches himself is an interesting story: a tough New York writer, living in the Village, who loved Martin and thought his biography would make for an interesting project—never dreaming he would spend four years of his life on an odyssey of research and investigation. We talked incessantly, swapping stories, asking questions, trying to divine answers, and then walked out into the February sunshine. Three grown men caught up in the aura and the legend of Dean Martin. We left Tosches at a corner of Sixth Avenue in the village. He said he was going back to his apartment to play some of Dean's records. Which is exactly what I did when I got home.

☆ ☆ ☆

For our twenty-sixth wedding anniversary, Joy and I took off on a working vacation to Southern California. Right back to where this book—and my career—began. Ten days of sunshine. We first visited San Diego where I guested on the local talk show that precedes ours on KUSI. Afterward, the station had a reception for me, and among the guests was San Diego County Sheriff Bill Kolender. He reminded me of his first television appearance as a San Diego cop on my old show in the sixties. He said I saved him. It's nice to have the town's sheriff beholden to you. We lunched at the La Valencia hotel in La Jolla with the Bill Rankins. (You remember Major Bill Rankin, who stuck his neck out for me when my worst Navy practical joke backfired, almost earning me a court-martial.) A tall blond woman approached our table and said she was the widow of Emil Karras, a linebacker for Sid Gilman's original San Diego Chargers team. I once did a feature story on Charger wives and she was terribly shy, but very attractive. Just before the story aired, she called me at the station and pleaded with me to kill her interview. I told her she had done great, and offered to send a cab for her to see the interview. When it finally ran, she was happy with it. Today she's married to Sheriff Bill Kolender, whom I'd seen just a few hours before. Strange how so many lives connect. Bill Rankin, now a retired colonel at seventy-five and still ramrod straight, laughed when we talked about our service days together over in Coronado. God, was that forty years ago? Later, Joy and I played tennis with Tom and Elaine Battista. Tom was the first director of my first show in San Diego—and we still talk about doing it again.

Back in Los Angeles, I reported to the NBC lot in Burbank to do a guest role on *The Fresh Prince of Bel Air* sitcom. (Didn't all of this start with me coming out west to play myself in a *Larry Sanders* episode?) The people at the *Tonight Show* got wind that I was on the premises and, at the last minute, I got booked to do a bit with Jay Leno, who's been riding high in the ratings. These late night guys won't leave me alone! Walking over to their studio, I passed Johnny's old parking space, now occupied with a different antique Leno car every night. (I remember accosting Johnny in his white Corvette for a rare interview there as though it was yesterday.) I found Jay onstage surrounded by his writers and staffers, trying to edit a taped piece involving celebrity lookalikes presumably on their way to a Hollywood premiere. Jay and I announced the mock arrivals after his monologue that night. He tried to keep up with me, hollering in what he called his best Regis Philbin voice. Sounded more like Dana Carvey to me.

Those hallways outside the cavernous NBC sound-stages reminded me of my aborted NBC morning show in 1981, the one nobody remembers, the one that should have been my network breakthrough show. Instead, all it did was break my heart. Fifteen years ago. Grant Tinker was upstairs then, engineering NBC's return to the top. Johnny was down the hall going over his monologue, continuing to make the *Tonight Show* a television institution. Now both of them are gone, but NBC's on top again. It's all cyclical in this business. Just like life itself.

I finished my work on the *Fresh Prince* show, which would end its six-year run a week later. The star, Will Smith, is moving on to a film career. It's a terrific cast, lots of spirit, lots of fun. They'll have a tough time saying goodbye at their wrap party. Alfonso Ribeiro is one of the supporting stars. His *Tap Dance Kid* was one of the first Broadway shows we saw as a family in New York. He was only twelve years old when he guested on our show.

Everywhere I see more reminders of the past. It's getting spooky. George Burns died while we were in town. He did our show only a few years ago. Looked like it would never end for him. At dinner on our last night in Los Angeles, at the restaurant Eclipse, I ran into Eddie Fisher, looking trim and alert and about to start another singing comeback. Wasn't his first NBC show in the fifties one of my earliest assignments as a page, back when television was all brand new and shiny?

It's now Sunday morning—sunny and bright—as Joy and I fly across America, back to New York. How many planes? How many trips? How much longer? The years keep going by. And so do the shows. Tomorrow Kathie Lee and I will meet again in our little studio at 67th and Columbus. One more show to do. One more host chat. One more time. But can I tell you a little secret? I can't wait to do it again.